Encountering
Jesus & Buddha

ENCOUNTERING
JESUS &
BUDDHA

Their Lives and Teachings

Ulrich Luz and Axel Michaels

Translated by Linda M. Maloney

Fortress Press
Minneapolis

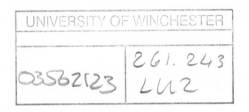
ENCOUNTERING JESUS AND BUDDHA
Their Lives and Teachings

Originally published as *Jesus oder Buddha: Leben und Lehre im Vergleich*, Becksche Reihe (Munich: Beck, 2002).

Cover image and design: Kevin van der Leek
Book design: Josh Messner

Library of Congress Cataloging-in-Publication Data

Luz, Ulrich.
  [Jesus oder Buddha. English]
  Encountering Jesus and Buddha : their lives and teachings / Ulrich Luz,
Axel Michaels ; translated by Linda M. Maloney.
      p. cm.
  Translated from German.
  Includes bibliographical references.
  ISBN-13: 978-0-8006-3563-3 (hardcover : alk. paper)
  ISBN-10: 0-8006-3563-9 (hardcover : alk. paper)
  ISBN-13: 978-0-8006-3564-0 (pbk. : alk. paper)
  ISBN-10: 0-8006-3564-7 (pbk. : alk. paper)
  1. Jesus Christ—Teachings. 2. Gautama Buddha—Teachings. 3.
Christianity and other religions—Buddhism. 4.
Buddhism—Relations—Christianity. I. Michaels, Axel. II. Title.
  BS2415.L8813 2006
  261.2'43—dc22
                              2006016211

The paper used in this publication meets the minimum requirements of American National Standard for Information Sciences—Permanence of Paper for Printed Library Materials, ANSI Z329.48-1984.

Manufactured in the U.S.A.

10   09   08   07   06   1   2   3   4   5   6   7   8   9   10

Contents

Preface

This book came out of a lecture series on "Jesus and Buddha" that the two of us gave in the summer semester of 1996 in Bern and in the summer semester of 2001 in Heidelberg. We wrote our individual chapters and replies separately, but they are the result of extensive conversations between us. Ulrich Luz wrote the chapters on Jesus and the replies to the chapters on Buddhism, while Axel Michaels wrote the chapters on Buddha and the replies to those on Christianity.

Many of the books cited in the text are found in the bibliography, which also contains some books we recommend for further reading.

Our audiences assisted us greatly by their questions, and we thank them. We also owe thanks to Ulrich Nolte for his editorial work and to Johanna Buss and Ulrich Dällenbach for their reference work. Axel Michaels also thanks Ute Hüsken for her critical reading of the parts of the text requiring a special knowledge of Buddhism.

Pronunciation of Indian Terms

Unless otherwise indicated or evident from the context, the foreign expressions come from Sanskrit. For the sake of coherence and comparability, expressions in *Pāli* are often also reproduced in their Sanskrit form.

The words are written according to the prevailing scholarly standard, to reflect the pronunciation of Sanskrit (skt.) and *Pāli (pā.)*. Three rules should be noted:

• A line over a vowel means it is long.
• A dot under a consonant (except *ṃ*) indicates a retroflexive pronunciation, whereby the tongue is bent slightly backward (as if there were a hot potato on it).
• An *S* with a diacritical mark (*ś, ṣ*) is pronounced "sh."

For more precise rules of pronunciation, see, e.g., Axel Michaels, *Hinduism: Past and Present,* trans. Barbara Harshav (Princeton: Princeton University Press, 2004), 48ff..

Fig. III.

Introduction

Buddha or Jesus? This book is about two of the most attractive religions of the present day, religions that are increasingly in competition with one another. A lot has been written about this, so right away let us mention three themes that will clarify what we want and do not want to do in this newest publication.

First of all, we do not intend to join in the popular chorus of interreligious dialogue, because we do not see ourselves as representatives of religions. It is true that Ulrich Luz is a Lutheran theologian (and therefore argues as a scholar and a Christian), but Axel Michaels is not a Buddhist, so he is not an equal dialogue partner in that respect. Neither of us is an apologist.

Second, we do not mean to offer a description of Buddhism and Christianity either. That would take us beyond our abilities in some ways. Axel Michaels explores Buddhism only in a short section of the book, and more as a student of the history of religions than as a philologist. Besides, in this book his focus is almost entirely on the early Buddhism associated with the historical Buddha. Ulrich Luz, as a New Testament scholar, is obviously no expert in the broader fields of Christian spirituality and the history of theology.

Third, we are not interested only in pointing out historical parallels between these two life stories or studying their mutual influences, for "the similarities between Buddhist and New Testament narratives have created a hotbed of dilettantism that has been living a blithe existence for some time now."[1] There may have been parallels, but they are mostly just that: parallels, lines that never meet.

Instead, what we have in common is an interest in the phenomenology of religion,[2] not for the sake of getting past the phenomena to religious "truth,"[3] but in order to understand religions in a way that takes them seriously on their own terms. Certainly, all functional questions—the kind that religious studies mainly asks today—are justified, but we find that only this most important aspect of phenomenology of religions—each religion's own self-understanding—makes it possible to appreciate a religion in its totality. We agree with Gerd Theissen that religion can best be understood as a cultural symbolic system.[4] This system must be interpreted as a whole, but there is no direct route from the symbol to what it symbolizes. So it is not a question of making symbols a vehicle for divine self-explanation; we know that we, as scholars, cannot decipher God. (Not even a theologian can do that, or wants to!) The shoemaker should stick to his last, and the interpreter to her symbols.

Within the framework of a study in religious phenomenology in this sense, we want to pose the question of the two "religious founders," Buddha Gautama and Jesus. Both of them achieved their significance in large part through what they became after their own time. Evidently the two religious founders belong within the context and the totality of the "semiotic cathedrals"[5] of Christianity and Buddhism. Christians constantly point to Jesus, and Buddhists refer to the Buddha, the so-called historical Buddha Gautama, although less often than Christians refer to Jesus. Inasmuch as we understand Jesus or Buddha Gautama, we hope to understand an important aspect of Christianity or Buddhism. But this often takes place only within the sphere of a particular (Buddhist or Christian) conceptual system, and comparing those systems must necessarily lead us into the language of religious studies.

We are also aware that the question of the so-called "religious founders" is altogether modern. The historian of religions Gustav Mensching distinguished between "organic" and "founded" religions; the latter he understood to be those "in which a distinguishable historical personality with a characteristic religious view had a decisive influence on the formation and spirit of the concrete religion for an indefinite period of time."[6] This seems to apply both to Jesus of Nazareth and to Buddha Gautama, although in very different ways. Neither man intended to found a new religion (and whether Buddhism is a religion at all is a long-disputed question), but both established a teacher-disciples relationship whose institutionalization resulted in the creation of the social body of a religion. It was the community that made the Holy Man (teacher, shaman, prophet, etc.) the founder of a religion, not the man himself.

So we will need to ask how much the essential differences between the two religions have to do with the differences between their founding figures. On the whole, Christianity is more clearly oriented to the world, more practical, more ethical in its direction. Buddhism, in contrast, is directed more to a letting go of the world. Christianity is centrally related to God's counterpart, who is Lord of the world and also Lord Jesus, while in early Buddhism the gods are really not much more than observers of the Buddha's path. In Christianity, centripetal tendencies triumphed. The movement devolved into church building and, connected with that, into severe intolerance and an absolutist claim. Faith became normative doctrine and an obligatory religious law. In

Buddhism, centrifugal tendencies won out. It remained in the loose form of an order, or a variety of schools. The individual monk and teacher on the path toward Buddhahood remains much more significant than in Christianity. Enlightenment is not subject to control, and what happens within it cannot be directly expressed in a normative doctrine.

But we want to do more than simply compare the founders. In our book, readers will continually encounter intriguing questions that take them beyond what is purely descriptive or interpretive. We want to use the convergences and divergences as reciprocal provocations to carry our thoughts beyond the ordinary, beyond what we already know. We want to let ourselves be provoked by the other to consider how it might be or could have been if the historical situation had been different. If the Buddha and Jesus could have met, they might well have avoided a dialogue.[7] But it is intriguing to ask what might have happened: Would the Buddha have been converted by Jesus and become his disciple? Would Jesus have gone into the desert and not to Jerusalem? Would Jesus have lost his belief in God? Would the Buddha have prayed to God?

Such questions, which sound fanciful at first, help a theologian think beyond the truth of his or her own religion, in this case Christianity. There are other questions that Jesus might ask of Christianity, and in turn there are questions to be put to Jesus in light of Christianity and its history. Then the theologian is doing his or her own work, for theology does not consist of offering criticism from within the secure haven of a supposed storehouse of truth, but of posing the truth question as a self-critical inquiry of one's own heritage, that of Christianity. The religious-studies scholar helps the theologian in this by asking provocative questions from the viewpoint of the Buddha.

So in this book a religious-studies scholar enters into dialogue with a theologian in order to transcend the boundaries of his own field of scholarship, which have become too constricting. The critical questions, by their very nature, are directed primarily at Christianity. Neither of us authors is a Buddhist; we are both Europeans and Christians—or at least shaped by a Christian and post-Christian culture. It is not our business to criticize or question Buddhism; at most we may now and then propose some cautious reflections along those lines.

If it should happen, at the end of our aggressive and contentious but always friendly discussion of "the Buddha *or* Jesus," that our readers should arrive at some form of "the Buddha *and* Jesus" without being unfaithful to either founder in his uniqueness, then we will have achieved more than we have dared to hope.

Part One
The Founders

1

One and Many Buddhas

Axel Michaels

There is only one Jesus, but there are many Buddhas. The individuality of Jesus contrasts with the elimination of individuality and singularity in the Buddha. This first significant difference is already apparent in the names and titles of these two founders.

The historical Buddha belonged to the tribe of the Śākyas (*pā. Sakya*) and the family Gautama. His first name was Siddhārtha (*pā. Siddhattha,* "he who has reached the goal"). But he was usually called Gautama (*pā. Gotama*) and later also *Śākyamuni* ("the sage from the tribe of the *Śākyas*"). Although this name is in poetic style, it has endured as the designation for the historical Buddha, even though, for reasons of simplicity and following convention, we usually speak of the Buddha (with the definite article) when we refer to the historical Buddha. His followers most often called him simply (skt.) *bhagava(n)t,* "Exalted One, Lord."

The traditions about Buddha *Śākyamuni* (after his enlightenment) called him *arhant* (*pā. arhat,* "holy one; one who has achieved enlightenment"), *jina* ("victor"), or simply *buddha* ("the awakened one, the enlightened one"). He also is supposed often to have called himself *tathāgata,* "the thus come one" or "the thus gone one" (i.e., like his predecessors, toward truth)[1]; both meanings are possible. In any case, the name already expresses an attitude: *tathāgata* is more a spiritual than a personal principle. Choosing this term for the Buddha meant understanding him as one of many Buddhas who appear in all ages of the world.

The designations for the illuminated *Śākyamuni* are not unique and unparalleled. Others could also bear them, but they express a special status.

The Buddha, like Jesus and other religious founders or saints, set aside the name given by his parents or was given additional names and titles of honor. The changes were necessary as a way to underscore these leaders' new beginning and the special character of their experience or their teaching. The names and titles of Jesus (*Kyrios, Christos,* Son of God, Son of Man, Savior) should be understood in much the same way.

Hence, when we speak of the Buddha, we must clearly distinguish the life of the founder, for which we have only indirect historical evidence, from the historical environment and the legend-enhanced life of a (particular) Buddha. Both pictures of the Buddha rest on written sources, but some of those come from historical periods separated by many centuries.

The Sources

Scarcely anything of Buddha Gautama's life can be historically tested; almost all of it is legendary. There are no contemporary sources. The first surviving testimonies were written at least three generations after the death of the Buddha. These are the inscriptions and cliff-carved edicts of the emperor Aśoka, who reigned from about 268 to 236/232 B.C.E. But even there, all we can detect are beginnings. A real biography of the Buddha, and thus most of what we associate with his life, was not written until hundreds of years after the Buddha lived. The *Pāli* canon contains, at best, the beginnings of a biography of the Buddha. The Buddha's *vita,* as it is widely known today, "exists" only in the legendary life stories written some eight hundred to one thousand years later (see table 1).

Table 1   **Sources for the Buddha's Biography**

Biographical sections in the *Pāli* canon and its parallels and translations: These include scarcely anything on the birth and youth of the Buddha, but sections describe his illumination and the establishment of the order.

Biographical inserts in the Vinaya texts: These contain no stories of his birth or youth, except in the Vinaya of the *Mūlasarvāstivādin* School.

The *Mahāvastu,* "[The Book] of the Great Events" (2nd–4th century C.E.) and the *Lalitavistara,* "The Complete Description of the Game [= earthly activities of the Buddha]" (c. 4th century C.E.): Docetic traditions, already marked by Mahayana tendencies, describe the Buddha as supramundane.

Independent biographies of the Buddha, especially the Buddhacarita, "The Buddha's Way of Life" by Aśvaghoṣa (c. 2nd century C.E.).

Comprehensive compilations of Buddha biographies, for example, the *Nidānakathā*, "Narrative of the Beginnings [of the Buddha]," written in Sri Lanka (7th century C.E.).

Source: Based on Étienne Lamotte, *History of Indian Buddhism: From the Origins to the Śaka Era* (Louvain-la-Neuve: Université Catholique de Louvain, Institut Orientaliste, 1988); and Hans-Joachim Klimkeit, "Die Heilsgestalten des Buddhismus," in Heinz Bechert et al., eds., *Der Buddhismus* (Stuttgart: Kohlhammer, 2000), 1:219ff.

The Buddha's discourses are transmitted in a variety of different canons. No single body of texts is normative for all Buddhist schools; rather, in a heterogeneous process, the different writings that were compiled soon after the death of the Buddha brought together individual collections of canonical texts in many languages (*Theravādins* in *Pāli*, *Dharmaguptakas* in *Gāndharī-Prakrit*, *Lokottaravādins* in hybrid Buddhist Sanskrit, etc.).

The canons are divided among three "baskets" (*piṭaka*), four or five collections (*nikāya*), or nine members (*aṅga*). In the wake of the mingling of regional traditions, the division into three baskets (*pā. tipiṭaka, skt. tripiṭaka*) prevailed. Thus, the canons contain collections of texts on monastic discipline (*pā. Vinayapiṭaka*), teaching (*pā. Suttapiṭaka*), and scholasticism (*pā. Abhidhammapiṭaka*). Different versions of these canons, or parts of them, have been handed down in the collections summarized in tables 2 and 3.

Table 2	The Canons

Pāli canon of the *Theravāda* school in the middle-Indian language of *Pāli*
> The only Buddhist canon that has been handed down complete in an Indian language. It therefore offers a point of reference for tracing the Buddhist traditions (see table 3). It was first handed on orally and was written down in what is now Sri Lanka at the earliest in the 1st century B.C.E. The version available today was authoritative for this school by the 5th/6th centuries C.E. at the latest.

Chinese canon (San-tsang = *Tipiṭaka*)
> The standard Taisho edition (2184) contains translations of the texts of many different Buddhist schools, including the *Dharmaguptaka*, the *Sarvāstivādin*, the *Mūlasarvāstivādin*, the *Mahāsaṅghika*, and others. With regard to the discipline of the orders, East Asian Buddhists follow the *Dharmaguptaka* tradition.

Tibetan canon (Kanjur)

Contains, among other things, translations of texts of the *Mūlasarvāstivā-din*, whose Vinaya tradition is also followed by Tibetan Buddhists.

Sanskrit texts of the *Sarvāstivādin,* the *Mūlasarvāstivādin,* and the *Mahāsaṅghika-Lokottravādin*

In manuscripts discovered in Central Asia and Tibet.

9 *Mahāyānasūtras*

Regarded as canonical in some places (e.g., Nepal).

Table 3 **Buddhist Writings**

Canonical Literature

Vinayapiṭaka ("basket of discipline"): Discipline of the Orders

Suttavibhaṅga with *Pātimokkha*: rules for the behavior of the monks and nuns of *Khaṇḍakā,* consisting of *Mahāvagga* and *Cullavagga* ("smaller" rules for monks and nuns, rules for behavior, formulas for legal actions, legends, accounts of councils) and *Parivāra* (lists, verses, etc.; systematization of the preceding parts of the *Vinayapiṭaka* from different points of view)

Parivārapāṭha: teachings and rules in question-and-answer form

Suttapiṭaka ("basket of discourses," *pā. sutta, skt. sūtra*): Teaching

Dīghanikāya ("collection of the long speeches"): 34 discourses

Majjhimanikāya ("collection of the unified speeches"): 56 groups of *suttas* (prose, verse, ballads)

Aṅguttaranikāya ("collection of speeches arranged in ascending order of number"): over 2,300 *suttas,* ordered according to the numbers of sequences of concepts

Khuddakanikāya ("collection of the [15] pieces"): 15 very heterogeneous groups of texts

Abhidhammapiṭaka ("basket of what relates to the teaching"): Scholasticism: Texts that, on the basis of lists, attempt to systematize, analyze, and explain the teaching

Kathāvatthu, a text refuting the views of a variety of persons holding other beliefs

Pseudocanonical Literature

Mahāyānasūtras and other *Mahāyāna* literature: a collection of new texts, including *Saddharmapuṇḍarīka* ("lotus of the good law"), *Laṅkāvatāra-*

or *Saddharmalaṅkāvātārasūtra, Suvarṇa prabhāsa*, and *Prajñāpāramitā* ("perfection of wisdom").
Vajrayāna literature, primarily Tantric texts (including the *Guhyasamājatantra*), hymns (*stotra*), and collections of magical formulas (*dhāraṇi*).

Noncanonical Literature
Pāli literature: commentaries, texts on the life of the Buddha (cf. table 1), *Visuddhimagga* ("way of purity") of the Buddhaghosa (Compendium of Buddhist Teaching), Milindapañha ("questions of Milinda = Menandros"), and chronicles (*Dīpavaṃsa, Mahāvaṃsa, Cūlavaṃsa, Bodhivaṃsa*)
Sanskrit literature, including further texts on the life of the Buddha, poems, stories of reincarnation (e.g., *Jātakamālā* of *Āryasūra*), Bodhisattva stories (*Avadāna*), philosophical texts (e.g., *Abhidharmakośa* of *Vasubandhu, Nyāyapraveśa* of *Dignāga, Yogacārabhūmiśāstra* of *Asaṅga, Madhyamikakārikās* of *Nāgārjuna, Nyāyabindu* of *Dharmakīrti, Śikṣāsammuccaya*, and possibly *Bodhicaryāvatāra* of *Śantideva*), and lexicographical texts
Source: For an overview, see also Thomas Oberlies, "Heilige Schriften des Buddhismus," in *Heilige Schriften*, ed. Udo Tworuschka, 167–96 (Darmstadt: Wissenschaftliche Buchgesellschaft, 2000).

The extent to which particular parts of the *Pāli* canon are words of Buddha *Śākyamuni* is extremely difficult to determine, so it is disputed. The canonical texts, which are almost impossible to date and whose authors are seldom known, do hand on oral tradition, as is also clear from the introductory formulas of the discourses ("So I have heard"). At councils and other meetings these texts evidently were examined and approved. But these texts are not the *ipsissima vox,* the authentic voice of the Buddha, for the Buddha spoke (*Ardha-*)*Māgadhī*, a North Indian idiom, while the earliest traditions (from about the first century c.e., some of them earlier) are in Sanskrit, *Pāli*, and Chinese. Still, even though we do not know the exact words the Buddha spoke, the texts give a pretty clear picture of his world.

Buddha Śākyamuni and His World

Gautama was born in Lumbinī, near the city of Kapilavastu (*pā.* Kapilavatthu) in the southern foothills of the Himalaya (Terai) in present-day Nepal. This information appears in an inscription in Lumbinī, near Kapilavastu, dated to

249 B.C.E. Kapilavastu, on the River Rohinī, was the capital of an apparently more or less autonomous province of the *Kośala* empire and may also have been a kind of well-to-do knightly estate with broad landholdings.

In nearly all the books on Buddhism we find the dates of his life as ca. 560–480 B.C.E. A lifetime of eighty years is unanimously given (which does not mean that it is certainly true), but there are serious doubts about the dates. The one thing that can be concluded with certainty from the ongoing debate is that the Buddha died between 420 and 350 B.C.E. Many scholars today accept the dates 450–370 B.C.E. (plus or minus ten years) as the duration of his life, but this conclusion, too, rests at least partly on assumptions.[2]

The borderland between India and Nepal where Siddhārtha grew up had fertile regions and others that were malaria-infested swamp, barely inhabitable. But rice cultivation was so intensively practiced that a surplus was produced. Siddhārtha's father was called Śuddhodana, literally "the one who grows pure rice," and was probably a landed nobleman; it is only the later sources that make him a universal ruler (*cakravartin*). Given the economic situation, republics were emerging, headed by a wealthy and proud nobility who had little political power. The empire of the *Śākyas* was this kind of aristocratic state with oligarchic rule. It was headed by an elected governor (*rāja*, literally "king"), who presided over the council. Only certain *Kṣatriyas*, members of the knightly and warrior classes, could be elected *rāja*.

Buddha Gautama's world probably included the brahmanic caste (*varṇa*) system, but it had less rigorous boundaries for *connubium* (marriage), commensality (table fellowship), and social hierarchy than the Brahmans allowed. Slaves were kept, but the social order was comparatively egalitarian and liberal, and it served as a model for the structure of the orders in Buddhism.

Life in these realms was fundamentally different from what it had been in the ancient Indian seminomadic Indo-Aryan tribes. We can offer only a short summary:[3] There was a transition from grain cultivation and animal husbandry (especially cattle and goats) to irrigation and rice cultivation, made possible by the construction of terraces and a complicated irrigation system. There is no archaeological evidence of iron plows or tools, but they are generally assumed because the vast clearings cannot be explained without them. The surplus that was produced led increasingly to the use of coins and an organized interregional commerce with planned routes capable of sustaining traffic and secured by military force.

Legal and political stability made possible the establishment of courts and city life, and these in turn supported the arts and sciences. A self-confident class of officials, merchants, and craftspersons was created; these were largely neglected by the Brahmans, whose clientele was only the aristocracy and themselves. The Brahmans regarded cities as strongholds of uncleanness. But it was in the cities that life was rapidly changing, and it was in the cities that Buddhism arose.

The Buddha probably came from an uneducated milieu. He may, over the years, have become acquainted with the Upanishads, the philosophical texts of ancient India, "but they did not shape his quest."[4] He spoke—in a popular tongue, not the sacred language of Sanskrit—to a society in which, for the first time in South Asia, there were such things as "individualism" and religious options. Greater mobility, occupational specialization, less dependency on the extended family, so vital for survival in purely agrarian conditions, offered the individual a spectrum of choices. Even if, as in the past, these were still restricted for most people, there were nevertheless alternatives to the sacrificial ritualism of the Brahmans. The Buddha's teaching was one of many in that period, which also saw the origins of Jainism. According to the tradition, the Buddha himself chose and tested a variety of religious paths before he developed his own.

Why was it especially the Buddha, among so many itinerant ascetics and preachers, who inspired such a response? One reason was that the Buddha did not simply teach a world-rejecting doctrine of liberation for what Max Weber would call the religious virtuosi, but (like Jesus) concerned himself with the "healing of souls" for all, almost independently of their social condition, origins, ritual connections, and abilities. The audience for his teaching was a society in which there was already a certain degree of social mobility. Buddha's opponents were not foreign rulers, Pharisees, and scribes, but for the most part priests and learned men, unbelievers, and radical ascetics. He contended with them, argued against them, polemicized at them, but never did this put his life in danger. The Buddha, who knew so much about suffering, scarcely suffered himself (apart from a—legendary?—life-threatening fast during his ascetic self-testing).

The Legends of the Buddha

It is significant that the legendary Buddha biographies pay special attention to his birth, life, and death, while the oldest strata of texts pay these topics scarcely any attention. The Buddha's disciples were attached to his teaching and followed his instruction not to make his person important. They handed on the teaching, not his life. The Buddha's first sermon is nearly identical in every *Pāli* and Sanskrit text, whereas the Buddha biographies are full of schematic variations, depending on their literary genre.

The Buddha biographies tend to show us either a realistic depiction of his birth (so in the early *Pāli* works, and perhaps still in *Aśvaghoṣa*), with father, mother, and the child Buddha, or an elaborated (docetic) Buddhology in which the father is not the begetter and the mother is only a vessel. These elaborated Buddha biographies had a more lasting influence than the realistic, religious-historical depictions and doubts about the historicity of the Buddha. In what follows we will deal primarily with the episodes that are relevant to a comparison with the life of Jesus.

The later birth stories speak of an angel, or bodhisattva, who is touched by the sufferings of humans, gods, and spirits and decides to take the form of a white elephant from the *Tuṣita* heaven (a sort of city of gods) and plant the seed of the future Buddha in the right side of the body of the chaste princess Māyā. There he remains for exactly ten months. Māyā gives birth while standing, her right arm clasped around a tree. Seven days later, she dies. Her sister Mahāprojāpatī Gautamī brings up Gautama. A brahmanic seer named Asita promises a great future for the boy. During his birth in the Lumbinī Park, flowers rain down from heaven, the music of the spheres is heard, a baldachin (canopy) sweeps through the air, worlds quiver, and an unimaginable glory attends the event. The great and unique one is accompanied by every kind of miracle story. The newborn takes seven steps in every direction and says (the child Buddha is immediately able to speak) that he will put an end to reincarnation, aging, sickness, and death. These legends are clearly grounded in ideas about emerging Buddhas, according to which bodhisattvas exist because of compassion for humanity and wait in the *Tuṣita* heaven for their reincarnation.

What is noteworthy in the legends about Siddhārtha's birth is that his father is excluded from begetting. Some sources speak of a vow of chastity spoken by both father and mother, but nothing is said about a virgin birth. The exclusion of biological processes of conception is a common feature of saints' legends in every type of religion. The same is true of pregnancy. The religious founder has a kind of phantom body, does not go through the impure embryonic phases, and comes into the world through the right (pure) side of his mother's body. All this is meant to emphasize both his purity within the mother's body and his difference. In the Lalitavistara, the Buddha even sits in a jewel-covered casket within his mother's body. Unbesmirched by blood or placenta, he comes (down) to earth. There was no development of a Buddhist *Māyālogy* comparable to Mariology.

Little is known about the Buddha's youth, just as no one knows what Jesus did during his early years. Holy people are not of much interest in the immature phases of their lives; when they are, their impetuous, hesitant, or protesting sides are usually glossed over. We may assume that Gautama's youth was carefree and protected: the parklands in Lumbini that archaeology has uncovered are vast, and the material in the *Pāli* canon speaks of three palaces, one for each season, with many servants. Everything else has been exaggerated by legend. Siddhārtha was unsurpassable in games and sports; he was always the first in archery, jousting, and fencing; he could kick an elephant over the wall with a single toe; no instructor could teach him anything; and according to the Lalitavistara he already knew sixty-four texts by heart when he began his schooling. Probably Buddha's youth is depicted as carefree, rich, and grand so as to make his decision to renounce everything and his revulsion for luxury and excess all the greater.

Gautama was married and had a son—at least, so the *Pāli* canon reports. But already in the Lalitavistara his marriage is portrayed as only pretended. In any case, it was arranged. According to one legend his father, Śuddhodana, decided to have his son marry at sixteen in order to prevent him from becoming a Buddha (as had been predicted at Gautama's birth). The marriage remained childless for thirteen years. In the night when the Buddha's wife, Yaśodharā, bears their son, Rāhula, the Buddha leaves her and becomes homeless. Beyond this, the wife of the later Buddha plays no part in the Buddha biographies, and the son only a minor role: He is taken into the order by the Buddha himself, but without making any great mark there.

The Buddha reached a crisis (according to the *Buddhavaṃsa* at the age of twenty-nine; in another source as early as age nineteen) in which he began to doubt the meaning of his life. This brought about a great life change: he became homeless. It is usual to associate four exits from the royal palace with the change in the Buddha's life. One after another, the Buddha encountered at these exits a helpless old man, a very sick person, a corpse, and a monk with a yellow robe and a shaved head.

Very early in the modern era (1881), Hermann Oldenberg described this part of the biography as legendary elaboration, saying it was developed in order to give concrete illustration of an internal experience, an inner change.[5] The Indologist Dieter Schlingloff showed that the early texts and illustrations reveal a number of impulses toward flight from the world:[6] the meditation under the tree, followed by passage near a cemetery, and a bedchamber full of women in unseemly positions that reminded the Buddha of a graveyard. Schlingloff concludes that of these, only the meditation under the jambu tree was genuine.

We never will be absolutely certain about the motif of flight from the world, especially since there are still other depictions of the Buddha's departure. In any case, the oldest strata of text are not yet acquainted with the legend of the four exits. Instead, they describe the Buddha's thoughts about fleeing from the world without elaboration and as the sign of an internal process.

The remaining episodes in the Buddha's life are essentially about his teaching. According to tradition, the Buddha tried various forms of asceticism for six years and placed himself under a number of teachers until, under a Bodhi tree in present-day Bodhgayā, after some temptations from Māra, the Lord of the world of the senses and the symbol of death, he achieved enlightenment. His spirit and mind were completely calmed, and he became totally absorbed into *Nirvāṇa*. From then on he has been regarded as "the Awakened One," that is, as Buddha.

A little later he went to Sārnāth (near Benares), and there, in the Grove of the Gazelles, he taught his first five disciples the Middle Way, the Eightfold Path, and the Four Noble Truths: the core of early Buddhism. Then followed forty-five years of itinerant preaching, which cannot be chronologically fixed. During this period occurred other episodes of temptation, the founding of the order, conversions, and missionizing.

Only the Buddha's death—or rather, his complete extinction (*parinirvāṇa*)—receives a fuller description. In Kuśinagara, on the road to his home country, he supposedly surrendered the last of his will to live, and he died after eating some spoiled food, but only after first giving some last instructions for the order and some additional teaching.

Historicity and Legend

What is true about the stories that have been and are still being told about the Buddha? We have only the earliest beginnings of genuine historical-critical research about him. The oft-criticized historical-critical study of the Bible is much more advanced. The credibility of the Buddhist sources for historical facts about the life of the Buddha has been sharply called into question, because most of them are stereotypical. Thus, the incarnation of the Buddha follows a pattern of twelve deeds that applies to every Buddha:[7] (1) The bodhisattva resides in the *Tuṣita* heaven, (2) decides to descend in order to save the world, (3) enters the womb of a chosen woman, (4) is born, and says, "I am the Lord of the world, I am the best of the world, I am the first of the world. This is my last birth. There is no further existence." (5) He becomes proficient in the arts and bodily exercises, and he marries. (6) Then there is a life spent in a palace or a house and the rejection of ordinary life, (7) flight from life in the house, (8) ascesis, (9) temptation and awakening, (10) illumination, (11) preaching, and (12) *Nirvāṇa*.

These life stories have a great deal of similarity; there is scarcely any difference between the disciples and the Buddha. For example, the life of the Buddha resembles that of his disciple Yasa down to the local details. Everything is hugely overblown and idealized. The places of the events are to be understood symbolically; they appear in the same form in many stories and myths. There was neither desire nor necessity for a Buddha biography oriented toward reality: "The concept of biography as such was foreign to the consciousness of the period."[8] Moreover, "If the doctrine of the Buddha had been just the saying of some person or individual, it would lack in compelling authority."[9] The Buddha was only one of many Buddhas in the revolving epochs of the world (*kalpa*), and the Buddha's life is only one of many in his own returning until his illumination. We are reminded of this by the pre-birth stories (*Jātaka*), the Buddha's deeds as bodhisattva, and the anticipation of future Buddhas—Maitreya, for example (see cover illustration).

This raises the problem of the historicity of the Buddha. The fixed points are so few that some have even questioned that he ever lived at all. They speak of a Sun hero or a foggy notion of God underlying the ideas about the Buddha. It is true that doubts previously expressed about the historicity of Gautama were eliminated, at the latest, by Hermann Oldenberg (1855–1920) and his influential book on the Buddha, which first appeared in 1881. All the same, even Oldenberg had only a "trust in the tradition."[10]

Buddhism itself sought quite early to "solve" the general problem of the incarnation of a savior by understanding it in terms of various forms or bodies[11] of a Buddha, thus making it possible to exalt and venerate the historical Buddha while at the same time leaving no doubt that an earthly Buddha constituted the lowest stage of Buddhahood. This is clear in the *Milindapañha*, in which King Milinda (Gr. Menandros) asks the monk Nāgasena about the Buddha's teaching:

"Honorable *Nāgasena*, does the Buddha (really) exist?"

"Certainly, great king, the Exalted One really exists."

"Is it possible, honorable *Nāgasena*, to say of the Buddha: 'Here he is, or there'?"

"The Exalted One is completely extinguished, great king, in the element of salvation (*pā. anupādisesa nibbānadhātu*), free from every trace of being. And therefore it is not possible to say of the Buddha: 'Here he is, or there.'" ...

"But, great king, through the body of the teaching (*pā. dhammakāya*) one may show the Exalted One. For the teaching was proclaimed by the Exalted One."

"You are right, honorable *Nāgasena!*" (*Mil* 73.9–22).[12]

A Buddha is extinguished and thus cannot be venerated, but an earthly Buddha can be a means on the path to Buddhahood.

Does Christianity Need the Historical Jesus?

Why does Christianity cling so tenaciously to the historical Jesus? The problems are scarcely smaller than those connected with the Buddha. The Gospels were not intended to be histories or to recount the life of Jesus. They do not tell us what Jesus looked like. They want to exalt him, to proclaim his message. They are scarcely interested in the earthly man Jesus, but are intensely focused on Jesus as Christ, *Kyrios,* Son of God. Consequently, the attempt to "rescue" Jesus from the sources appears to be useless as well as impossible. The appeal to Jesus as a historical person is itself post-Jesus and is legitimate, at most, as a feature of the history of theology. No matter where one takes hold of the question, the Jesus who is recovered is the Jewish, the early Christian, the Hellenistic, the Gnostic, the Catholic, the Protestant ... but not the historical Jesus.

In contrast, the mythical images of Jesus are being increasingly suppressed, it seems. While Rudolf Bultmann, for example, rejected every attempt to perceive the historical Jesus behind the kerygmatic (proclaimed) Jesus, a multitude of newer books looks to discover Jesus above all in his historical, primarily Jewish context. But we may ask, against this trend: Does Christianity really need Jesus as a historical person? Could not being a son/child of God (e.g., Meister Eckhart's "being-son") correspond to the Buddha-nature of every human being? Should not the quest therefore be to discover the Jesus-nature (or divinity) in the individual? How much of this idea of the divinity (and therefore immortality) of the human person can Christianity or Christian theology accept?

The Buddhahood of the Buddha is both intimate and distant.[13] Transcendence is possible only in this identification; therefore, to the extent that such concepts are legitimate at all for Buddhism, it must be that the human being can also be "God." For Christianity, God stands above the world, but could Jesus—apart from all theological and church-historical reservations—not also be regarded as a refutation of this distance?

Response / *Ulrich Luz*
Christianity Needs the Man Jesus!

Does Christianity need the "historical Jesus"? The answer must be yes and no! The "historical" Jesus is a modern scholarly construct, the child of the Enlightenment. Throughout many centuries, believers knew nothing of the "historical" Jesus, but they did know the man Jesus, the one who is true God and true human being, the Son of God, the Incarnate One. The modern question about the "historical Jesus" was posed in recent centuries—originally more at the fringes of the church and rather outside it than inside—at the point at which people no longer recognized their own faith in the church's teaching about the two natures of Christ. They attempted to get around this problem by looking for the "historical Jesus"—what he was really like and not necessarily the way he was taught about in the church's systems of belief.

The people who ask about the historical Jesus in this way of course *need* Jesus. The market continues to be flooded with books about Jesus; they attract crowds of readers and are highly valued. It appears that these books are needed because they link people's own guiding imagery with Jesus: Jesus is the teacher of true humanity, the one who proclaims an immediate and genuine relationship to God, the preacher of a new way of interpreting existence, the revolutionary, the complete man, a dropout, a marginal or model Jew. Jesus is different; he is a Jewish-Cynic peasant philosopher, the embodiment of a new humanity, someone who trod the boundaries between the religions, who went to India. For me, as a Christian theologian in a post-Christian and religiously pluralistic world, it is amazing how many people today still choose Jesus as their guiding figure. This gives us a preliminary answer to the question posed: present-day people evidently need the so-called historical Jesus because they need guiding images.

But this response rouses an objection: if the so-called historical Jesus continues to function as a guiding image today, in one way for some people and in a different way for others, what is "historical" about him? In view of the multitude of different images of Jesus, can we still discern anything at all about the historical Jesus? At this point, the answer can only be given in the most general terms: Yes, we can. The state of the sources is not all that bad! We have a great number of different sources from various circles of tradition that were written down within a single century. The state of the sources is better than for Buddha Gautama. There is only a single person in antiquity who was significant in religion and philosophy yet wrote nothing, about whom we know more than we know about Jesus, and that is Socrates. The difficulty in saying something about the historical Jesus is not so much a matter of the sources as it is that so many people have linked their own guiding images with Jesus, and in so many books. Jesus-research is about disengaging one's own guiding images from historical reality, as far as possible. Of course, that is never a complete success, but we can hope to come close to it. Otherwise, we could never come to any agreement about images of Jesus.

If the modern question about the historical Jesus arose more on the fringes of the church than in the church itself, does Christian faith really need Jesus? If the gospels themselves were unacquainted with the notion of the "historical" Jesus, if Christians through all the centuries before the Enlightenment got along without him, why does Christian faith today have any need of him? Of course, Christians do not need the historical Jesus as the direct basis for their faith. That would be impossible, because then Christian faith would be based on a hypothetical construction that might look different from the point of view of a scholar or change when new sources are discovered. Rather, today's Christians need the historical Jesus because they, too, are thinking people shaped by modernity. Christians, too—or Christians especially!—draw their guiding images from Jesus. They, too, have to learn to distinguish between their own images of Jesus or favorite ideas about him and the historical reality. They, too—they especially—have to come to terms with other people on the subject of Jesus. If they do not do all that, they absolutize their own image of Jesus. That is precisely what the question of the historical Jesus aims to avoid. That is, it has a self-critical function.

But beyond that, Christian faith also needs images of Jesus. Jesus linked his own work with God, so God will always be present, in some way, in Christian images of Jesus. We may speak of "myth" here, we may recall traditional Christologies (which are also among the "images of Jesus"), or we may construct new images of Jesus, such as Dorothee Sölle's picture of Jesus as representative for the absent God.[14] There will always be something of God in Christian images of Jesus. This is appropriate to Jesus himself, for his concern was with God and God's reign. Such "images" are necessary for every person of the past, because people from the past live in us only through images. Fundamentally, therefore, I do not want to close myself off from the ideas that Axel Michaels proposes—that transcendence happens through such images and that Jesus should be understood in this sense "as a refutation" of the "distance" between God and the human. Rather, such a thought is very close to Christian belief. Christian theology has spelled out the christological "model of exchange" in endless variations: "God became human so that the human might become God."[15]

However, we also find here a fundamental difference between Christianity and Buddhism: The christological "model of exchange" presumes that the divinity of the human is not something that is somehow given and only needs to be discovered. Rather, the human being, in Christian belief, is a creature and therefore fundamentally different from God. Humans have lost their divine image and even their ability to know God (cf. Rom 3:23). Therefore any "divinity" of the human is preceded by soteriology: Before "Christ lives in me" as a new self, he must have "given himself for me" (Gal 2:20). God, or Christ, in Christian faith is something outside me, a precondition out of which I live. Therefore, Jesus has never been seen in Christian tradition as a refutation of the distance between God and the world. He is not about refuting, but rather *overcoming* this distance.

However, in my view, if we are really talking about an image of Jesus, it is not possible to reduce the man Jesus to something merely internal, e.g., to the birth of the Son of God in the soul,[16] which might then correspond to the Buddha-nature. Such a reduction would by no means correspond to the thought of medieval mysticism either. For the medieval mystics, the Jesus-image of the church's teaching—the doctrine of the two natures—was anything but irrelevant. These medieval mystics shared in the piety of the "imitation of Christ," oriented to the life and especially the death of Jesus. For them, the historical Jesus was always a model of life, constitutive not only for redemption but also especially for how to live. Christian faith always was and is multidimensional. Within that multidimensionality, the historicity of Jesus functions to secure the application of faith to practice.

Admittedly, I have not been talking about the historical Jesus, but associating him with our myths, guiding images, and projected hopes. The question of the historical Jesus serves here only as an aid: it is meant to help us distinguish between Jesus and our images of him, between what stems from Jesus and what comes from us.

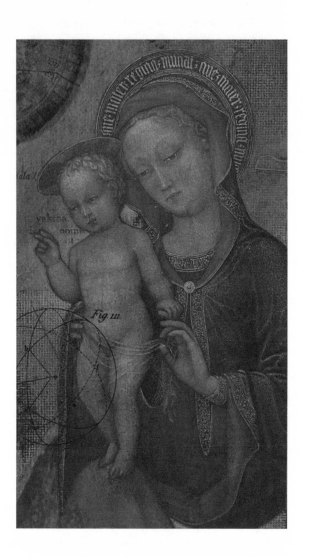

2

Jesus: His Life and His World

Ulrich Luz

C hristianity, like Judaism and Islam, is in great part a religion of the book. This is connected to the fact that there are certain historical events constitutive for Christianity that had to be told again and again, and interpreted again and again. Buddhism also is a religion of the book. But in its canonical texts, the life of Buddha Gautama plays nothing like the role played by Jesus' life in the New Testament canon. What is crucial, rather, is the Buddha's teaching. Furthermore, the Buddhist canon does not have the same fundamental significance as the canon in Christianity. Even in the history of the creation of the New Testament canon, we can see unique features that are important for the way Jesus is understood in Christianity.

Unique Features of the Development of the New Testament Canon

In comparison with the writing down of the traditions about Buddha Gautama, those about Jesus were recorded with lightning speed. Fewer than eighty years passed between the death of Jesus and the presumed date of completion of the latest New Testament writing, the Second Letter of Peter. This may have been something of an accident: Jesus himself did not write, any more than Gautama did. But in the Roman Empire of that time, written texts were much more common than in India at the time of Gautama. In addition, Paul and his letters contributed a great deal to the swift creation of the New Testament canon.

Nevertheless, it is striking that as early as the fourth decade after Jesus' death there was a clear need to secure the basis of the Christian proclamation, namely, the accounts of Jesus' work and his preaching. Mark's intention was to safeguard the *archē,* that is, the "beginning" or the "basis" of the church's preaching, through a written account of Jesus, similar to a biography (Mark 1:1). That he was not alone in his concern is evident from the fact that very quickly Matthew and especially Luke pursued the same course. Quite soon, about sixty years after Jesus' death, the Gospel of Matthew identified the church's proclamation, the "gospel," with Jesus' preaching: Matthew speaks of the "preaching of the kingdom" (Matt 4:23; 9:35), referring to Jesus' preaching, which is to be further proclaimed by the church. Jesus' life and preaching constitute the enduring basis for the church. Luke, the author of a two-volume historical monograph for educated Christian readers, aimed in his first book, about Jesus, to give assurance of the "reliability" of what Theophilus (his addressee, to whom he dedicated his book) had learned when he was being instructed. That is why he wrote a historical monograph (Luke 1:1–4). Matthew and Luke begin their accounts with the birth of Jesus; thus, in terms of their material, they are already offering a full-blown "biography." All three give evidence of a clear understanding that the concrete circumstances of Jesus' activity, his deeds and his death, are foundational for the church. Thus, there came to be an exclusive link between the church's preaching and teaching and the person and life of Jesus. These three writings, then, together with the Gospel of John, stand at the beginning of the canon in all its early forms.

In Buddhism the development was different. The process of writing down the tradition took place over a number of centuries. At the beginning and at the center were *not* the texts that speak of the Buddha's life.

The process of canonization of the gospels was essentially complete by the end of the second century. Except in Syria,[1] the canonicity of the four Gospels was established throughout the early Catholic Church around 200 C.E. From the late second century onward, the canonization of the texts also served as a marker of internal church divisions. The Marcionites had a different canon than the early Catholic Church. For Christian Gnostic communities and schools there were other gospels alongside the four canonical texts. The establishment of the wording of the canon coincided with the process of setting its limits. The history of texts in the late second and early third centuries shows us how the words of the New Testament, originally handed on rather freely, were increasingly stabilized through textual recensions.

Early interest in the biblical text is impressively documented by the very many manuscript fragments of the New Testament we possess from as early as the second and third centuries. Since the end of the second century, the discipline of "exegesis" has become more and more important in the church. The interpretation of Scripture, its literal and its spiritual-allegorical meaning, presupposes a stable and secure wording of the text. Origen, the great ecclesiastical exegete of the early third century, was therefore also a textual critic.

In Buddhism the development was not only much slower, but in part also very different. A unified canon was never established, and a final stabilization of the wording came very late.

Sources

The non-Christian sources for Jesus are sparse. A few ancient writers and a few passages from Jewish rabbinic texts mention him by name. The most important non-Christian source is the witness to Jesus by the Jewish historian Josephus (*Ant.* 18.63–64). This passage was edited by Christians, but in my opinion its original form can be reconstructed.[2] In any event, the non-Christian testimonies to Jesus show that Jesus was a historical figure who really lived. They give us important information on certain points, especially regarding his execution.

Most sources of information about Jesus are Christian—the canonical Gospels, as well as the other gospels listed in table 4.

Table 4   **The Christian Sources**

Biographical Gospels	
Gospel of Mark	
Before 70 C.E., from Rome	Little teaching material
Author: God-fearer or Gentile Christian	Emphasis on miracles, lack of understanding on the part of the disciples,
No infancy narrative	discipleship of suffering, Passion
No post-Easter appearance stories	
Gospel of Matthew	
80–90 C.E., from Syria	Infancy narratives and post-Easter
Author: Jewish Christian	appearance stories different from
Matthew apparently uses Mark and Q; has little special material	those in Luke
Sharp conflict with Israel's leaders (Matt 23)	Five discourses with teaching Jesus fulfills the Law and the prophets

Gospel of Luke

80–100 C.E.; place of composition uncertain (Rome?)

First part of a two-volume historical monograph (Luke-Acts)

Author: educated God-fearer

Luke uses Mark, Q, and other traditions

Infancy narratives and post-Easter appearance stories different from those in Matthew

Extensive special material; Luke is the most important source for Jesus

Jesus gathers the people of God, Israel.

Emphasis on miracles

Gospel of John

90–100 C.E., written in Asia Minor

Jewish-Christian in origin

Independent type of piety

Depends on the Synoptics only in concept and a few pieces of material

Logos Christology

Discourses, "I am" sayings

Author presents a "high" Christology: Jesus is the Father's Son coming "from above"

Of secondary significance as a source for Jesus

Other biographical gospels

Only fragments preserved, early 2nd century

Gospel of Peter

Jewish-Christian gospels

Papyrus Egerton 2

Of little importance as sources for Jesus

Sayings Gospels

Sayings Source Q

"Final version" c. 60 C.E.; successive growth

Origins: Palestine–Syria

Q comes from a Jewish Christianity that failed in its mission to Israel

Not a simple collection of sayings; rather a "half-gospel" with "biographizing" introduction

Individual collections and texts sometimes given a biographical introduction

No Passion narrative

Collection of traditional sayings for didactic and missionary purposes?

Son of Man sayings and final judgment emphasized in the structuring of the source

Was there a "Q community" with an individual profile, or is Q an "auxiliary" collection?

Important source for Jesus

Gospel of Thomas

Original Greek text, retained entirely in Coptic	No narratives
Final version early 2nd century, with successive growth	No apocalyptic sayings; very few sayings about the Son of Man; mystic-pantheistic Jesus-piety, with Gnostic features in the final phase
Earliest phases in 1st century, partly independent of the canonical gospels	Of secondary significance as a source for Jesus
Purely a collection of sayings	

Gospels of the Risen One

Teachings of the Risen One to selected disciples in instructional or dialogue form, e.g., *Dialogue of the Savior, Apocryphal Letter of James, Gospel of Mary*	Typical Gnostic form of gospel
Time: 2nd century and later	Of no importance as a source for Jesus

Infancy Gospels

E.g., *Protevangelium of James, Infancy Gospel of Thomas*	Important for popular piety, literature, and art
Time: end of 2nd century or later	Of no importance as a source for Jesus
Legendary	

Passion Gospels

E.g., *Gospel of Nicodemus, Acts of Pilate*	Important for popular piety, literature, and art
Time: 3rd century and later	Of no importance as a source for Jesus
Legendary	

The most important source of controversy among New Testament scholars is the significance to be given the noncanonical Gospel of Thomas as a source for reconstructing the preaching of Jesus. One current in research, which includes the majority of German-speaking scholars, emphasizes the Gnostic character of the final form of this gospel and suggests that it was written down in this form only in the second century.[3] These scholars are also inclined to emphasize the dependence of the Thomas tradition on the canonical gospels and the Sayings Source, Q, or at any rate to regard its traditions as secondary. Another trend in scholarship—represented primarily, but not exclusively, by

American exegetes—stresses that the traditions and literary character of the Gospel of Thomas mark it as independent of the canonical gospels. They emphasize that the preliminary stages of this gospel are to be found in the first century.[4] I do in fact accept that the tradition available to this gospel was not influenced to a great extent by the Synoptic tradition. However, it is difficult to reconstruct the preceding layers of the tradition found in the existing, Gnostic Gospel of Thomas. The piety of the communities behind the Gospel of Thomas is so unusual that I consider it similar to that behind the Gospel of John; both adapted the Jesus tradition to their own piety and used it only selectively. Thus, for me, the Gospel of Thomas is not a primary source for reconstructing Jesus.

The other important controversial question has to do with the Sayings Source, Q. Here it is striking that Jesus' sayings about the Son of Man or about judgment often stand at the end of separate complexes of tradition. They also form the conclusion of the whole source (Luke 17:23–37). Some scholars have concluded from this that they were added secondarily, that is, that the Jesus tradition was apocalypticized at a later stage.[5] This fits what we find in the Gospel of Thomas, which contains almost no judgment or Son of Man sayings. These scholars' explanation for this is that the early Christian Jesus missionaries, who were the source for Q, reacted to the rejection of the Jesus preaching in Israel with apocalyptic threats of judgment. The original Jesus tradition, they say, was generally free of such traits. Many other scholars, myself included, find this unlikely. We cannot guess, from the position of individual texts within Q, what their age may be. A secondary apocalypticizing of the Jesus tradition would be contrary to the history of development of early Christianity, in which, generally speaking, the expectation of an apocalyptic end faded, the anticipation of an imminent end was transformed into awaiting the end-time, and apocalyptic images and ideas became increasingly rare. Moreover, other studies have shown that a considerable number of the judgment and Son of Man sayings may very well go back to Jesus.[6]

Present State of Research

These different evaluations of the sources yield different pictures of Jesus. In the United States, currently the center of Jesus research, two basic types of Jesus images stand in opposition to each other. On the one side there is the generally unapocalyptic Jesus of the Jesus Seminar. Here Jesus is regarded as a "new human being,"[7] a rebel, a nonconformist Jewish rural philosopher, a kind of Jewish Cynic.[8] The counter-position, in a number of different ways, sets Jesus' eschatological preaching in the foreground—that is, his message of the coming reign of God, the coming restoration of Israel, God's unalterable love, and the approaching judgment. Here we find the important Jesus books by Geza Vermes, E. P. Sanders, John Meier, and Dale C. Allison.[9] One might say that this trend in scholarship reveals the revived and increasing influence of the Jesus image in the so-called religious-historical school, such as that of Albert Schweitzer.[10]

Jesus research on the European continent, especially in German-speaking countries, also generally emphasizes the dominance of the eschatological in Jesus' preaching: The in-breaking reign of God is manifested as love for the disadvantaged and poor of Israel; God's judgment shows the reverse side of this when it is rejected.[11] German-speaking Jesus scholarship shows the continuing influence of the interpretation presented by Rudolf Bultmann and his students, whereby Jesus' apocalyptic and eschatological statements are studied for their significance for human existence; this, of course, drained them of some of their strangeness.[12]

I have no intention of drawing a complete sketch of the life of Jesus here. That would be difficult, simply because outside the Passion account we do not know the "framework of Jesus' story,"[13] and the numerous individual episodes familiar to us from the Gospels cannot be put in chronological order. Therefore, I will simply point to some individual items that are important for a comparison to Gautama Buddha.

Jesus in His Political and Social Context

Unlike the Buddha, Jesus did not belong to the upper class. According to Mark 6:3, he came from a large family in the little village of Nazareth and was an artisan by trade; thus, he was somewhere in the lower or middle classes. Jesus' connection to the "little people" appears, for example, in his healings and exorcisms. In the society of that time it was primarily the poor, who could not afford doctors, who depended on miraculous healers. It appears also in the choice of imagery in his stories. They mainly tell about small farmers, housewives, fisherfolk, fathers, day laborers, tenants, small and middle-layer capitalists, people who build houses, and the great dreams of little people (Matt 13:44–46).

Like the Buddha, Jesus also gave up his orderly life, his trade, and his family and led an itinerant life in poverty. He certainly did not leave his family because he was sated with luxurious living; correspondingly, he does not reveal any ascetic tendencies in the strict sense—apart, perhaps, from a brief phase as disciple of John the Baptizer. Nevertheless, it is clear that his abandonment of family and profession was a free decision and was not done under the direct pressure of a social crisis. Jesus, as an artisan, probably did not come from utterly insecure social circumstances. A village artisan was more certain of an income than were the small farmers, who were constantly threatened by high land taxes, drought, bad harvests, and the greed of large landowners. In Galilee at that time, with its population made up primarily of very poor small farmers, there were already signs of evasive tendencies (for example, a man might become a "robber," that is, a Zealot), but nothing indicates that Jesus' dropping out was brought on by poverty.[14] Jesus' family then made an attempt to bring him back home, where he apparently would have been assured of support.

Jesus was not a city dweller. He worked in rural upper Galilee, an area populated by Jews. During his public activity he does not seem to have entered the Hellenistic or Hellenized cities in the near vicinity, such as Tiberias, Sepphoris, Ptolemais, or Scythopolis. That is striking, because he apparently was not interested in drawing boundaries between Israel and non-Jews, a division that was reinforced, for example, by male circumcision or the purity laws. He evidently knew nothing of any city other than the holy city Jerusalem. Jesus' origins in rural Galilee played a distinct part in various aspects of his preaching—for example, in his attitude toward the Temple and the purity laws. It was not that Jesus, or Galileans as a group, were hostile to the Temple! But there is evidence to show that apparently, among the poor people of Galilee, the Temple with its array of taxes was regarded as a financial burden and that tithes were not always treated with great exactitude.[15] Likewise, prescriptions for purity and purification were not so easily carried out in villages as in city dwellings, quite apart from the fact that they were often simply unknown. On the whole, Jesus appears to have distanced himself quite clearly from ritual ordinances. The Temple was not the center of his piety. In all that, he is not so different from Gautama Buddha.

Special Aspects of the Life of Jesus

We do not know the exact dates of Jesus' life. The year of his birth is uncertain because we remain unsure whether we should accord greater credibility to the birth stories in Matthew or those in Luke. According to the former, Jesus was born under Herod the Great, thus prior to 4 B.C.E. (cf. Matt 2:1, 16); according to the latter, he was born at the time of the first Roman tax census, probably the one that took place after the deposition of Herod's son Archelaus in the year 6 C.E. (cf. Luke 2:1–2). Both the birth stories are legendary and lack historical credibility; there are almost no overlaps between them.[16] The year of Jesus' death depends on whether one gives preference to the (more probable) Passion chronology in the Gospel of John or the one in the Synoptic Gospels: either 30 C.E. (the most likely date) or 27 C.E.

According to Luke 3:23, Jesus was about thirty years old when he began his public activity, which lasted only a very short time, perhaps as little as a single year. Unlike the Buddha, Jesus died while still a young man. The short period of his activity did not permit him to consolidate and institutionalize his movement. The process of consolidation was hindered not only by his expectation of the imminent coming of the reign of God, but also by the brevity of his life.

It is also important that the Jesus movement bears many of the features of a youth religion. The Jesus traditions speak of a conflict with the father and mother, not, as with the Buddha, a conflict with children (Matt 10:35). Jesus' sayings about discipleship deal first of all with leaving father and mother (Luke 14:26; Mark 10:29; cf. Matt 8:21).

Corresponding to this is the fact that there are also reports of a conflict between Jesus and his parents and family. It is true that we do not have such marvelous stories about that as in the legends of the Buddha's departure from Kapilavastu. The most important tradition is the little pericope in Mark 3:21, 31–35, which tells how Jesus' mother—his father may already have died—comes with his siblings and tries to take him back to the shelter of his family, because they say he is crazy. They evidently did not agree with Jesus' unusual religious path. This fits also with the rejection of Jesus in his home village of Nazareth, where people knew him (Mark 6:1–6).

All the gospels report that Jesus' activity began in association with John the Baptizer. That is, we know his "teacher." John was an ascetic and prophet of the end-time who preached in the desert, proclaiming the imminence of God's judgment (Luke 3:7–9) and sealing those who repented with a "baptism for the forgiveness of sins." Jesus was baptized by him. But his relationship to John is not simply that of a faithful disciple: On the one hand he took up John's preaching of judgment and carried it further, but on the other hand he deliberately distanced himself from John by doing his work not in the desert but in the land of Israel itself. Above all, however, he spoke of the coming reign of God and of his own work as its beginning. John, in contrast, did not yet belong to the time of the reign of God (Luke 7:28; 16:16).

Jesus' activity as exorcist and healer of the sick is also part of the reign of God. These are among the best-attested facts known about his life. They are confirmed not only by the abundance of tradition about them, but also by the fact that they come from very different strands of tradition.[17] Thus, Jesus was a charismatic. In contrast, we have no tradition of healings by John the Baptizer—an indication that the tradition did not confuse the two figures.

Jesus gathered disciples around him. With them he moved through Galilee as an itinerant preacher (cf. Luke 9:58), proclaiming the reign of God (Luke 9:60, 62; cf. Mark 1:18). According to the tradition in Luke 10:1–16 (cf. Mark 6:7–13), parts of which are ancient, Jesus also sent his disciples throughout Israel to preach the reign of God. Thus, they were more colleagues than disciples. The audience for Jesus' preaching was the whole people, especially the simple, uneducated women and men of Galilee. The people appear to play a greater part in the Jesus traditions than in the traditions about the Buddha.

Unlike Gautama Buddha, Jesus was single. This is very remarkable for a Jew, because marrying and begetting children was considered a commandment of obligation. What does his single status mean? Jesus was certainly no misogynist, and he did not exclude women from his inner circle. He did not reject marriage; rather, he regarded it as so holy that he forbade divorce (Matt 5:32; Luke 16:18). Most helpful, I think, is a reference to Matt 19:12: "There are eunuchs who have made themselves eunuchs for the sake of the kingdom of heaven." This is about freely chosen celibacy for the sake of God's reign. This fits with Mark 12:25, according to which there will be no more marriages in the reign of God after the resurrection of the dead. Thus, we can understand Jesus' celibacy in terms of his eschatological proclamation of the reign of God. I interpret it as a kind of "symbolic asceticism," similar to his and his disciples' poverty and their refusal to practice a trade or profession.

At the end of his brief public activity, Jesus went with his disciples to the Passover feast in Jerusalem. Probably he did not do so without a purpose, and he was most likely aware of the risk he was running. There are many reasons to believe that we must interpret his death as part of his mission. It is different with the Buddha: at a great age, after surviving a severe illness, he entered into *Parinirvāṇa*.

Jesus as an Individual

The time of Gautama Buddha in India was a period of incipient religious individualization. The same is true for the time of Jesus. Jesus' spiritual ancestors were the prophets, who as individuals commissioned by God stood up against the rulers and the dominant trends. At the latest since the encounter with Hellenism in the third to second centuries B.C.E., there was a dispute in Israel about what being a Jew meant; the confrontation with Hellenistic pressures to assimilate led to conflicts within Judaism. The religiously motivated Zealots and the orders at Qumran are examples of how, at that time, one might become a rebel for the sake of fidelity to God. Other religious groups as well, such as the community of the Pharisees, called for a deliberate decision: people had to join them or accept their interpretation of the Torah. Alongside them were apocalyptic groups, which we can imagine as a type of "pietistic" circles of the devout, who in faithfulness to God awaited the end of the evil world. Thus, there was a spectrum of religious choices.

Jesus' biography bears some clearly individual traits. They are attested by his break with his family, his activity as an itinerant charismatic, his refusal to exercise his trade or to live in a family, his special claim to authority, and finally his path to Jerusalem and to death. In his marked individuality he matches other great figures who, posthumously, became "religious founders."

The path Jesus chose for himself within his world of multiple religious possibilities was not that of asceticism. Jesus did not stay with John the Baptizer at the Jordan; he abstained from marrying, but not from eating and drinking. His food was not locusts and wild honey (cf. Matt 11:18–19). It is true that he stopped practicing his trade, gave up his fixed abode, and went preaching and healing throughout the land, but he did not return to the desert. Rather than joining a group of the utterly pure or the utterly obedient, he lived among the people and preached the reign of God to them. In his interpretation of the Torah, too, in which he insisted on righteousness, mercy, and fidelity and not on tithing (Matt 23:23–24) or purity regulations, he applied the will of God to ordinary people.

In many ways this recalls the Buddha's "Middle Way." Jesus and Gautama Buddha had in common that they turned away from those who had been the religious elite; they democratized religion. Both also turned away from the radical-elite path of asceticism. With Jesus this turning to the people had to do with a new experience of God that could be described in terms of "the reign of

God" or "God as Father." At first glance I do not see anything comparable to this in the Buddha. Nevertheless, the path they followed and the way to which they invited people are similar in many ways.

Response / *Axel Michaels*
The Word of God and the Silence of the Buddha

The process of canonization took place in Buddhism much more slowly than in Christianity. Probably it was the monastic praxis associated with a command to preach that developed the need for a formally regulated textual tradition. The *Pāli* canon, written in a language that is probably an artificial mixed dialect formed from a number of middle Indo-Aryan languages that are not yet sufficiently studied, is only one—though the oldest one—of many canons from the various Buddhist schools. There is no primitive canon, as was previously supposed. In addition, *Pāli* is not a unified language that can be given a close regional definition; the concept itself comes from the seventeenth century.

However, what is crucial in this process is that Buddhism never developed a unifying sacred scripture like the Bible for itself. Buddhist teaching is a product of the ancient oral art of debate, in which there was a constantly renewed struggle for truth conducted—with the approval of the founder—in regional languages rather than in the sacred language of Sanskrit. The Buddha, like Jesus, could not write, and unlike Jesus, he probably had no written alphabet available.[18] Still, none of that was sufficient to prevent a reliable tradition from developing, because the art of oral transmission of texts had developed to the utmost, precisely in India. Above all, however, the Buddha was not an essentialist or a narrow-minded dogmatician. Someone like him, who denied the existence of a soul or a self, could scarcely insist on the eternal truth of some formulation of words. An enlightened one, he said, neither agrees nor disagrees; he does not discuss; he has no standpoint (*MN* I.500.32–34; *SN* III.138.27–29). A popular parable speaks of teaching as a boat that one leaves behind after crossing the river. Consequently, he also foresaw the end of his teaching: it will endure a thousand years, or only five hundred years if women are admitted to the order (*Vin* II.256.13–16). Therefore, the Buddha did not insist on fidelity to the letter of his teaching, which for him had only one flavor: that of redemption.

Gautama Buddha and Jesus see the supreme reality—the reign of God or *Nirvāṇa*—as not really accessible to human understanding, but they could not agree on the form in which this supreme reality is perceptible and communicable. In Christianity the Word, the *Logos*, is probably still part of the supreme reality, which is expressed through it. In contrast, in Buddhism the word also and in particular belongs to what is conditioned, mortal, suffering. Thus, the Buddha is not silent for reasons of inability, but for epistemological reasons. For him, the supreme reality does not need words, neither God's word nor human word. If it were dependent on those, it could not be the supreme reality. Mystical movements in Christianity, too, as we know, opened themselves to similar ideas. Therefore, in both religions silence has a high status, and it is only in (meditative) silence that Buddhism and Christianity may ultimately find each other.[19]

It is true that the Buddha did not desire to conceal anything, even God (*DN* II.100.2–4). He was no Cynic. What he said was all that he had to say. But neither is his silence nihilism. He did not mean to say that beyond or in the hereafter there is nothing, for he did speak about *Nirvāṇa*:

> Wrongly, meanly, falsely, and baselessly some ascetics and Brahmins accuse
> me, saying that Gautama, the ascetic, is a nihilist and preaches extinguishing,
> destruction, and nothingness [of the self]. I am not that at all, and I do
> not say such things. Today, you monks, as before I preach only the one
> (teaching): Suffering, destruction of suffering… [then follow the Four Noble
> Truths] (*MN* I.140.10–15).

The Buddha could not and would not preach a world that is not from this world, because he thought that this (or that) world (and thus God) cannot be grasped in words. His silence about this world was, as Raimundo Panikkar and Claus Oetke rightly indicate,[20] often an ontic and eloquent (Oetke calls it a "significative") silence.

Part Two
The Reign of God and Nirvāṇa

3

Jesus' Preaching
and the Reign of God

Ulrich Luz

According to the Gospel of Mark, Jesus began his preaching this way: "The time is fulfilled, and the kingdom of God has come near; repent, and believe in the good news!" (Mark 1:15). This summary is the work of the evangelist and shows where he sees the center of Jesus' preaching to be.

The Hebrew/Aramaic expression *malkut,* normally rendered in Greek as *basileia* and in English as "kingdom," does not mean a kingdom in the sense of a territory. It ought to be translated in a more dynamic and functional way; its intent is to say that God reigns and people are subject to God's rule. The closest translation is "reign." This is not a detail, but an expression in words of the fundamental fact that the Old Testament biblical and Jewish tradition makes no statements about God's being, God's existence, essence, or characteristics. Rather, it speaks of God's dealings with human beings, the people Israel, and the whole world. Nearly all the fundamental statements about God in Jewish tradition are dynamic expressions about God's actions, and at the same time they are statements of relationship applying to God *and* human beings, God *and* the people, God *and* the world. "The reign of God" is a prime example of this, but the same is true, for example, of the expression that is so central in Paul's writings, "the righteousness of God." Jesus, then, belongs within this Jewish biblical tradition. He can only talk about God by saying what God *does.* Therefore, history and experience are fundamental categories of biblical thought.

Malkut Yhwh, God's reign, is a biblical-Jewish core statement. Of its very nature it is closely bound up with the Temple in Jerusalem, where God was King, enthroned on the cherubim:

> The Lord is king; let the peoples tremble!
>   He sits enthroned upon the cherubim; let the earth quake!
> The Lord is great in Zion. (Ps 99:1–2)

Therefore, sayings about God's reign or the description of God as ruler or king in the Psalms and liturgical texts such as the Sabbath Songs of Qumran[1] are very frequent. In rabbinic texts "the reign of God" is quite often linked to the speaking of Israel's fundamental confession of Yhwh, the only God (Deut 6:4). Confessing God, the one God, who from the time of the Babylonian exile was increasingly regarded as ruler of the entire world, now means "taking up the yoke of the reign of God."

Jesus combined many statements about the reign of God with indications of imminence in time: it "has come near" (Mark 1:15). "Your kingdom come," the Our Father prays (Matt 6:10). One saying of Jesus even proclaims that the reign of God "has come to you" (Luke 11:20). Thus, for Jesus the reign of God is the central expression of the hoped-for and longed-for future. Jesus shared that hope with most of the Israelites of his time, who experienced the present as a time of oppression, foreign rule, and their own powerlessness. Therefore "the reign of God" became an expression of hope, especially in prayer. Thus, for example, in the Eighteen Benedictions, prayed daily, the eleventh reads:

> Bring back our judges as of old
> and our counselors as in the beginning,
> and swiftly become king over us, you alone.[2]

Here the "reign of God" means especially the restoration of the good old primeval time of Israel. The Kaddish prayer, which Jesus' "Our Father" prayer apparently emulates, formulates this more openly and urgently:

> May his reign come in your lifetime
> and in your days and the life of the whole house of Israel
> swiftly and soon.[3]

Here, as with Jesus, we find intense expectation of the coming end. Above all in apocalyptic texts, the hope for a future reign of God becomes anticipation of something wholly new. The Most High will appear, shake the earth, cast down the mountains, darken the sun, push back the sea; he will appear openly, punish the Gentiles, destroy idols, and elevate Israel to the heavens (*As. Mos.* 10). Even belief in creation is no longer of any significance here: The coming of the reign of God means the coming of a new world.

Gershom Scholem sees Judaism as a whole as a tension-filled interaction between tradition and new revelation, and Jewish messianism as an interweaving of restoration and utopia.[4] In some streams of Judaism the weight falls on the side of tradition and restoration, in others on that of new revelation and utopia. In Temple-centered Essene Judaism the balance lay on the side of tradition and restoration, but the same was true of Torah-centered Pharisaism and later of rabbinic Judaism. The balance tended toward new revelation and utopia for many prophets, and again later for apocalypticism or Jewish mysticism. John the Baptizer and Jesus also belong within these two strands of Judaism. For John, the preacher of judgment, the election of Israel and descent from Abraham no longer offered security, for God can raise up children of Abraham even from stones (Matt 3:9). For Jesus, too, God's fundamental ordinances of salvation in history are much less weighty than God's hoped-for new future. He scarcely ever speaks of the Exodus and says very little about Israel's election. In his antitheses, he goes beyond God's ancient revelation at Sinai. Even the Temple, for him, is among the things that will be destroyed (Mark 14:58). Torah and prophets belong to the former age that ended with John the Baptizer (Luke 16:16). But with himself, Jesus, something new is beginning—the reign of God.

The Future of the Reign of God

Like others, Jesus also prays for the coming of the kingdom (Matt 6:10). Unlike the Eighteen Benedictions, his prayer does not speak of any concrete hopes he associates with the coming of the reign of God. But that does not mean his hope lacked concreteness. First let me indicate where the center of Jesus' hope for the reign of God did *not* lie. It was not associated with the idea of Israel's rule over the nations and the elimination of foreign rule, so important in many Jewish texts from Daniel 7:9–25 to the Eighteen Benedictions. Rather, Jesus formulates much more generally and broadly: "The first will be last" (Mark 10:31); "Those who humble themselves will be exalted" (Luke 14:11). So it is about a reversal of the current power relationships. The "last" are the little people—for example, the children, who in the ancient world were for the most part not even regarded as full persons

(Mark 10:15).[5] The "last" are the poor, to whom the reign of God belongs; the weeping, who will find consolation; and the hungry, who will be filled (Luke 6:20–21). The rich will find it harder to get in than for a camel to pass through the eye of a needle (Mark 10:25). Jesus' participation in the life of the poor probably accounts for the fact that the most important image of hope he adopts from the biblical tradition is that of a good meal. In the future reign of God, people will dine (Matt 8:11–12). Even during his last meal with his disciples, Jesus looks forward, full of hope, to his next meal in the reign of God: "Truly I tell you, I will never again drink of the fruit of the vine until that day when I drink it new in the kingdom of God" (Mark 14:25). Jesus compares the reign of God to a banquet at which poor nobodies surprisingly receive a fine repast (Luke 14:16–24). Related to this is the image of the marriage feast that Jesus uses in his so-called parable of the ten virgins (Matt 25:1–12). The reign of God reflects the hopes of little people, the underdogs of their society.

The Future Reign of God Is Already Beginning

What makes Jesus so unusual, in comparison with other Jews of his time, is his conviction that God's longed-for future is already breaking through. His conviction was not rooted in the cultic piety of the Temple; Jesus did not speak of a God who is forever enthroned in the Temple upon the cherubim, and whose presence can be experienced in the Temple's worship. For him, rather, the world is ruled by the Evil One, the Devil, by demons, sickness, and injustice. Luke 10:18 probably recalls Jesus' visionary experience: "I watched Satan fall from heaven like a flash of lightning." Elsewhere Jesus speaks of the devil who has been conquered by one stronger than he and has lost his armor (Luke 11:21–22). The demons are the devil's bodyguards. Therefore Jesus can say, "If it is by the finger of God that I cast out the demons, then the kingdom of God has come to you" (Luke 11:20). Because the devil has been conquered and the reign of God has broken in, Jesus can drive out the demons. In this way people will be healed and reintegrated into society, since the poorest people suffer illness both as a loss of identity and a loss of community. In Jewish hope there will be no sick, infirm, or possessed people in God's new world.[6] Jesus was an exorcist and a miraculous healer. (Miracles are also reported of the Buddha,[7] but in contrast to the stories of Jesus, these miracles are for the most part not, or only indirectly, in service to poor people. Rather, they express the power of meditation.)

Thus, the great reversal in the world, the future reign of God, has already begun. Jesus sees here the decisive difference between himself and John the Baptizer. The old, the time of the Torah and the prophets, lasted until John (Luke 16:16), but then the time of the reign of God began; and the least in the reign of God is greater than John (Luke 7:28). God's reign is visible in signs in the work of Jesus, and in this sense, the reign of God is "among you" (Luke 17:21) (*not* "within you!").[8]

Apart from exorcisms and healings, there are other signs of the in-breaking of the reign of God. It is constantly said of Jesus that he ate with other people; in fact, in contrast to the ascetic John, he was labeled a glutton and a drunkard (Luke 7:34). In the post-Easter traditions, people transferred to him stories about the feeding of gigantic crowds of people with an abundance of bread fit for Paradise, as in the time of Elisha (Mark 6:34–44 and in several other places).[9] The anticipation of the reign of God in the Last Supper shows that he associated his meals with the coming of the reign of God (Mark 14:25): in them everyone will be full and happy. Jesus indicates the degree of happiness by using the image of a marriage: "The wedding guests cannot fast while the bridegroom is with them, can they?" (Mark 2:19). A wedding means celebrating, eating, drinking. Here the image is applied to Jesus' own work, but he also uses it for the coming reign of God (Matt 25:1–12), which is beginning with him.

The future reign of God is open to everyone. Jesus shares the Jewish expectation that in the end-time the Gentiles will make pilgrimage to Zion and there pay honor to God and Israel: "Many will come from east and west and will eat with Abraham and Isaac and Jacob in the kingdom of heaven" (Matt 8:11). However, in contrast to most Jewish texts, he shifts the accent by *not* speaking of Zion and *not* saying that the Gentiles who come will pay homage to Israel. Apparently, as far as he is concerned, there will be no boundaries in the coming reign of God between Israel and the Gentiles. That is not yet the case in his own activity. Only by way of exception is the barrier overcome by people like the Syro-Phoenician woman (Mark 7:24–30) and the centurion at Capernaum (Matt 8:5–13). That is why they were so clearly remembered afterward.

But it is significant that Jesus drew no boundaries within Israel itself. He placed Israel's marginal people—the poor, the disadvantaged, women, toll collectors, and prostitutes—at the center; he integrated sick people, unclean people, and possessed people, and he apparently even included Samaritans within the people of God. All this is a symbolic indicator pointing to the future openness, the lack of boundaries, within the reign of God.

Jesus' Activity as the Beginning of the Reign of God

In all this, Jesus took up the experiences of little, marginalized people, the people on the margins of Israel, the great majority of little people—their sense of exclusion, their deep longings. In his work he lifted them up and joined them to the magnificent hope for the coming of the reign of God. That is why they are of such overwhelming importance: "Blessed are the eyes that see what you see! For I tell you that many prophets and kings desired to see what you see, but did not see it, and to hear what you hear, but did not hear it" (Luke 10:23–24). This new beginning is happening in his own work.

There is something illusionary in Jesus' assurance: he expands the significance of his own symbolic actions to infinity by linking them to the coming reign of God. After all, a couple of exorcisms do nothing for all the other sick people beyond a glimmer of personal hope! A couple of meals for poor down-and-outers do not resolve the social question, and a couple of impressive stories do even less. Jesus himself must have known how tiny this beginning was and how inadequate to the mighty thing that is coming, namely, the universal reign of God. A hint of this knowledge is reflected in two parables of a kind Jesus rarely told, relating directly to the reign of God: the parable of the mustard seed and the parable of the leaven (Luke 13:18–21). From something very tiny, a mustard seed, grows a huge bush that recalls the world-tree. From a very ordinary bit of leaven kept by a housewife comes a giant quantity of bread dough, enough to feed a whole village. The image of the leaven is especially alienating because it was not found in the tradition and is totally unfitting for comparison with the longed-for reign of God. Jesus must be thinking of his own work when he speaks of the mustard seed and the leaven, so he inserts his work into the coming of the reign of God.

Immediate Anticipation of the End

The Gospels often say that the reign of God "is near" (Mark 1:15; Luke 10:9, 11). Does this formula come from Jesus? Jesus would, in that case, have anticipated that the end would come soon, as many of those around him also did. In terms of the criteria of context and plausibility of the effect,[10] this is highly probable. There had always been an expectation of a rapid end in various Jewish groups, from the book of Daniel through the *Assumption of Moses* and John the Baptizer to the Zealots. It flamed up again and again, especially in crisis situations. An imminent end was expected in early Christianity, too, especially expressed by Paul (1 Thess 4:13–5:11, among other passages), the book of Revelation, and some sayings in the Synoptic tradition. I leave open whether the clearest testimonies—namely, the so-called predictions of the end in Mark 9:1 ("There are some standing here who will not taste death until…the kingdom of God has come with power"), Mark 13:30 ("This generation will not pass away until all these things have taken place"), and Matthew 10:23 ("You will not have gone through all the towns of Israel before the Son of Man comes")—go back to Jesus, or only to the early communities. But a clear indication that Jesus also shared this kind of imminent expectation comes from two other passages. One is the parable of the fig tree in Luke 13:6–9, in which the barren fig tree is granted one more year of grace before it is cut down, that is, before the judgment. The other passage is the eschatological anticipation at the Last Supper (Mark 14:25), formulated as a kind of vow of renunciation. Such a vow would be remarkable if Jesus had not felt assured that he would soon again drink of the fruit of the vine with his disciples.

Such assurance is impressive. How did Jesus come by it? Something else is striking in what Jesus says about the reign of God: he talks of it as if it were an active subject. It "has come near" (Mark 1:15). It "has come to you" (Luke 11:20). "Your kingdom come" (Luke 11:2). It "is among you" (Luke 17:21). Apparently for Jesus the reign of God is an event in itself, something that affects human beings but is not determined or brought about by them; it has its own power. The little parable in Mark about the seed growing by itself makes this especially clear. After the farmer has thrown the seed on the ground he goes home and sleeps and wakes, day and night, and the seed grows without his knowing it. "The earth produces of itself" (Mark 4:26–29). What does that mean? The coming of the reign of God, apparently, cannot be a human task or a matter for human concern. It comes by itself. God brings it, and God alone. There is an amazing trust in God within such ordinary-looking statements. This trust appears in a similar fashion in other parts of Jesus' preaching—for example, in his unconditional assurance that God hears prayer (Matt 7:7–11).

Jesus as Preacher of Judgment

Jesus speaks remarkably often about the approaching final judgment. Quite a few of his parables are about a reckoning or a harvest, both of them traditional images for judgment. Others warn of the day of judgment that comes suddenly and surprisingly. Add to these a great many words of warning and other sayings about judgment. This side of Jesus' message is not very popular; many people are only too glad to suppress it, for example, by saying that such sayings do not come from Jesus.[11] But it is absolutely impossible to dispute that the core of the numerous sayings about the end-time and the judgment stems from Jesus.

The approaching judgment is closely connected to the coming reign of God. In some parables it is the reverse side of God's reign. In the parable of the great feast, the guests who were first invited remain, at the end, outside the door (Luke 14:24), just like the so-called foolish virgins in the parable of the bridegroom at the marriage feast (Matt 25:11–12). Jesus speaks prophetic words of warning that are quite pointedly about judgment—for example, the saying about the Son of Man in Luke 17:26–30, which compares the coming of the Son of Man with the catastrophes of the Flood and of Sodom and Gomorrah:

> Just as it was in the days of Noah, so too it will be in the days of the Son of Man. They were eating and drinking, and marrying and being given in marriage, until the day Noah entered the ark, and the flood came and destroyed all of them. Likewise, just as it was in the days of Lot: they were eating and drinking, buying and selling, planting and building, but on the day that Lot left Sodom, it rained fire and sulfur from heaven and destroyed all of them.

It is obvious that Jesus thinks of the final judgment as a cosmic catastrophe, not simply as a judgment within history. He seldom reveals how he imagines the judgment of the world; the little we have retained has apocalyptic and cosmic dimensions, as in the dreadful warning in Matthew 24:40–41: "Then two will be in the field; one will be taken and one will be left. Two women will be grinding meal together; one will be taken and one will be left." The righteous will evidently be taken away, the unrighteous destroyed on the earth. Jesus probably thought of the judgment as the portal to the fulfillment of the reign of God.[12] In any case, for him the reign of God is not simply the continuation, improvement, and perfection of the world; its accomplishment involves the world's ending.

Interestingly, we can observe some features in the judgment sayings that are very similar to the sayings about the reign of God. I want to draw particular attention to two of these:

First, the judgment, like the reign of God, is in a certain sense already present. It, too, is being symbolically accomplished by Jesus and his disciples. In the mission discourse, the disciples Jesus sends out with the message about the reign of God are not only instructed to heal the sick, drive out demons, and so make visible and tangible the *shalom* of the coming reign of God (Luke 10:9), but also, wherever they are not received, to publicly shake the dust from their feet as a sign of judgment (Luke 10:11): "On that day [that is, on the day when the reign of God comes] it will be more tolerable for Sodom than for that town" (Luke 10:12). Jesus himself acts in much the same way: From him we have "woes" against, for example, Chorazin, Bethsaida, and Capernaum, places that did not allow themselves to be brought to repentance by his miracles (Luke 10:13–15). A woe is more than a threat or an announcement of judgment; in a certain sense it anticipates the evil to come. Thus, with Jesus, the symbolic presence of the approaching reign of God and the symbolic presence of the coming judgment correspond.[13]

A second feature of the judgment sayings is that not only the coming of the reign of God, but also the judgment itself, is connected to Jesus' present activity. This is first evident from the fact that it depends on one's decision about *Jesus* whether one will withstand the judgment or not. The people of Chorazin, Bethsaida, and Capernaum come to judgment because they did not let themselves be moved by *Jesus'* miracles (Matt 11:20–24). According to the parable of the two who built houses (Luke 6:47–49), withstanding the final judgment depends on not only hearing Jesus' words, but also following them. Thus, the response to Jesus is decisive for the judgment. Jesus says the same thing in his Son of Man saying in Luke 12:8–9: "And I tell you, everyone who acknowledges me before others, the Son of Man also will acknowledge before the angels of God; but whoever denies me before others will be denied before the angels of God." So it appears that his own work is inaugurating the world judgment. There is a structural analogy between his proclamation of the reign of God and his proclamation of judgment.[14] In all this, the distance from the Buddha is very great indeed.

The Reign of God and Nirvāṇa

When we compare Jesus and the Buddha, at first only contrasts appear:

First, Jesus' concern is with *God's* reign. He is sustained by an unconditional trust that *God* will bring about God's reign. God's action precedes Jesus' own action and sustains it. Jesus' mission rests on the experience of and hope for the working of another, God, a counterpart. This experience and hope give Jesus an immediate assurance that he himself is not responsible for, that he need not verify for himself. *God* loves human beings, especially the underprivileged and those who are, religiously speaking, the "least" in Israel. *God* hears their prayers. *God* gives healing and breaks the power of the demons. All that is the beginning of God's coming reign, when God will make the lowest to be the highest and the last to be the first, when tears will be dried and the hungry satisfied. All this is what God will do. God's reign will come by itself.

In Buddhism it is entirely different. The gods are mere spectators of the Buddha's path. Since they *are* and live in a happiness that is imagined as almost earthly in nature, they themselves are in need of redemption.

Second, with Jesus the reign of God is connected to the fullness of life. It is precisely not the extinction of life, but hope for its fulfillment. Jesus' proclamation of the reign of God reflects the deep longings of poor and marginalized people—longings for health, wholeness, self-identity that is not determined from without, community, satiety, openness, the removal of boundaries, righteousness, *shalom*. It is no accident that its meaning was described in the early Jesus tradition, perhaps even by Jesus himself, as "life" (cf. Mark 9:45; 10:17; Luke 16:25; etc.). For individuals, in any case, the reign of God meant "gaining life" (Mark 8:35).

How distant from this does *Nirvāna* appear to be, when described, as it must be, as liberation from life, the extinction of life!

A third contrast is that hope for the reign of God has a cosmic dimension. The hope that individuals associate with it for themselves is at the same time expanded into a hope for the whole world. "The reign of God" means that God—who in Israel's belief is the only God and ruler of the whole world— takes possession and accomplishes that rule. It is the question of world rule, which in the face of the present experience of reality is answered contrary to fact. Therefore, the hope for the reign of God is much more than an individual perspective.

In early Buddhism the question of world rule in particular was an illusionary and preliminary question that faded and vanished in the face of *Nirvāna*. In contrast to Jesus, the Buddha's ambitions were much narrower and more realistic. He shows individuals a not impractical path out of the constraints of the world.

Fourth, Jesus understood his own actions as the symbolic anticipation of the reign of God. In doing this he inflated his work enormously and attributed to himself an immense significance by linking himself with the reign of God.

In this he is far more than simply one in the long series of prophets, more than a perhaps quite successful minor exorcist, more than a gifted Wisdom teacher or a charismatic in direct contact with God. By regarding his own actions as the symbolic beginning of the longed-for reign of God, he ties God to himself.

In contrast, the attainment of Buddhahood probably means ultimately that the Buddha himself becomes unimportant. His path is simply the demonstration of the path for all. His answers to the questions posed to him could ultimately be nothing more than indications that the questions people ask are preliminary.

Finally, Jesus' preaching of judgment also is enormously far from Buddha's teaching. The end of history and of human existence is not only life in the reign of God, but the *duality* of life and destruction. Neither of these things has anything in common with extinction, with *Nirvāna*.

In light of the idea of judgment, the retrospective effects on present life of what is to come also are completely different. While the Buddhist experiences the provisionality of earthly life and especially of himself or herself in contrast to *Nirvāna*, the thought of judgment intensifies the significance of *this* life and *this* world. While the perspective of *Nirvāna* draws the Buddhist away from this world, the thought of judgment sharply reminds the Christian that what matters is what people do here and now.

Also related to the idea of judgment and to *Nirvāna* is the fact that the meaning of Jesus Christ and that of Gautama Buddha are completely different: While the latter goes before others on the path to *Nirvāna* and there is dissolved as a self, the exalted Christ is enthroned as Lord and judge of the world. The distance between him and the Buddha could not be greater.

Self-Critical Questioning of Christian Faith

For me, Jesus' preaching of the reign of God poses critical questions for Christianity. It seems clear that we cannot go on preaching the coming of the reign of God with the assurance that Jesus showed. It is not only the problem of imminent expectation; it is also that Jesus' hope for the coming of the reign of God has remained completely unfulfilled. The reign of God has not come.

The earliest post-Easter Christianity lived out of the fundamental experience that God had said yes to Jesus in a different way than Jesus had expected. Faith in Jesus' resurrection meant a fundamental transformation of Jesus' hope for the coming of the reign of God.[15] God said yes to Jesus in such a way that this hope remained unfulfilled. Thus, Jesus' certainty of the in-breaking of the hoped-for reign of God became the essence of an unfulfilled and still existing hope. That hope is not less true or deep because it has not been fulfilled. And it remains a hope that lives because of God and can only be a *sustaining* hope by remaining hope in God alone. Jesus showed this impressively in his life and actions. To that extent, he remains fundamental and the agent of hope for many.

But at the same time, it seems that his failure is an indication that we ourselves must also let go of Jesus. We cannot simply remain with him and make him, just as he was, the way, the truth, and the life (cf. John 14:6), without reflecting on his failure. Did his failure consist in this, that he, who saw his own work and the coming of God as so closely united, in fact linked himself too closely to God and therefore, paradoxically, became one of those who exalt themselves (cf. Luke 14:11)? Then we need to learn from the Easter accounts that in the resurrection God answers very differently from the way Jesus himself had thought and hoped it would be. Albert Schweitzer was one of the few who really took that seriously and had the courage, inspired by Jesus, to take a different path from the one Jesus himself took.

Response / *Axel Michaels*
The "Buddhist" Nearness of the Reign of God on Earth

Early Buddhism and Christianity separate on the matter of "God." God, the absolute God, the rule and reign of God, the scarcely separable combination of judgment and salvation, an expectation of the imminent end, and the delay of the Parousia—nothing in early Buddhism corresponds to any of these ideas. Nevertheless, I will (as a lay theologian) attempt, from a Buddhist perspective, to approach the concept of the reign of God.

Let us be clear about one thing from the start:[16] The Buddha never said that there really are gods or that there are none. In particular, he had very little to say about a reign of the gods; in Buddhist teaching, the gods are located in the lowest of the three worlds, the passing world of the senses (*kāmaloka*). Therefore, he neither could nor would have said anything about an in-breaking of divine rule, either close at hand or distant. Neither did he (despite the ancient Indian teaching about the cyclic destruction of the world) emphasize the dynamic aspect, so important for Jesus and for Israel.

Jesus, in contrast—and in his historical context this was something new—regarded the reign of God as already beginning. This produced a clear "relation to the present," a loving attention to human beings and the world, something the Buddha fundamentally regarded (in love as in all things) as passing away and therefore filled with suffering. But for Jesus it was essential to introduce a new sense of God and the world that centered on care for the poor and the experience of love.

Indeed, the reign of God is "among you" (Luke 17:21) or "within your field of operations,"[17] that is, present, even though not yet completely. At any rate, with Jesus it is there, like a mustard seed. It was already disputed within the earliest Jesus movements and is still disputed in New Testament theology[18] how Jesus linked the already-beginning reign of God (the present perspective) with the future of the reign of God (the future-utopian perspective). If the present perspective is given preference, the question arises—from a "Buddhist" point of view—whether "reign of God" cannot be understood as an individual, personal reign of God. In any case, says Herbert Braun, "the preaching of the nearness of the kingly rule is meant to warn people to disregard themselves."[19]

Because the reign of God has already begun, because it is not merely a distant occurrence, because it is effective in and through Jesus as a human being, because it is a new experience and at the same time the in-breaking of salvation—for all these reasons I question whether the reign of God cannot also be understood as an entirely personal reign of God during one's own lifetime, as the liberation that the human being already has within herself or himself, which Jesus wanted to help us attain, as love for others, but also for oneself, as a rejection of the handicapped, possessed, demonic part of the self. It is true that Jesus proclaimed the reign of God as "among you" (Luke 17:21)—as Ulrich Luz says, "not *within* you!"—but he also said that it is realized in an individual (that is, himself), and not only in the community, the people, the neighbor.

I say this in order to prepare for the idea of salvation within one's own lifetime, but also in view of the evil that has befallen humanity because of Christian expectation of the end and its apocalypticism in the name of God. It is only when Christianity decisively rejects as mistaken this anticipation of the end and the threat of judgment,[20] as Luz does, that talk about the reign of God can have any meaning today, even for most Christians, as an ethical appeal to repentance and a call to a new inner reflection.

Certainly, in spite of all the twisting and turning of the matter, we have to say that God is missing from Buddhism, and Jesus demanded that we turn to God. Does Buddhism have to "pass" on this point? Ultimately it would seem so, yet if God is thought of (and experienced as) emptiness (*śūnyatā*), there is in Buddhism that certainty and absoluteness that for Jesus and for Christianity are at the beginning of all things. But which "God" is this? That is the question, but this question is certainly un-Buddhist and probably un-Christian as well.

4

Self, Nonself, and Nirvāṇa

Axel Michaels

In memoriam Inge and Water Wiemann[1]

B uddhism is regarded as the doctrine of the nonself. Only where there is no self is there deliverance and enlightenment (*nirvāṇa*). For Christianity a denial of the self is scarcely achievable. Such a thing would make impossible any personal relationship between God and the individual, would contradict the idea of creation, and would allow for scarcely any autonomy of the subject, free will, and thus Christian ethics (key to which are human equality and the associated dignity of the human being). Moreover, modern Western people (strongly shaped as they are by Christianity) are repulsed by being forced to admit that the thing they love most—namely, the self—ought not to exist. Self-realization, self-development, self-awareness, self-confidence, self-determination, self-reliance—all these are important goals in the West. Can this world cope at all with the thesis of denial of the self?

Self and Nonself

Scholars of Buddhism have also had difficulty in acknowledging, without reservation, the doctrine of the nonself.[2] Essentially, there are three reasons for this.

First is a problem of translation. The central Sanskrit concept of *ātman* (*pā. atta*) can be translated as a noun, "the self," or as a reflexive pronoun, "oneself," sometimes even as "I" or "substance, soul." But when Max Müller's sentence *attā hi attano nātho* (*Dhp* 160) is translated "Self is the lord of the self," it suggests to the reader that there is a self. But when the word is translated as a reflexive pronoun we get the thoroughly Buddhist sense, reiterated in the Buddha's preaching until the very end, "One is the master of oneself," meaning one should choose oneself as refuge and light, that is, rely on oneself in the search for truth: "Therefore insist, Ānanda, that you are your own light and your own refuge, that nothing else is your refuge, that the teaching is your light, the teaching is your refuge, nothing else is your refuge" (*DN* II.100.20–24 = Oldenberg, *Reden des Buddha*, 144–45). Misreading the text in this way, one could also accuse Matthew of teaching denial of the self by translating Matthew 16:24 as "Whoever would follow me should deny his Self [instead of "himself"] and take up his cross and follow me."

A second difficulty is that the Buddha himself was often silent regarding questions about the self and thus did not contribute much to the clarification of this problem:

> The monk Vacchagotta asked the Exalted One: "Is there, O Gautama, an *Ātman*, a true self?" Addressed this way, the Exalted One remained silent. [So Vacchagotta asked again:] "Then, O Gautama, is there no true self?" Again the Exalted One remained silent. Then the monk Vachagotta rose from his seat and went away. Afterward, *Ānanda* asked the Buddha why he had not answered the question. The Buddha said: "If, *Ānanda*, I had answered the question of the monk Vachagotta, 'Is there a self?' by saying 'There is a self,' I would have taken the side of the ascetics and Brahmans who teach the doctrine of eternity. But if, *Ānanda*, I had answered the question of the monk Vacchagotta, 'Is there no self?' by saying 'There is no self,' I would have taken the side of the ascetics and Brahmans who teach the doctrine of destruction. And if, *Ānanda*, I had answered the question of the monk Vachagotta, 'Is there a self?' by saying 'There is a self,' would that accord with my knowledge that all *dhammas* are without self?"

> "Certainly not, Lord!" [answered *Ānanda*].

> "And if, finally, *Ānanda*, I had answered the question of the monk Vachagotta, 'Is there no self?' by saying 'There is no self,' that would have thrown Vachagotta, who is already confused, into still greater confusion, for he would have thought: I used to have an *Ātman*, but now I have none." (*SN* IV.400.10–401.11)

The Buddha created for others the confusion he sought to spare the itinerant monk Vachagotta. For people continue to ask, "Is there a self or not?" This very silence has sometimes been understood to mean that the Buddha did *not* deny the existence of a self.[3] It is true that the Buddha teaches what the self is not, but he leaves open the question of what it is. Nevertheless, it would be a mistake to conclude from this that there is no such thing as a self. The unspoken words of a founder are also subject to exegesis.

It is not easy to find an unequivocal answer to the basic question of the self in any of the canonical texts,[4] because while the various statements can be attributed historically to individual schools, arranging them chronologically still remains difficult in many cases. According to a general, though not very well secured consensus, the original community divided around 350 B.C.E. into *Theravādins and Mahāsaṅghikas*. The *Theravādins* are said then to have divided again into—traditionally—eighteen schools (in fact, there were far more). Of these, the *Puggalavādins* or *Vātsīputrīyas*, the *Sārvāstivādins*, and the *Sautrāntikas* have left the clearest traces.

The *Sārvāstivādins* and the *Sautrāntikas* (as well as the *Mahāyānist Yogācāra* school) maintained the apparently majority-supported position that the *ātman* is to be denied, theoretically and philosophically, but they still questioned, as did the others, how then the given identity of the "I" was to be understood. The *Sautrāntikas* were probably close to what the Buddha himself meant when he disputed the *ātman* as self with the following argument: If the *ātman* is unchangeable, it cannot be the cause of the action, the agent, because the unchangeable lacks the criterion of identity. Two different things that are supposed to be the same (such as *ātman* and *brahman*) must have undergone change, or else they would not be different, but in that way they would have shown themselves to be changeable, and to that extent subject to suffering.

The minority counterposition was that of the *Vātsīputrīyas*, also called *Puggalavādins* because they do not question the existence of a personality (skt. *pudgala*, pā. *puggala*). They say that an *ātman* (which they call *puggala*) exists, but it is indefinable, for the following reason: The *ātman* cannot be identical with the other constituents of life, nor can it be different from them, because otherwise it would be either mortal or eternal. But if it is eternal, it cannot possibly be mortal, and then there also could be no rebirth; hence the person is indefinable (skt. *avaktavya*).

All the schools, of course, recognize that in daily life and consciousness of oneself, there is an "I" and a self. They speak of the "I" (*aham*) and oneself (*pā. atta*) and also of persons (*pā. puggala*), people (*pā. purisa*), or living beings (*pā. satta*). But the self of daily experience is highly deceptive, especially if one regards it as spirit, consciousness, or soul. The Buddha thought it would be better to see the body as the self, because it changes less swiftly than the spirit (*SN* II.94.21–95.4). Even the individual stored memory (skt. *ālayavijñāna*),[5] so closely bound to the person, which is significant especially in *Yogācara*, is ultimately not recognized as the self.

Practical Application of the Teaching about the Nonself

Even if it cannot really be denied that the Buddha maintained the doctrine of the nonself, the questionable passages remain contradictory, murky, and mysterious. One reason for this is to be sought, as Tilman Vetter and Lambert Schmithausen in particular have shown,[6] in the applicability of the teaching to spiritual practice. Vetter demonstrates this in what is probably the most ancient passage in the teaching on the nonself: *Vin* I.13.18–37 (*Mahāvagga*). This is a discourse following the first sermon, which—according to the tradition—converted Buddha's five skeptical disciples and made them the first monks.

First the Buddha speaks about five *skandhas* (literally "groups, heaps"), usually called "factors of being," but better translated "accumulated components":[7] *rūpa* ("form and body"), *vedanā* ("sensation"), *saṃjñā* ("sensation, perception"), *saṃskāra* ("act of will, spirit formations"), and *vijñāna* ("consciousness"). All these *skandhas* are the constituents of being that is subject to suffering and therefore to deliverance, but they are not its self, because they are unstable (*pā. anicca*), subject to suffering (*pā. dukkha*), and tied to change (*pā. vipariṇāmadhamma*). From this came (later) the fundamental teaching of Buddhism, that all conditioned or existing things have three characteristics: they are mortal (*anitya*), suffering (*duḥkha*), and not the self (*anātman*).

What is unstable, subject to suffering, and changing, continues the Buddha, cannot be the self. When one looks at things with the right consciousness—Vetter calls it the ability to distinguish (*pā. sammappaññāya*)—it must be recognized that this is not my self. One should look with "wisdom" upon what is visible in the here and now, within and without, gross and fine, and so on. Then one will be freed from desire, then knowledge will come to be, and then rebirth will be destroyed. After the five ascetics had heard this discourse, they, too, were completely freed from *āsava*, i.e., the "inflowings"—for example, of "sensory drives" (*pā. kāmāsava*), "the drive to exist" (*pā. bhavāsava*), "the desire to be well thought of" (*pā. diṭṭhāsava*), and "the drive of ignorance" (*pā. avijjāsava*).

Vetter thinks that all these points indicate a practical goal—namely, abandoning the false, nonredeeming identification of the self with the *skandhas*.[8] But in neither *Vinaya-* nor *Suttapiṭaka* is there a theoretical discussion about the existence or nonexistence of a suffering-free, enduring self.

Probably the Buddha experienced a transformation in regard to this question. While in his early years, he still took an explicit position on the (Brahman) theories of *ātman* of his contemporaries, so he may also have spoken about the (*vijñāna* as) self; in his later, more mature years he increasingly avoided such hairsplitting. These, said the Buddha, are only a "path of opinions, a thicket of opinions, a wilderness of opinions, a stage-play of opinions, a spasm of opinions, a fetter of opinions, full of suffering, full of corruptibility, full of excitement, full of torture" (*MN* I.485.28–31 = Oldenberg, *Buddha,* 218). Consequently, the Buddha repeatedly rejected false teachings that proclaimed the eternity of the self and the world with this observation:

> "The views that are stated in this way, and to which people cling in this manner, will lead to this and that rebirth, and with regard to the beyond will have these and those consequences." This the Exalted One perceived, and he also perceived what follows from it. And he did not cling to this knowledge. And as one who does not cling to it, he truly knew extinction for himself. After he had known the coming to be and the passing away, the joys and the suffering of the feelings, just as they are, you monks, the Thus Gone One *(tathāgata)* was released, because he did not hold fast. (*DN* I.16.33–17.4)

Thus, for the Buddha, everything that does not serve deliverance is irrelevant. He did not fight about truth, but when he did so at all it was for the sake of deliverance. Just as the sea has only one taste, namely, that of salt, "so also, you disciples, this [my] teaching is saturated with only *one* flavor, the flavor of deliverance" (*Vin* II.239.23–33). This application to deliverance implies a pragmatic procedure directed to the practice of meditation. The Buddha therefore took little part in the quarrels of the learned. Those who believed him—here is a parallel to Jesus—had to go with him and change not only their minds, but also their lives.

Of course, the question remains: Why did the majority of Buddhists over time adopt the doctrine of the nonself? One reason may be that many monks posited an enduring, nonsuffering unity they called *Nirvāṇa*, but they did not want to link it to the changeable self. For both teachings—enduring *Nirvāṇa* and also the time-conditioned self—to coexist, the two sides could not touch; consequently, the self could not be *Nirvāṇa* or participate in it. That, according to Vetter, was a logical reaction to doctrines about the eternal core of the person, and the contradiction could only be resolved as (meditative) praxis, not as knowledge.

Later, in the noncanonical literature, it is unmistakably taught that there is no *ātman*. This became a core statement for all Buddhism.

Self and Rebirth

The teaching about the nonself enabled Buddhism to overcome a difficult problem: how could the transmigration of souls, an idea generally accepted in the Buddha's time, be explained if there is no self? What, then, is migrating, if not something like a self? It is difficult to conceive of rebirth without notions of substance and a personal core. Can there really be rebirth without a transmigration of souls?

To explain this paradox, the Buddha tended to use more images than theoretical answers. An example is the image of the cubes piled upon each other. Each cube functionally qualifies the one above it, but they are not identical. Neither are the pearls on a string, linked only by that thread. The *Milindapañha* chooses the image of a self-devouring flame. The flame in the first night watch is different from that of the second, etc. It is the same, yet it is always different; it arises from the same material and so burns the whole night long: "So also, great King, the chain of the *dhammas* (beings) hangs together: the one arises, the other departs. Without beginning, without end it hangs together; therefore it is neither the same being nor a different being that attains to the last phase of its knowing" (*Mil* 40.28–32).[9] Thus, there is no self, no soul, only a flow of changing factors of being, the *skandhas*, that join together for a brief time. Even for early Buddhism, the All was almost unintelligible. Each shapes its own rebirth through its deeds, yet the new being is not altogether identical with the previous one. All beings have a pre-empirical "I" but no eternal self. Buddha's polemic against the self or the "I" went to the extreme of completely denying an agent. Instead, it is the *skandhas* that, constantly changing, permit impressions of an agent to arise.

Nonself and Nirvāṇa

Not only the doctrine of rebirth, but also that of *Nirvāṇa* demands the thesis of the nonself, because people asked: If the self does not wander from rebirth to rebirth, is it then at least in a position to enjoy *Nirvāṇa*? What is this

Nirvāṇa (*pā. nibbāna*), which literally means "extinguish, blow out"? The parallel to Latin *spiritus* and Greek *pneuma* is obvious. To this very question posed by a monk named Sāriputta, the Buddha answered, "The end of desire, the end of hatred, the end of blindness: this my friend, is what one calls *Nirvāṇa*" (*SN* IV, p. 251).[10] But that is only one of many sayings of the Buddha about *Nirvāṇa*, not all of them by any means totally alike, so even this key concept is also shrouded in obscurity. Nevertheless, many scholars thought it possible to say something about *Nirvāṇa* (without having achieved it), so it is said that *Nirvāṇa* is Peace, Security, Blessing, Silence, the Sphere, Deathlessness, Truth, Purity, the Most High, the Eternal, the Uncreated, the Endless, the Good, the Enduring, or a mixture of all these. It is possible, more or less, to find citations supporting all these opinions, especially in poetic texts. The systematic portions of the texts and the sermons yield—in summary—the following statements about *Nirvāna*:

- It is unnameable: "No eye, no tongue, no thought can reach the Holy One in utter *Nirvāṇa*" (*SN* IV.52.29–53.4). Cf. 1 Corinthians 2:9: "What no eye has seen, nor ear heard, nor the human heart conceived."
- It is without qualification, i.e., it is the passing away of the factors of being and thus the end of rebirth (*SN* IV, pp. 378–79): "The destruction of becoming is *nibbāna*."
- It is unification with the god *Brahmā* (*DN* I.235.1–253.2).
- It is the end of suffering, and that means the end of becoming and passing away, of mortality:

    You monks, there is a sphere that is neither earth nor water nor fire nor air; it is neither the sphere of endless space nor the sphere of endless consciousness nor the sphere of nothingness, neither the sphere of perception nor the sphere of non-perception; it is neither this world nor another, neither sun nor moon. I deny that it is coming or going, enduring, death, or birth. It is only the end of suffering. (*Ud* 80,10–16)

- It is, above all, negatively described, but it is not nothingness: It would almost be heresy to equate *Nirvāna* with nothingness, says Constantin Regamey;[11] no school asserts such a thing. *Nirvāṇa* is not conditioned, it is not absolute, but it is like a soul: without a self.

"Is *Nirvāṇa* happiness?" the monk Udāyi once asked Sāriputta, previously mentioned. He answered: "Dear friend, *Nirvāṇa* is happiness (*sukha*), *Nirvāṇa* is happiness." Not believing him, Udāyi counters: "But friend Sāriputta, what kind of happiness can it be if nothing can be felt any more?"

Sāriputta responds: "Just that is happiness, that there is no more feeling" (*AN* IV.414.25–415.4).

Thus there is a crucial difference between *Nirvāṇa* and the reign of God, as the theologian Paul Tillich recognized:

> If in Paul the Kingdom of God is identified with the expectation of God being all *in* all (or *for* all), if it is replaced by the symbol of Eternal Life, or described as the eternal intuition and fruition of God, this has a strong affinity to the praise of Nirvana as the state of transtemporal blessedness, for blessedness presupposes—at least in symbolic language—a subject which experiences blessedness.[12]

For that very reason, *Nirvāṇa* is not "only" happiness.

Moreover, *Nirvāṇa* is not the result of something, because then it would be linked to a cause and so would be conditioned, which means suffering and mortality. *Nirvāṇa* is truth, and nothing comes after it, not Paradise, not eternity, and not happiness. The usual expressions, that Buddha entered into *Nirvāṇa* or *Parinirvāṇa*, a complete extinction, are thus deceptive, because a Buddha does not go anywhere, but simply ceases to be, is extinguished.

Nirvāṇa is truth, and nothing comes after it. But *Nirvāṇa* also, because it is truth, does not come only later, only after this life. Salvation in Buddhism is not transcendent, not beyond. *Nirvāṇa* is also possible during one's lifetime. But there is no subject that can perceive this *Nirvāṇa*, not even in one's lifetime.

Salvation without Heaven?

Without prejudice, one scarcely could come to the conclusion that Buddhism acknowledges a self as ultimate basis. Therefore, we should not attempt to impose a transcendent self on it for the sake of interreligious harmony. Walpola Rahula, a scholar and high-ranking monk, has expressed this very clearly:

> It is better to say frankly that one believes in an *Ātman* or self. Or one may even say that the Buddha was totally wrong in denying the existence of an *Ātman*. But certainly it will not do for any one to try to introduce into Buddhism an idea which the Buddha never accepted, as far as we can see from the extant original texts.[13]

And Rahula rightly notes that if the Buddha had believed in God and the soul, he surely would have said so, because these doctrines were certainly taught in the milieu in which he lived. On the contrary, he did not accept such teachings:

> "O bhikkus [monks], accept a soul-theory [*pā. attavāda*] in the acceptance of which there would not arise grief, lamentation, suffering, distress and tribulation. But, do you see, O bhikkus, such a soul-theory in the acceptance of which there would not arise grief, lamentation, suffering, distress and tribulation?"

> "Certainly not, Sir."

> "Good, O bhikkus. I, too, O bhikkus, do not see a soul-theory, in the acceptance of which there would not arise grief, lamentation, suffering, distress and tribulation." (*MN* I.137.24–31)[14]

The denial of the soul represents the sharpest and probably the most irreconcilable contrast with Christianity. This question is the breaking point, as was evident when Pope John Paul II described Buddhism as an "atheistic system."[15] When he visited Sri Lanka in 1991, there was a storm of indignation, and high dignitaries within Buddhism refused to meet with him. Apart from some incomprehensible misinterpretations of Buddhism, such as the designation of this religion as "negative soteriology" and the depiction of *Nirvāṇa* as "a state of perfect indifference with regard to the world,"[16] the Pope finds it beyond question that withdrawal from the world is permitted only "in order to unite oneself to that which is outside of the world—by this I do not mean nirvana, but a personal God." He elaborates:

> Union with Him comes about not only through purification, but through love.... *Christian mysticism* from every period . . . is not born of a purely negative "enlightenment." It is not born of an awareness of the evil which exists in man's attachment to the world through the senses, the intellect, and the spirit. Instead, Christian mysticism is born of the *Revelation of the living God*.[17]

At first glance, the Buddhist doctrine of the nonself is indeed alienating, and because of their strange terminology, the Buddhist explanations are not much help. But when we reflect on terms like *self, individual,* or *I* in terms of the history of philosophy, the Western perception of the self also is rendered somewhat shaky. For the feeling of personal identity is not at all as certain as we believe it to be. One is not a self, and one does not have a self. Who, then, can be it, and who can have it? The self itself? And what can this self be, other than that by which it is named, what characterizes it? But in Western philosophy, a substance or essence has been attributed to the self. A distinction was made between *esse morale* and *esse rationale,* on the one hand, and *esse naturale* on the other. These distinctions first made possible the dichotomies that are typical of the West—spirit/matter, subject/object, human/nature, freedom/determinism—none of which make much sense in Buddhism, because there the self, or the soul, also participates in the changeability of the body. This rests for the most part on the notion that the soul has a fine-spun substance. But as soon as one no longer contrasts the soul with the mortality of the body, and instead links the two together, it becomes clear that it (the self) cannot be salvation, if salvation is seen as permanent and immortal.

As plausible as the Buddhist notion of the self may be, it leads, as we have said, to some basic divergences from Christianity. Not only is a personal relationship between God and the individual—that is, faith in God—vastly limited, and not only must creation, the reign of God, and life beyond the world (including every form of heaven) almost necessarily be denied, but also ethical problems are created as regards freedom of the will and sin.

From the point of view of Christianity, especially apologetic theology, Buddhism is amoral and egoistic because it sets saving oneself in the foreground. Moreover, it is seen as presumptuous, because salvation is possible without the action of another (God). Gustav Mensching called this "self-salvation";[18] Max Weber dubbed it "self-divinization,"[19] not without a disparaging undertone. No wonder theologians who tried to mediate between Buddhism and Christianity repeatedly sought to construct a kind of "grace of enlightenment." Nathan Söderblom called enlightenment "a gift of grace without a giver," and for Rudolf Otto, enlightenment is "a mysterious event that lies not in human hands."[20] But in India, as Wolfgang Schluchter rightly says, "salvation" is "exclusively the consequence of the 'achievement' of the individual."[21]

However, from the point of view of Buddhism one may just as well ask whether Christianity is not "immoral" because it places salvation entirely beyond the world. The reign of God is—except for a very few voices, such as in the Fourth Gospel—indeed near, but always future: "Your kingdom come!"

(Matt 6:10), so it comes in a certain sense after death. But what if one does not believe in a (self living) life after death?

Response / *Ulrich Luz*
Christianity and the Self

For Christianity a denial of the self is scarcely possible, while Buddhism is a doctrine of the nonself. That is how Axel Michaels sees it. My counterthesis would be this: It is precisely in regard to the question of the "self" that there are a very great many points of contact between Christianity and Buddhism. Certainly, I know that the modern West talks constantly about self-realization, self-assertion, self-presentation, self-determination, self-reliance. But how "shaped by Christianity" is this modernity if the "self" is its "best beloved"?

Let us suppose that the Buddha had met Jesus and asked him what he thought about the self. The scene is absurd, because Jesus' mother tongue had no word for the self. So the scene would have to begin with the Buddha's interpreter laboriously explaining the question to Jesus. And in spite of all the explanations, Jesus has still not understood it. The Buddha, wise and practiced in dealing with strange people, asks again, "Young man, then what are *you*?"

Jesus answers, "Honored strange rabbi, I am flesh." The interpreter, a Jew learned in philosophy, explains, "He means that he is a creature of God, a body full of life, fellow creature and fellow human being." Buddha asks, "Young man, what is life?" But Jesus does not want to get into a discussion with the foreign holy man. To bring the conversation to an end, he answers with one of those polished sayings he likes to use because he knows that his conversation partners usually have no comeback: "Those who try to make their life[22] secure will lose it, but those who lose their life will keep it" (Luke 17:33).

We no longer know the original context in which Jesus used this saying. He may have said it to people like the wealthy grain farmer whose story is found in Luke 12:16–21, that is, to people whose death will interrupt their profit planning. Perhaps he said it to his disciples while they were on their way to Jerusalem and were beginning to suspect that this might be the last journey for their master and for themselves. If at that time his disciples had asked him what kind of life he was talking about, a life one would hope to keep secure, he might well have answered with a reference to life in the reign of God. And if they had gone on to ask him what that life would look like, perhaps so as to be able to correctly estimate the risk they were running, he would have said something harsh to them, such as, "Whoever does not carry the cross and follow me cannot be my disciple" (Luke 14:27).

Thus, there does indeed seem to have been for Jesus something analogous to the Buddhist question about the self. But in his case, it is not about the abstract question of the "self." Rather, with him it is, again and again, a question of "life." Life is concrete, embedded in social relationships. Life means health, wealth, power. Jesus knows that one has to let go of life in that sense in order to gain the true life that corresponds to the reign of God. Certainly he is thinking as well of what we today call "eternal" life, but the eternity of the reign of God begins for him in the present. Unlike the Buddha, he reflects very little on the causes of suffering. The analogy consists rather in the fact that for Jesus Christ, as for Buddha, the issue is letting go of life that is not true life. There is also a convergence in that the question of true life cannot be resolved by changing one's theoretical opinion about life; it can be accomplished only by changing one's life.

Beyond Jesus, I see contacts with the Buddha in early Christianity, especially in Paul. Paul is especially well suited for comparison with the Buddha because we find in him a high level of individualism, similar to that of the Buddha, and an equally high capacity for abstract reflection. I see similarities to the Buddha especially in his "mystical" interpretation of baptism and the Christian life.

Early Christianity as a whole regarded baptism as a total break within a person's life. Paul interprets it as dying and rising with Christ (Rom 6:3–11; Col 2:12), the Fourth Gospel as a second birth "from above."[23] The baptized regarded themselves as "a new creation" (Gal 6:15; 2 Cor 5:17). They have been incorporated into a new sphere of life, namely, "the body of Christ" (1 Cor 12:13).

Paul interpreted and deepened these convictions as applied to individuals. He was probably moved to this by his own experience; the vision of Christ before Damascus that was so fundamental for him meant a total turnabout. He sees baptism as a change of person. A key text that comes very close to Buddhist statements and at the same time distinguishes Paul's thought from them is Galatians 2:19–20: "For through the law I died to the law" (Gal 2:19). The law, the valid will of God, makes it clear to him that he is governed by the active power of evil and is "dead" to God's will. Paul formulates that death most impressively in his great text about the "I" under the rule of sin in Romans 7:7–25. The death of the "I" is not a physical death, nor is it divine punishment for sin; rather, it is complete unfreedom through being enmeshed in evil. This is comparable to the Indian-Buddhist concept of an eternal circling in *Samsāra*, even though Paul is thinking of the key concept of sin and not of mortality. There is also a strong affinity to the Zen Buddhist idea of the great death.[24]

Rescue happens only when this "I," entangled and ensnared in evil, takes leave of itself. "I have been crucified with Christ," Paul continues in Galatians 2:19. His next statement is famous: "It is no longer I who live, but it is Christ who lives in me" (Gal 2:20). A "change of ego" has taken place in baptism. Christ is the new subject of the human being. Baptism therefore means the death of the ego and the gift of a new, different "I." The Japanese New Testament scholar Seiichi Yagi speaks here, from a Buddhist perspective, of the death of the ego and of "Christ in me" as "self-ego."[25]

The nearness to and distance from Buddhist concepts are obvious. The idea of letting go of the "I" is as central in Christianity as the idea that the ego that must be let go of is not autonomous, as it thinks it is, but is nothing but the sum total of dependencies of an "I" that is unfree and thus dead. Buddhism and Paul also have in common that the person who is no longer determined by his or her own ego is experiencing new life already, here and now, in the world. For Paul, of course, this does not mean the elimination of suffering, but suffering in anticipation of life (2 Cor 4:10–11). The most profound difference from Buddhism is that for Paul a new, strange self takes the place of my "I." The experience of the change of self in baptism is for him an expression of an utterly radical experience of grace. Paul speaks this way because his experience is that he owes everything he is, not to himself, but to another (1 Cor 4:7). Is this experience of grace specific to Christianity, or is it meaningful or perhaps even necessary to interpret the experience of enlightenment (which cannot be "achieved" through meditative techniques and is not an attainable goal of human efforts) as a Buddhist experience of "grace"?

Part Three
Love and Tranquility

5

Jesus' Ethics

Ulrich Luz

A first glance at Jesus' ethics and those of early Buddhism reveals a great many convergences. For Jesus, as for the Buddha, the fundamental moral commandments are in the foreground. The Ten Commandments play a major role for Jesus (Matt 5:21–22, 27–28, 33–37; Mark 10:19), and the Buddha's five commandments for laypersons[1] broadly correspond to the second table of the Decalogue. For both of them, sacrifices and ceremonial take a backseat. Jesus places love at the center; for Buddha, goodwill and compassion are very important. The love commandment, goodwill, and compassion are universal in scope, for the Buddha as for Jesus. Jesus, like the Buddha, makes some overtures to a two-level ethics; for Jesus this is in the form of commandments that apply only to disciples. Thus, the similarities appear to be many.

In describing Jesus' ethics, I will attempt to highlight points that possibly indicate differences, namely, the questions of the radicality of Jesus' ethics, of Jesus' own authority, and of what love is understood to mean.

With regard to all three of these questions there is also a problem of interpretation that is "internal to Jesus." This is the problem of the relationship between the proclamation of the rapidly approaching reign of God, including judgment and the end of the world, and Jesus' ethics. It has always been observed that Jesus' ethical statements appear to stand alongside, but unconnected to, his announcement of the reign of God. Jesus' ethical preaching is deeply influenced by Jewish wisdom. One genre that dominates his teaching is that of the wisdom admonition, e.g., "Give to everyone who begs from you; and if anyone takes away your goods, do not ask for them again" (Luke 6:30). Many principles take the form of the wisdom saying called *mashal*, e.g., "No one can serve two masters...you cannot serve God and mammon" (Matt 6:24). Many of the parables also are important for Jesus' ethics. Some of his ethical statements contain references to the Torah, most of them indirect. References to the coming reign of God are very few. Jesus' judgment sayings and judgment parables present the grand alternative, but they seldom contain concrete instructions for action.

Unfortunately, Jesus did not leave us his preaching in the form of a systematically arranged textbook, and the Jesus tradition lacks the kind of helpful didactic and systematic texts found in the Buddhist series.[2] Therefore, it is always Jesus' interpreters who construct the unity of his eschatological and non-eschatological sayings. This has been done by moving either the ethical or the eschatological sayings into the background.[3] There have been attempts to reinterpret Jesus' eschatological sayings.[4] The sayings about the coming judgment of destruction by the Son of Man have been, preferably, declared ungenuine.[5] Or interpreters speak of Jesus' two lines of utterance, one eschatological and one theological, whereby the former serves only an auxiliary function to the second and more central line.[6] In my description of the reign of God,[7] I have not adopted any of these escape routes, so in this chapter I am obligated to give at least a brief answer to the question of how I harmonize the two lines of utterance.

The Radicality of Jesus' Ethics

Jesus seems to have sharpened and radicalized quite a lot of traditional sayings from Jewish hortatory preaching, especially those from the wisdom tradition. This sharpening shows itself sometimes in a polished rhetorical style. The Jewish tradition, like Jesus, knows two concepts of purity, the ritual and the ethical: "There is nothing outside a person that by going in can defile, but the things that come out are what defile" (Mark 7:15). In Jesus' formula the two concepts—the uncleanness of foods and the "uncleanness," that is, untruth or lovelessness, of words—are set in exclusive opposition. Other passages (for example, Matt 23:23–24) show that Jesus was most probably thinking of a radical priority of the moral over the ritual, and was not yet proposing a fundamental abrogation of the purity laws. Paul was the first to interpret him in that sense (Rom 14:14). The famous saying about the speck in the brother's eye and the log in one's own (Matt 7:35) also is first and foremost *verbally* radical; only in the context of the Sayings Source, where it is preceded by the absolute command not to judge (Matt 7:1–2), does it acquire a deeper and ironic dimension. In that context every judgment about specks in a brother's or sister's eye, where applicable, is now rendered impossible.

Other wisdom sayings of Jesus are so radical that they utterly contradict experience. Everyone knows what happens to someone in a fight who offers the other cheek to the opponent: he or she will get hit again (cf. Matt 5:39b). Jesus himself experienced that obviously enough in his passion. The same is true of the next saying, about the shirt and the cloak (Matt 5:40): what kind of jerk would sue a poor man for his shirt? The Bible explicitly forbids taking his cloak as well, because the cloak is the blanket with which the poor man can cover himself at night (Exod 22:26). Here we have exaggerated formulations of a demonstrative renunciation of violence that have nothing to do with realistic steps toward reconciliation. Rather, this is about radical symbols contrary to all violence, a symbolic protest against it. The Passion Narrative again shows that Jesus is completely serious in making these demands.

Another example of Jesus' radicality is his command to love our enemies. There are many similar commandments; the examples extend from Egyptian wisdom through Greek (especially Socratic) tradition to Buddhist texts.[8] Characteristic for Jesus are the sharply contrasting phrases. It is precisely enemies whom one should love, in all their brutality: "Love your enemies; do good to those who hate you" (Luke 6:27–28). Gerhard Lohfink has, not unjustly, called this a "contrast ethics."[9]

In Jesus' interpretation of the Torah, his antitheses show how he radicalized traditional Jewish ethics, including especially the Decalogue. What Jesus demands in these antitheses—namely, refusal to use a single word in anger against any fellow human being and rejection of any lustful glance—is nothing new in the tradition. What is new is the absolute obligation attached to his demand: "If you are angry with a brother or sister, you will be liable to judgment; and if you insult a brother or sister, you will be liable to the council; and if you say, 'You fool,' you will be liable to the hell of fire" (Matt 5:22). The field of things subject to condemnation is here expanded to include what is internal to the person; a word in anger is equal to murder. Similarly, Jesus—again taking up Jewish principles—can forbid oaths because every word should be truthful (Matt 5:33–37). In one of his admonitions, formulated like so many of these in the second person plural, he says, "Do not judge, so that you may not be judged. For with the judgment you make you will be judged!" (Matt 7:1–2). The admonition is very general; Jesus leaves it to his hearers to establish its breadth. It was only his interpreters who first came to the conclusion that Jesus "obviously" was thinking only of relationships between human beings.[10]

The consequences such commands might have—for example, for the poor, for legal affairs, or in the case of Jesus' prohibition of divorce, for divorced women who could not remarry (cf. Matt 5:32)—do not appear to have interested Jesus. His commands tend toward an otherworldly maximum. When we hear them, we are impressed and struck by them, because they are true in themselves and express something of what the human being might be in the eyes of God. But they are uninterested either in what is possible or in the consequences that might follow if they were made into generally applicable maxims. For Max Weber they were parade examples of a pure ethics of conviction, completely devoid of any ethics of responsibility that would weigh the consequences for those affected.[11] To that extent they are often not based on experience, in the sense of wisdom, but are in fact contrary to common experience. They say nothing about the coming reign of God. But I think they are formulated in light of it. This is how the true human being who is gripped and transformed by the reign of God would act. The tendency to radicality in Jesus' demands has to do with the in-breaking of the reign of God.

Jesus' Sovereign Authority

According to Luke 16:16, the time of the Torah and the prophets ended with John the Baptizer; after that comes the reign of God, which many are seeking to enter. We would expect from this saying that Jesus' relationship to the Torah, which for Israel is *the* pledge of God's election, was not a direct and simple one. In fact, on the one hand the Torah, especially the Decalogue, is important to him. It cannot be shown that Jesus deliberately violated it. His interpretation of the Sabbath commandment in favor of human need (Mark 2:27) is, in fact, within the framework of current Jewish understanding of the Sabbath and represents one possible reading in that context.

Nevertheless, it is striking that Jesus almost never appeals to the traditional authority of the Bible. He certainly knew many biblical themes, a lot of biblical material, and biblical characters, but he does not argue exegetically. Only in the case of marriage, which for him is absolutely sacred, does he appeal to the order of creation in Genesis 1:27 (= Mark 10:6–9). It may be that he had—again in harmony with other Jews of his time—turned against the permission to divorce that was given by Moses (Mark 10:5–6). His complicated relationship to the Torah is best illuminated by the introduction to the antitheses: "You have heard that it was said to those of ancient times, 'You shall not murder'; and 'whoever murders shall be liable to judgment.' But I say to you…" (Matt 5:21–22). I presume that here Jesus is contrasting his own words not with some other Jewish interpretation, but with the Torah itself.[12] In doing so, he takes seriously the fact that the Torah in Judaism at that time was a living thing, not yet codified to the very letter. Not only was there a living, oral Torah alongside the written one; no, the written Torah itself is living and can be newly formulated. One example of this is the Temple Scroll found at Qumran, which in part rewords the canonical fifth book of the Torah (Deuteronomy) as direct address of God to Moses.[13] Jesus links his words to this living Jewish Torah. But what is striking in his case is that he does not hide his own authority behind that of Moses; instead, he contrasts it to what Moses says: "but *I* say to you." What Jesus then says is by no means a contradiction of the Torah of Moses; it is a deepening and radicalizing of it. In doing this, Jesus appeals to nothing but his own authority.

The introductory formula for the antitheses corresponds to the contrast between the reign of God and the time of the Torah and the prophets in Luke 16:16. It also corresponds to the sovereign authority just described: Jesus formulates wisdom admonitions that, at least in part, transcend the evidence of experience, but without appealing to any authority for his radical demands. Sometimes he precedes his words with an emphatic "truly, I tell you," a usage that is scarcely attested at all in Judaism and that Christians who handed on his words evidently regarded as typical of Jesus. All this corresponds to Jesus' role in the in-breaking of the future reign of God and his claim that hearing and following his words about how to be and how not to be would be decisive for the judgment (Luke 6:47–49). Jesus evidently claims for himself a great deal of authority, but he does not appeal for it to any other source, not even what he himself may be (for example, as Messiah or Son of Man). His authority is direct and relies on the power of what is spoken.

The authority Jesus claims for himself gives his hearers a clear direction but does not lay down the law. Jesus' demands are not binding legal ordinances; they are not *halakot*. Jesus often speaks in terms of incentives and examples. The three sayings about turning the other cheek, going to court over a shirt, and going the extra mile (Matt 5:39–41) are *examples* of radical nonviolence.

They do not mean less than they say, but rather more. They appeal to the hearers' creative imagination to invent similar examples of provocative nonviolence in other situations. The appeals to reconciliation (Matt 5:23–24, 25–26) are also examples, illustrative statements that indicate a direction for action and the radicalness of such action. This is where we should locate, for example, openly formulated maxims of the type "those who humble themselves will be exalted" (Luke 14:11). Each person must discover for herself or himself what these maxims mean concretely in one's life. In the same way, ethically oriented parables like the story of the Good Samaritan (Luke 10:30–37) cannot be directly translated into instructions for action; we are meant to allow them to move us to act.[14] All these texts count on a great degree of freedom and creative imagination.

Centrality of the Love Command

Early Christianity was unanimously convinced that the center of Jesus' ethical preaching and their own ethics was the love command, especially the command to love enemies: "Love your enemies, do good to those who hate you, bless those who curse you, pray for those who abuse you" (Luke 6:27–28). Three things are clear:

1. Love is understood first and foremost as deed, as praxis. It is by no means *merely* a feeling or internal affection. It encompasses a person's whole praxis, internal and external, praying for others and doing good things for them. It thus corresponds to the first two antitheses. There seems to be no distance in this love, but rather an all-too-extreme engagement of intense empathy.

2. The group of those thought of as "enemies" is not limited, for example, to one's personal enemies. "Abuse" would probably have meant torture. In Matthew's version (Matt 5:44), Jesus speaks of praying for persecutors, thus making clear that he includes religious enemies of the community in the love command.

3. The brutality of hostility is not in the least belittled. Jesus does not argue that enemies are people, too, or that those who appear to be enemies may really be people of goodwill. Instead, he clearly says what they actually do: they hate, they curse, they abuse. These are the people, above all, whom one is supposed to love with the most extreme intent and purpose.

This focusing of love represents, on the one hand, an enormous simplification and, on the other hand, an enormous sharpening of the divine will. It is a simplification because in every situation the person who needs love becomes the canon of interpretation of the will of God. The Samaritan understood this when he took up and cared for the one who had fallen among robbers; the priest and Levite did not (Luke 10:30–37). Jesus practiced it when he fulfilled the Sabbath commandment by helping others, healing the sick, and doing good (cf. Mark 3:4). This is behind the statement that what comes out of a person—angry words—"makes unclean" (Mark 7:15). The book of people in need is one that everyone can read and understand. There is no need to be learned in scripture or adept in religious practices. Jesus' command to love represents a sharpening of the divine will because it is understood to be hugely radical: One must forgive seven times a day or seventy-seven times (Luke 17:3–4; Matt 18:21–22). One must begin already to practice the coming reversal of power relationships in the reign of God: "Whoever wishes to be first among you must be slave of all" (Mark 10:44). This last text also makes clear once again the indirect relationship between love and the approaching reign of God.

It is in the nature of every demand to love that it cannot be limited to particular cases and a specific maximum amount. Jesus focused that demand by removing all limits, concentrating on enemies, and understanding the love thus demanded as the means to the will of God. The question arises whether this focusing of the love commandment is not an excessive demand. The history of Christianity is full of examples of how this command has been suppressed or instrumentalized by the church.[15] Jews in particular are more than correct when they ask critically whether Jesus, had he not set the bar so high, might have produced more solid results under which they, among others, would have suffered less.[16] The New Testament itself raises some critical questions. What happened to love of enemies in Matthew's violent and consequential reckoning with the "hypocritical" Pharisees and Scribes in Jesus' woe-discourse (Matthew 23)? How do we reconcile the fear-drenched images of the final plagues and the horrors of the sea of fire in the book of Revelation, a book certainly influenced by a desire for compensation, with Jesus' boundless love?

What, then, is the basis for this demand, and how viable is it? In Jesus' preaching it is the reference to the goodness of God, who is merciful and whose example makes human compassion possible (Luke 6:36). It is God who forgives sins without measure (Matt 18:23–35), is as close to human beings as a loving father (Luke 11:2; 15:11–32), and hears people who pray to him (Matt 7:7–11; Luke 11:5–13). It is, above all, the arrival of the coming reign of God, already, now: All around Jesus, people are being made healthy and are being fed, being freed from demons and coming to themselves, being transformed from outsiders to central figures, becoming important because they are important to God. Is that enough? In the later post-Easter traditions Jesus himself is experienced as the essence of divine love: "The love of Christ urges us on, because we are convinced that one has died for all" (2 Cor 5:14), and "God's love was revealed among us in this way: God sent his only Son into the world so that we might live through him" (1 John 4:9). Above all, early Christianity found the essence of God's love, which sustains human life and love, in the death of Jesus, which it interpreted in manifold fashion as a redemptive death, a sacrifice that brings life, a gift of freedom, the basis for reconciliation with God, etc. In fact, on the basis of this experience these Christians came to the sharply focused formulation that God is love (1 John 4:8).

The basic structures of Jesus' ethical preaching thus correspond in many ways to his preaching of the reign of God. Radical love of enemies corresponds to the unconditional love of God. The retreat of the Torah corresponds to the new action of God in the in-breaking of God's reign. The radicality of Jesus' commands corresponds to the clash between the reign of God and the world ruled by the Evil One. That Jesus' ethics is comprehensible and open, appeals to everyone's ability to make choices and to imagine, and is not intended to be an ethics for elites—all this corresponds to the certainty that the reign of God is coming for all human beings. The unconditional authority of Jesus, the speaker, that becomes evident in his teachings corresponds to the role he plays in the in-breaking of the reign of God. Therefore, my thesis is that Jesus' ethics is shaped by the reign of God. It presumes the experience of the arrival of the reign of God and experiences of the love of God. It appeals to all people to act in a way that corresponds to the reign of God.

Jesus' Command to Love and Buddhist Compassion

I understand the Buddhist ethics of compassion as a preparatory stage on the path to serenity (*upekṣā*). "Serenity" in any case has to do with letting go, with taking back empathy, which, after all, as com*passion* is a part of passion, of suffering, from which the human being needs to be freed. I understand serenity as similar to what later in *Mahāyāna* is called emptiness (*śūnyatā*). In this, however, love itself, which is always a tie to something, is transcended and surrendered. Serenity is "being untouched,"[17] not empathy. "Therefore avoid feeling love for anything" (*Dhp* 211). Compassion appears to be something temporary.

Can an ethic of compassion in Buddhism be more than a stage, to be deliberately transcended on the path to salvation? Or is there something like an enduring tension between compassion and serenity? What would it look like? Or is there, besides the compassion of the one who is on the path to "serenity," also another, perhaps deeper form of compassion and love, namely, a compassion derived from the experience of enlightenment and emptiness? That would be the compassion of the Buddha, or of every enlightened one.

In any case, it appears that here we must acknowledge a difference between Buddhism and the New Testament. Compassion is not the center of life for Buddhism. For the New Testament, in contrast, God's very self is love. The biblical God has nothing to do with the passionlessness (*apatheia*) that perhaps would come closest to resembling the Buddhist serenity, which then in the ancient church, under Greek influence, came to be seen as an important attribute of God.

Questions for Christian Faith

If I see things correctly, the Buddhist concept of compassion is far less expansive and less demanding than Jesus' concept of love of enemies. But at the same time I have the impression that in the history of Buddhism this concept has, on the whole, been lived out in a very impressive fashion. Buddhism did not lead to the construction of a church that made ruling claims for itself that were incompatible with love of enemies. The love command was not powerfully subordinated to organizational claims to the possession of truth, as was the case in Christianity. As far as I know there have never been any wars fought in the name of Gautama Buddha.

In the response to the preceding chapter I indicated that belief in Jesus' resurrection means accepting not only God's yes but also God's no to Jesus' hope for the definitive arrival of the reign of God. Faith in the resurrection implies a transformation of Jesus that includes a kind of farewell to him. The same necessity of saying good-bye, in part, to Jesus applies to Jesus' ethics. In the history of Christianity one repeatedly encounters new attempts to interpret Jesus' ethics; I see these as transformational concepts. Examples include a two-level ethics, the distinction between office and person, ethics of conscience, ethics of responsibility, and so on. I will not evaluate them individually here but only say that such transformational concepts are necessary for very basic reasons. In the search for new ethical concepts that may take their fundamental directions from Jesus, the question of bases is especially important. This led to the circumstance that in the history of Christianity the radical command to love has always been subject to being misused for other purposes or even suppressed. This was often connected to Christianity's claim to absolute truth and the related inclination to dualism.

What I find especially challenging in the Buddhist concept of compassion is that Buddhism does not regard human compassion as the response to a divine gift of love. Let me, for the moment, take up the disputed (and in my opinion false, because formulated in Western terms) proposition that Buddhism is a religion of "self-redemption" and speak provocatively: compassion in Buddhism is a step on the path of "self-redemption" and *for that very reason* has had impressive and beneficial effects. That should give us pause.

Despite all the need for transformation, however, Jesus' ethics of the reign of God is not done away with by the fact that the reign of God has not come. Jesus' utopian ethics contains so much longing for genuine humanity, so much power, and so much truth that we cannot do without it as a counter to the daily order of things as we find it in our world. Precisely *because* the reign of God has not come, Jesus' ethics remains necessary as the counter to the world. We need people who live in light of the hope for the reign of God that remained unfulfilled for Jesus—minority groups, nuns, monks, communities, individuals whose lives are shaped by that hope. Otherwise, the power of the factual would be almighty. Jesus' utopian ethics remains an ethics of hope.

Response / *Axel Michaels*
Love of God and Love of Enemies

It is tempting to follow up on Ulrich Luz's self-critical reflections and, from the point of view of Buddhism, call into question the radical nature of Jesus' ethics. Luz himself has called Jesus' ethics a form that can hardly be practiced, an "otherworldly maximum." It seems to me that this radicalness has to do with Jesus' radical identification with God: As love of God in the sense of God's love for human beings, Jesus' command to love has to be unconditional, and since Jesus tied himself so closely to God, his demand to love must also, it seems, be "superhuman." What I want to address is whether the serene love urged by the Buddha represents a less radical opposite pole.

For the Buddha, actions are first and foremost false and at the same time immoral if they are not motivated by goodwill, compassion, joy, and serenity.[18] This brings me to a critical challenge to Christianity. I will shape it as a conversation between Jesus and the Buddha:

Jesus: "Ancient sage, your form of unaffectedness and compassion is something remarkable in itself. I see here a deep indifference to the suffering, the weak, and the sick. What kind of lovelessness is this! What self-centeredness! My love, in contrast, goes out even to enemies. If someone strikes me, I offer my other cheek as well. In wrath, I take the part of all who are humiliated. For them, I even give my life."

Buddha Śākyamuni: "Oh, you hotheaded son of God! You speak of nonviolence, yet you only arouse new violence. Wrath is a poor leader. Angry compassion, after all, is only passion. How provocative it is to offer the other cheek! It positively demands a second blow. I, on the other hand, prefer to go away and so reduce the amount of anger in the world."

Jesus: "But, oh, orange-robe-wearer, with all respect, that is no help to the poor sufferers. Someone has to stand with them, so God's love can come to them through me."

Buddha Śākyamuni (turning away): "I do not contend with the world; the world contends with me. What other sages teach, that I also teach" (*SN* III.138.26–32).

This placidity in argument is characteristic of the Buddha and of Buddhism. The Buddha, according to most of the sources, did indeed teach out of compassion for beings that are not yet redeemed, but only to those who were willing to listen. His compassion was neither missionary nor dedicated to the improvement of the world. Ultimately, there is no absolute ethics because there is no absolute teaching. Ultimately, only the individual can help herself or himself.

The regularity with which one encounters this peaceableness in countries influenced by Buddhism is captivating. As a rule, a Buddhist will neither defend his or her conviction by force nor seek to force others to turn away from their religion. In the face of innumerable attacks and humiliations, Buddhists have, in fact, scarcely ever staged religious wars.[19] Even so, Buddhism has been practically expelled from its land of origin, and Tibet has endured a hideous fifty years of religious persecution. The attitude of the present Dalai Lama to this enduring conflict is significant:

> We Tibetans lament that the Chinese have attacked our country and
> made us their colony. But it is not because we hate the Chinese. On the

contrary: We are grateful to them that they have given us the opportunity to practice patience, tolerance, and forgiveness. In doing so, they have tested our courage to the utmost.[20]

Buddhism has no need or canonical authority for defensive church construction, dogmas, or centralization, even though there is, of course, a full complement of Buddhist organizations. No explicit legitimation of war can be found in its canon, not even a legitimation of defensive war or self-defense. Of course, there is also no explicit prohibition of making war. The killing of any living thing is, in the first place, an obstacle to one's own spiritual perfection, so soldiers cannot achieve salvation. The same is true for fishers, hunters, butchers, and executioners, all of them lower occupations. Instead, nonviolent submission is to be preferred; the Buddhist monks who burned themselves to death during the Vietnam War are a symbol of this attitude.

Of course, Buddhist countries are not free of violence and more recently of fundamentalism. Of course, in the division between *Mahāyāna* and *Vajrayāna,* they have developed the bases for violence and even a legitimation of war, even the growth of militarized sects and monasteries, as well as Nichiren's defense of Buddhist teaching by force of arms. But compared with the postulated and realized peacefulness of Buddhism, these violent initiatives are rather marginal.

In the ethics of Buddhism and Christianity, too, faith stands over against knowledge. What would happen if, parallel to Japanese Amida-Buddhism, the "Buddhism of faith"[21] in which redemption is awaited from Amidea (skt. *Amitābha*) Buddha (which in itself is almost Christian), a "Christianity of unbelief" were to develop, such that God would no longer be thought of and felt to be a personal Father and Thou, but as a power that effects a liberating, saving change in—indeed, a dissolution of—the self? Then the ethical motto would be: "(Non)self love instead of love of enemies," or better, "Love your neighbor, including your enemy, as little as you love yourself." Most of those who have wanted to improve the world (as the history of Christianity, not least, shows) have remained dissatisfied with themselves and so have, in many cases, caused terrible harm. Had they pursued only their own salvation instead of the salvation of the world, had they loved themselves more than their enemies, perhaps a great deal of injustice might have been avoided.

This is true not only for the people who fought for Christian righteousness with good intentions, who nevertheless brought about evil. It is true of all who desire good deeds at any price, even that of giving themselves. It is no accident that Albert Schweitzer and Mother Teresa have become the supreme models of modern Christianity. These are two people of action, tireless in their admirable struggle against suffering. The case is very different with the supreme authority in Buddhism today, the fourteenth Dalai Lama, an image of personal integrity but not by all means a man of selfless good deeds. The Buddha even set those who seek their own salvation above those who care "only" for the salvation of others.[22] Certainly this is also a maximum ethical demand, from monks for monks, without regard for an ethics for family and state, or even for the neighbor.

I will go one step beyond this observation and ask (in Buddhist fashion?): Does the human being become good, or is she or he already good? Fear and suspicion, toward oneself and others, are sources of the mistrust produced by ethical systems. Where these no longer exist, but instead (here I am almost preaching a Buddhist sermon) goodwill, compassion, joy, and serenity—that is, the immeasurable (*apramāṇa*)—stream forth in every direction, or where (here I am thinking in Pauline and Reformed fashion) the human being is completely accepted by God and need not prove himself or herself, there is an end to the form of self-denial that is always the most helpful source of ethics.

6

Ethics in Early Buddhism

Axel Michaels

Buddhist ethics consists in large part of norms that appear in almost identical wording in Brahmanic and Jainist writings and are also at the center of every system of Christian ethics, for instance, the Decalogue: one must not kill, commit adultery, steal, give false witness, injure others. An example comparable to the Ten Commandments is the list of the ten actions that either are contrary to salvation or affect karma (*AN* V.303.19–22):

1. Killing living things
2. Theft
3. Unchastity
4. Lying
5. Speaking coarsely
6. Speaking foolishly
7. Calumny
8. Greed
9. Malice
10. False perception

The ethical prescriptions are directed to all, not only to religious specialists, even though already in Matthew 19:21 and fully evolved in the writings of Thomas Aquinas we see the development of a two-level ethics: the Decalogue is for everybody, but the *consilia evangelica* (Evangelical Counsels), with their demand for poverty, chastity, and obedience, are only for nuns and monks.

In similar fashion, Buddhism universalized ethical norms that at first applied only to monastic life—that is, in principle they were opened to the whole world because all barriers related to birth status were removed. This thesis has been emphatically proposed by the Oxford Indologist Richard F. Gombrich.[1] According to him, the Buddha's "success" was that he ethicized the Brahmanic doctrines of reincarnation and karma from the period of the Upanishads, to the extent that what counted for salvation was no longer only the deed (that is, the right sacrifices), but also the intention. For Gombrich, this ethicizing constitutes a turning point in the history of civilization whose importance can scarcely be overestimated.

The Buddha's radical turn consisted in his not damning every action (as did the Hindu and Jain doctrines of salvation) or every thought, but only those thoughts and actions that do not lead to salvation because they lack the right intention. This led to an increased emphasis in Buddhism on deliberateness, awareness, and attention. As for Jesus, everything must come from within. Thus, the Buddha is not against actions—not even, in principle, against recitations, rituals, or sacrifices—but against actions done in a false and immoral state of mind.

This internalizing of Brahmanic-Vedic religion had three revolutionary effects that are comparable to the origins of Christianity. First, it was denied that the Brahmanic priesthood was the primary and only ethical authority; instead, each person was responsible for himself or herself. Second, what was decisive was no longer belonging to a class, family, or tribe (so-called relational dharma), but again the individual self. Third, the whole universe (instead of a privileged class) was ethicized, although certainly this only applied to beings that can have conscience or intentions—thus essentially gods, people, and animals.

Despite some commonalities with Christianity, the ethics of Buddhism differs from Christian ethics on two points. It is principally derived from an intensive monastic spiritual practice, and it includes animals and nature.

Early Buddhist Ethics and Spiritual Praxis

Ethics in more ancient Buddhism was, because of its basis, focused neither on life nor on the self. Neither offers scope for redemption in the sense of *Nirvāṇa*. Early Buddhist ethics was associated more with meditative spiritual praxis than with right action. Right behavior is always also right spiritual behavior, which should lead to the elimination of suffering. This is expressed, among other texts, by the Noble Eightfold Path:

> And what, O monk, is the noble truth about the path that leads
> to the elimination of suffering? It is this noble eightfold way (*pā.*
> *āryāṣṭāṅgamārga*): 1. Right view (*samyagdṛṣti, pā. sammṣḍiṭṭhi*),
> 2. right decision (*samyaksaṃkalpa, pā. sammāsankappa*), 3. right
> speech (*samyagvāc, pā. sammāvāca*), 4. right behavior, action (*samyak-
> karmānta, pā. sammākammanta*), 5. right way of living (*samyagjīva,
> pā. sammā-ājīva*), 6. right effort (*samyagvyāyāma, pā. sammāvāyāma*),
> 7. right remembering (or awareness or attentiveness) (*samyaksmṛti, pā.*
> *sammāsati*), 8. right meditation (or collectedness, or concentration)
> (*samyaksamādhi, pā. sammāsmādhi*). (*DN* 311.28–313.27)

This eightfold way, according to tradition, consists of three groups: knowledge (*prajñā*, numbers 1 and 2), morality (*śīla*, numbers 3 through 5), and collectedness (*samādhi*, numbers 6 through 8). Buddhist scholasticism has given content to these doctrines, but in this context, what is important is the sources and context of the ethical norms.[2] At the beginning of Buddhist teaching stands the Buddha's immediate knowledge of conditioned becoming (*pratītyasamutpāda*), which attempts to explain in almost legal terms the becoming and passing away of all of what we would call psychic and physical phenomena. This knowledge he gained from a deep meditation and formulated as the Four Noble Truths, perhaps the sole dogma of Buddhism. According to these—this is the First Truth—all is suffering, and all is passing away and without a self, including the human being. Five groups of attachments or factors of being (*skandha*) are formed in each rebirth, each time anew, but there is no soul that moves from birth to birth. The reason for this painful rebirth is—this is the Second Truth—the thirst, the hunger for life, that arises out of the law of the conditioned origins of new life. Only when the thirst is abandoned is there an end to this circle and an escape from suffering, *Nirvāna*; this is the content of the Third Truth. The destruction of the thirst for life is the Noble Eightfold Path. It is right mental, moral, and spiritual behavior— and the Fourth Truth.

Thus, spiritual praxis presupposes an insight into the necessity to change one's life. Meditation prepares the way for salvation. In this way knowledge is linked clearly to morality and immersion. But right knowledge is achieved only when the spirit is prepared through right deeds.

Hence nearly all ethical norms are derived from monastic spiritual praxis. Thus, the five normative rules (*pañcaśīla*) that in some Buddhist traditions are taught to a layperson upon conversion are also part of the rule that novices, monks, and nuns must observe:[3]

1. The commandment not to harm any living thing (*ahiṃsā*), including animal sacrifices
2. The prohibition of theft, not only of material possessions, but also of spiritual (the basis for the principle of not wasting time)
3. The prohibition of adultery and the commandment of celibacy
4. The prohibition of lying
5. The prohibition of alcohol and drugs

The five prohibitions, as the first half of the ten bases of instruction (*pā. sikṣapāda*), are also part of the ten general moral rules, that is, they apply to those actions contrary to salvation (*pā. akuśalakarmapatha*) that monks and nuns must renounce. Added to these are prohibitions against mindless talking, calumny, greed, malice, and a false point of view. Three further rules that laypeople are also supposed to observe on special Buddhist feast days are also found in the codex of behavior for monks and novices: a commandment to fast in the afternoon and evening; the avoidance of dancing, music, singing, jewelry, perfume, makeup, and other means of beautification; and the avoidance of high beds.

Ethics and Everyday Life

These primarily monastic norms have far-reaching consequences even today, because people refer to the words of the Buddha even for the answers to modern questions.[4] Attempts are made to resolve the ethical problems of divorce, communism, capitalism, governance, war, or fundamentalism by recourse to the canon, and similar approaches are applied to questions of bioethics (abortion, manipulation of embryos, euthanasia, etc.).[5] In particular the *Sigālovā-dasutta,* the sole discourse that treats of the ethical norms for the laity, is cited. But concrete statements by the Buddha also are helpful—for example, that one should consume a quarter of one's income, invest half in business, and reserve another quarter for emergencies (*DN* III.188.17–22). Interestingly, the Theravadan Buddhaghosa (fourth to fifth centuries C.E.) counts generosity, especially giving to monks, as reinvestment: in a sense, there is a payoff after death.

Despite the primarily monastic roots of this ethics, the Buddha also indirectly taught virtues for daily life. Six such norms are listed, each arising out of a particular personal relationship (*DN* III.188.23–192.6): (1) from the relationship of husband and wife in marriage is derived the virtue of mutual attentiveness; (2) from the relationship of parents to their children, the virtue of gratitude; (3) from the teacher-pupil relationship, the virtue of knowledge; (4) from friendships, the virtue of partnership; (5) from the relationship of master and servant or king and people, the virtue of justice; and (6) from the relationship between monk and layperson the Buddha derives no distinctions in principle, but the virtue of the equality of all human beings.

Gustav Mensching thus rightly observes that Buddhist ethics is ascetical and turned away from the world, but at the same time is also turned toward the world because the Buddha did not expect everyone to take the final step of becoming a monk; he acknowledged a variety of stages of perfection.[6] From this arose a recognition of social obligations, and it is astonishing what a social force Buddhism became when it was carried to other countries. For the most part, deep-seated renewals in those places stem from Buddhism. Not only was Buddhist ethics for everyone, independent of caste status and gender, it often also meant democratization. The inscriptions of Emperor Aśoka (third century B.C.E.) are the earliest witnesses to the social-revolutionary power of Buddhist ethics. Here the ruler—in a way that remains remarkable in one so powerful—expresses his regret for misdeeds committed, renounces all violence and conquest, rejects animal sacrifices, and requires of himself and his subjects nonviolence, calm judgment, and gentleness.

Buddhist Love

In comparing Buddhism with Christianity, one is drawn especially to Buddhist love or kindness, better "goodwill, friendship" (*maitrī, pā. mettā*), and, closely related to it, compassion (skt./*pā. karuṇā*). Significant differences are evident here, as Hermann Oldenberg had already noted:

> One may compare the great figures here and there. Here Saint Francis or Vincent de Paul, who practice love of God and love of neighbor to help the least of the lowly, the most deeply suffering of all sufferers, out of the warmest personal attachment. There Sariputta or Ananda, who sits down in the loneliness of the Indian forest to contemplate the *maitri* and out of the cool quiet of Nirvana, to which he knows himself close, extends his good

will toward people, animals, and all creatures from one region of the world to another—the good will of one who has sought and achieved "not to love anything in the world." Are these not the citizens of two different worlds?[7]

Buddhist love is the first part of the Four Divine Conditions of Abiding (*brahmavihāra*), also called the Four Immeasurables (*apramāna*), which the saint can experience and that are explained thus:[8] (1) love (*maitrī, pā. mettā*), (2) compassion (*karuṇā*), (3) joy (with) (*muditā*), and (4) serenity (*upekṣā, pā. upekkhā*). The enlightened one is so filled with these attitudes that his deeds incur no further karma and thus no new rebirth.

Love

A classic text for all-embracing Buddhist love—or better, goodwill or kindness (*maitrī, pā. mettā*)—is the following passage from the *Mettāsutta:*

> As a mother watches over and protects her only child, even to the endangerment of her own life, so one should lovingly embrace the whole world with beneficent, unlimited kindness. Whether walking or standing, sitting or lying, as soon as one has awakened one should attentively practice this thought and realize it in such a way as to live in the highest way. Whoever has surrendered unknowing and acquired the deep inner vision, free from sensual desires and founded on virtue, is perfected; for such a one there will be no more rebirth. (*Sn* 149–52)[9]

This feeling of friendship is marked by gentleness and indifference, however, not by empathy. *Maitrī* is in a sense nothing more than an indifferent goodwill or liking. Thus, it is clearly a different love from what Paul describes, the love that is greater than faith and hope and without which each of us would be like a clanging cymbal, even if we spoke with both human and angelic tongues (1 Cor 13:1). Nor should one love enemies and neighbors as oneself; rather, one should love or hate neither oneself nor enemies nor neighbors. Instead, one should show no strong arousal of feeling at all, receiving everything with the same gentleness and kindness. Only in this way can one avoid the egoism of action, which causes suffering even in love:

> All pains and laments, all the suffering in the world of every form, comes through what is dear to one; where there is nothing beloved, these also will not occur. Therefore those are full of joy and free of pain who have

nothing in the world that they love. Therefore whoever strives to be where there is neither pain nor gloom should love nothing in this world. (*Ud* 92.18–23)[10]

There should be no loving, because that implies the expectation of a reign of God; rather, compassion is the necessary consequence of a right spiritual attitude. Unlike New Testament love (Greek *agapē*), Buddhist love is not given and received from God, but is the result of a meditative process of self-redemption.[11]

It is true that in early monastic Buddhism the love and compassion thus demanded were not necessarily followed by works of charity. (Buddha himself did not heal as Jesus did; at most he pointed out the way and the stages on the way. If Jesus was a healer, Buddha was a psychotherapist.) Nevertheless, lay Buddhism and *Mahāyāna* Buddhism developed an ethics that is quite comparable to Christian *caritas.* Here and elsewhere Buddhists have engaged themselves on behalf of the poor, those in need, and the disadvantaged. They have assumed responsibility in society and politics and have demonstrated and agitated against injustice, violence, and cruelty.

Compassion

After the one seeking salvation has realized all-bountiful love (*maitrī*), "love of neighbor, fellow-feeling, compassion" (*karuṇā*) enters in, for now one has the ability to recognize oneself, "free from grudge and from ill-will," in all things and all persons. Associated with *karuṇā* is the self-sacrifice that is found over and over again in Buddhism. It has its mythological predecessors in the prebirth stories (*Jātaka*), as when the Buddha in his early existences throws himself before starving animals to be their food. Especially in *Mahāyāna* Buddhism, *karuṇā* was developed into the ideal of the bodhisattva. According to this, those who are capable of redemption should renounce their redemption in order to free other beings from the painful cycle of rebirth.

One consequence of *karuṇā* is the virtue of generosity (*dāna*), which is also praised in Brahmanic dharma-texts. This was especially for Buddhist laypeople, not least because the monks depended on this generosity for their survival. Gifts to monks could transfer religious service, so that even those who practiced trades and professions through which they accumulated negative karma, and who—strictly speaking—constantly violated the ethical norms of Buddhism, especially the prohibition against killing, could participate in religious blessings.

Joy

Out of love of neighbor or fellow-feeling arises the "common joy" (*mudita*) over having sought salvation and found the way to the elimination of suffering.

Serenity

At the end of the search for salvation is serenity (*upeksa*), which is exercised toward all beings and from which is derived, among other things, a universal tolerance. This serenity encompasses the soteriological necessity of letting go, selflessness, indifference, or detachment. This can be confused with egoism, since it appears that one's own search for salvation is always primary, but the consequences of serenity are not at all selfish. Letting go is based on knowledge of the Four Noble Truths, especially knowledge of the mutability and passibility of everything conditioned that comes to be. This includes also all motives, all characteristics connected to self-centeredness and love of self. No wonder that, in consequence, the Buddha always spoke also against pride, arrogance, hatred, anger, avarice, greed, and lust. Letting go demands other characteristics, such as humility, gentleness, patience, self-control, lack of desire, modesty, truthfulness, and wisdom.

Serenity and gentleness are closest to Buddha's preaching of the Middle Way and the avoiding of every kind of violence, even in knowledge, even in regard to the good. Nevertheless, there is a tension between serenity or detachment (*upeksa*) and compassion (*karuna*). The two are possible, according to a later text, not simultaneously, but only successively:

> When, with the Buddha, the great detachment is actualized, all the living beings of the world could be burned before his eyes like dry twigs: he would not notice it. When he actualizes the great compassion, the sight of a single suffering being is enough to cause his unbelievably strong and unshakeable body to tremble like a banana leaf in a storm. (*Vibhasa* 428 c17–21)[12]

Buddhist Ethics Regarding Animals and Nature

Unlike Christian love, Buddhist love from the outset is directed to all living things, although not really to plants. The result is a special ethics of care for living things—especially humans and animals, less so for plants—and nature, which is required by the commandment not to wound, *ahiṃsā*.

Lambert Schmithausen, the scholar who has done the most fundamental study of this theme,[13] has shown not only that "the first and probably also the most important element of right behavior (*śīla*) and right, healthful action (*kusala*)"[14] is the self-commitment not to kill other living things, but also that this renunciation of killing and destruction is broad in scope. Thus, even dangerous animals, insects such as mosquitoes, or tiny things like ants are to be protected. Dangerous beasts are to be met with the demeanor of kindness (*maitrī*) already described (*AN* II.72.9–73.10). Monks and laity are to cultivate a special reverence (*lajjā*) for life and a sympathy (*dayā*) and concern (*anukampā*) for the good of living things (*DN* I.63.20–22; *MN* I.287.27–29; *AN* V.266.22–24). Torture of animals, hunting, and the willful damaging of plants are thus forbidden. Soldiers, hunters, and farmers have opportunities to compensate—through donations to a monastery, for example. The ideal of Emperor Aśoka, who gave up hunting and counseled peaceableness, was constantly being worked out. Even gifts to despised animals, such as dogs, are considered creditable. Special measures of protection are commanded—for example, straining water through a filter cloth in order to spare the tiniest animals.

It is well known, of course, that Buddhism has not been as radical as Jainism, which developed the strictest precautions for the protection of all living things. Thus, certain Jainist monks had to go naked so as not to withhold from stinging insects the skin that is theirs to attack. Likewise, eating meat and fish was forbidden to Buddhist monks only when the animals were killed especially for them and they knew of it (*MN* I.369.5–7). Early Buddhism also took a middle course on this question.

In early Buddhism the ethics of protecting living things applied to human beings and animals, but only in exceptional cases to plants. It derived in part from fear of the vengeance of the living things that were killed, perhaps also from a feeling of relatedness (cf. *SN* V.353.29–354.5), and increasingly from compassion.[15] After all, the ability to suffer is a precondition for the ability to be redeemed. Buddhahood is in all living things, so Buddhas do not kill any living thing. On the contrary, they help them on the way to redemption. This is the consistent development found in the bodhisattva principle of *Mahāyāna*.

Of course, neither life nor nature represents a value of its own in early Buddhism, certainly not the highest value. A Buddhist ecology can be derived only in a limited sense from the ancient layers of the texts. Thus, for example, one can only indirectly derive the protection of species, since compassion always extends only to individual animals.[16]

Love and Kindness

Jesus' ethics is shaped by love of God and human beings, Buddha's ethics by knowledge and kindness. Jesus aimed at the heart, Buddha at the head. Jesus wanted to combat evil; Buddha's target was painful transitoriness. In the New Testament, the highest virtue is *agapē*; in Buddhism it is serenity. These divergences—distorted by exaggeration—should be noted. In large part they can be explained by the particular social and historical situations of Jesus Christ and Gautama Buddha. However, in a universal, globalized ethics (as represented, for example, by the "Declaration of Human Rights" (the UN declaration), it appears increasingly necessary to draw from Buddhism its more comprehensive rejection of violence, which also includes the protection of animals and plants,[17] and thus to combine Christian and Buddhist ethics.

Jesus' intention was, through his ethics, to prepare people for the reign of God. Thus, mercy and care for others are at the top of the list. In his eyes, would the Buddha have been prepared for the coming reign of God? Probably not! It is true that in his actions he fulfilled the criteria of honesty, sincerity, and purity of heart, but he would have been lacking—once again—in faith in God, who (in contrast to the Pharisees' mere following of the law) was central for Jesus. But for the Buddha, even faith is too much of a good thing and thus incapable of redeeming. He might have asked: What good are faith and good works if they are impelled by the thirst that causes suffering?

Response / *Ulrich Luz*
Love and Grace

Axel Michaels has pointed to faith in God as the decisive difference between Jesus and Buddha: "But for the Buddha, even faith is too much of a good thing and thus incapable of redeeming. He might have asked: What good are faith and good works if they are impelled by the thirst that causes suffering?"

These concluding remarks on ethics in early Buddhism signal a misunderstanding of Jesus and Christianity. Jesus did not want "through his ethics to prepare people for the reign of God." That was, more or less, the opinion of

Hans Windisch. According to him, Jesus' sharpened demands were essentially "conditions for entrance" into the reign of God.[18] That was, in a sense, the thesis also held by Albert Schweitzer, according to whom Jesus presented a radically intensified "interim ethics" for the short time until the coming of the reign of God.[19] My thesis, following Jürgen Becker, is that Jesus' ethics is shaped by the rule of God. His call for decision "lives out of the experience of the offer of salvation from that same God; it is a grateful response...a shaping of life out of joy experienced."[20]

Let me illustrate this with the reign-of-God parable of the treasure in the field: *First* someone finds in a field his or her lifelong dream, a golden treasure. *Then* the person sells everything she or he has and buys the field (Matt 13:44). *Finding Is the First Act* is the title of a wonderful book that draws out precisely this feature of the parable.[21]

This basic feature recurs in later interpretations of Jesus in the New Testament. "God is love," because he sent his Son into the world (1 John 4:8–9)— and that is the basis of life in this world. The Son of God "loved me and gave himself for me." Only in that faith can Paul say, "It is no longer I who live, but it is Christ who lives in me" (Gal 2:20). Among those aspects of Christianity that correspond to what Buddhism calls thirst is what Paul means by "justification by the works of the law" (Gal 2:16), namely, the firm will of a human being to stand justified before God on the basis of one's own deeds. This very thing, according to Paul, comes to an end if I "through the law have died to the law" (Gal 2:19). Christian faith thus understands law precisely *not* as impelled by "thirst," but as sustained by the underlying nearness and love of God, which leads to the death of the "I" that is focused on itself and the experience of a new "I," which is "Christ in me."

In early Buddhism, by contrast, kindness (*maitrī*) and compassion (*karuṇā*) appear to be essentially steps on the way to serenity and emptiness as "kindness" and "compassion" are both practices on the path to serenity and selflessness. Therefore, in Buddhism it never can be a matter of an empathetic, engaged loving of the neighbor "as myself."[22] Kindness and compassion are, rather, ways of practicing the letting go of one's own self. It seems to me, then, that the place of love in Buddhism is different from its place in Christianity. Christian love comes from the experience of the love of God and of grace. Compassion in early Buddhism is, rather, an attitude of fundamental importance on the way to serenity.

Probably for this reason, Axel Michaels has interpreted early Buddhism as a "meditative process of self-redemption." I suggest that, as regards Buddhism, we avoid using the word *self-redemption*, because that would be handing it to cheap Christian apologetics on a plate. Redemption consists, in Buddhism, precisely in the knowledge that the self is not, as in Western philosophy since Descartes, a given entity, but rather is something to be overcome, something that dissolves in the process of liberation from the cycle of becoming and ceasing to be. In early Buddhism it may be a matter of redemption from the self, but by no means redemption through the self. The expression "self-redemption" is, rather, a category of Western, Christian-influenced study of Buddhism.[23]

This brings me again to my basic question: Is there an experience in early Buddhism corresponding to what Christians understand as grace? Lambert Schmithausen speaks of the "compassion of the Buddha," meaning the compassion that comes from the experience of enlightenment, which is distinct from what "one practices within the framework of the way of redemption,"[24] and that aids one's own redemption. If there had been such a practice in early Buddhism, it would represent a very deep convergence with early Christianity. Christian love that lives out of the gift of grace corresponds to the love of the enlightened one who, after all, continues to live after his or her enlightenment in a world overflowing with suffering and lovelessness. But perhaps this is an idea that appears only in later *Mahāyāna* Buddhism.

Part Four
Passion and Suffering

7

Suffering in Early Buddhism

Axel Michaels

The Suffering of the Buddha

Jesus' suffering, with the crucifixion as its primary image, is familiar to most people. It is less well known that Buddha *Śākyamuni* also is supposed to have suffered much after leaving the palace, according to the legendary sources. Accompanied by five disciples, he is said to have practiced severe ascesis in Uruvelā (south of Patna, near Bodhgayā). The tradition attributes the following account to him:

> When, Aggivessana, I tried to take hold of the skin of my belly, I grasped
> my backbone, and when I wanted to grasp my backbone, I took hold of
> the skin of my belly: that is how closely the skin of my belly was sticking
> to my backbone as the result of this meagre intake of food. And when,
> Aggivessana, I tried to defecate or urinate, I fell over on my face as a result
> of this meagre intake of food. And in order to bring life to my body,
> Aggivessana, I rubbed my limbs with my hand. And when, Aggivessana,
> I rubbed my limbs with my hand, the hairs, whose roots had rotted, fell
> from my body as a result of this meagre intake of food. (*MN* I.246.3–12)[1]

The Buddha tries to compel knowledge, both physical and mental, by putting himself in a breathless trance—with resulting headaches and buzzing in his ears. He also practices every kind of mortification. He goes about naked or wrapped only in animal pelts or shrouds, fasts or eats only a single food, does not cut his hair or shave, stands and sleeps without a roof over his head, does not wash, exposes himself to extreme heat, and even eats his own feces. The result is that he grows thin and almost starves (a well-known motif in representations of the Buddha). But the discourse always ends, as in the preceding quotation, with a reference to the fact that this experience of pain led to no result.

Thus, the Buddha—at least according to the legends—endured extraordinary tortures on his way to knowledge, but they did not bring him to his goal. On the contrary, he rejected these ascetic methods, which are still in wide use today. He began to eat again and, strengthened in body, went through four contemplative immersions, through which he achieved the highest enlightenment. A yearlong intensive phase of pain and suffering was followed by the first mystical experience, the meditation under the Aśvattha tree, later called the Bodhi tree.

In the Buddha legends, the preparation for what for all Buddhists was probably the decisive event or experience in Gautama's life (through which he ultimately became the Buddha) is elaborated and adorned with symbolic elements that promise well. The path to the River Nairañjanā near the village of Urubilvā is shown him, gods accompany him, his body becomes radiant, a throne is prepared, etc. The Buddha sits down under a tree in Bodhgayā to meditate and decides, "May my body wither here on this place, may my skin, bones, and flesh disappear; until I have achieved the enlightenment that is so difficult to acquire in four ages of the world, I will not move from this seat" (*Lalitavistara*).[2]

The Buddha achieved this enlightenment for himself, despite temptations and errors. It is not an action of grace, not a revelation, not an experience of call. It is knowledge obtained without a message from another, without appeal to a previous authority. Unlike Jesus and many other religious founders, the Buddha did not desire to be more than a human being, nor did he want to preach or prophesy, but only to help people on the path to knowledge, to show them the way: "One is the master of oneself; who else can be one's master? You will never find better masters than when you have made yourself master of your own self" (*Dhp* 160). This truth is the subject of the Buddha's first sermon; it thus follows immediately after his own (self-imposed!) experiences of suffering. With this first sermon the wheel of teaching was set in motion, and the Middle Way was proclaimed. Accordingly, in the *Pāli* canon the biography of the Buddha ends with this first sermon, which contains the teaching of the Four Noble Truths. In these truths, which Hermann Oldenberg has rightly described as the "core and corners" of Buddhism, the concept of suffering (Skr. *duḥka, pā. dukkha*) appears four times.

The Concept of Suffering in the Four Noble Truths

These, you monks, are the Four Noble Truths. Which four? Suffering, the origin of suffering, the cessation of suffering, the path leading to the cessation of suffering.

What is the Noble Truth of Suffering (*duḥkha*)? Birth is suffering, aging is suffering, sickness is suffering, death is suffering, being united to what is distasteful is suffering, separation from the loved is suffering, not to get what one wants and strives for is suffering: in short, the five categories affected by clinging (*upādānaskandha*) are suffering. This is suffering.

What is the Origin of Suffering (*duḥkhasamudaya*)? It is the thirst (*tṛṣṇa*) that leads to rebirth, that, accompanied by relish and lust, relishes this and that. This is the origin of suffering.

What is the Removal of Suffering (*duḥkhanirodha*)? It is the complete rejection and removal of this thirst that leads to rebirth, accompanied by relish and lust, relishing this and that: It is the removal and the suppression of this. This is the removal of suffering.

What is the Way Leading to the Cessation of Suffering (*duḥkhanirod-hagāminī pratipat*)? It is the Noble Eightfold Path, that is to say: Right View, Right Intention, Right Speech, Right Action, Right Living, Right Effort, Right Mindfulness and Right Concentration. This is the path that leads to the removal of suffering. These, you monks, are the Four Noble Truths. (*Mahāvagga* I.6.10ff.)[3]

The very first truth is "the truth of suffering." In this, first of all, biological and physical processes—birth, aging, sickness, and death—are equated with suffering. It should not be overlooked that birth, as rebirth, was regarded in early Buddhism (but not only there) as part of a chain of suffering. It was experienced more as pollution than as a promise of happiness. The processes of decay in the life and body of a human being constitute the basic anthropological experience of suffering. This is expressed in an infinite number of sayings and discourses:

> If there were three things, you monks, that did not exist in the world, the Perfected One would not appear in the world, the holy, highest Buddha. Without them the teaching and order that the Perfected One proclaims would not enlighten the world. What three things are these? Birth, aging, and death. (*AN* V.144.6–8)

The next sufferings are, we might say, psychic in nature: separation in time and space, the loss of beloved persons or things, unfulfilled wishes. Everything rests on the knowledge that even the most beautiful and joyful experiences and things can cease to be or may be lost.

Physical and psychic suffering belong to the five factors (*skandha, pā. khandā*) or elements of all being that is subject to redemption (see chapter 4). Physical and psychic suffering are tied to cause and effect, for they reveal three characteristics of the conditional: beginning, passing away, and existence-and-change. As long as human beings cling to their physicality and the other factors, they cling to what is unstable, that is, subject to suffering, and thus resemble a dog tied to a stake and constantly running in a circle (cf. *SN* III.150.7–23). For the *skandhas* are empty, without self (*anātman, pā. anattam*), and unstable (*anitya, pā. anicca*)—and therefore are subject to suffering.

The *skandhas* are also described as categories of appropriation (*upādāna*), because greed or desire, literally thirst (*tṛṣṇā, pā. taṇhā*), draws one to them. Only Arhats and Buddhas, who have conquered this desire, are free from them. What is this desire, this thirst? The Buddha taught, "It is the thirst that leads to rebirth, including joy and lust, which finds its pleasure here or there: the thirst for lust (*pā. kāmataṇhā*), the thirst for being (*pā. bhavataṇhā*), the thirst for power (*vibhavataṇhā*)" (*MN* I.299.18–20).

The Suffering of Beginning and Ending

The second Noble Truth is closely linked to another chain of concepts that is fundamental to Buddhism: the formula of origins in dependencies (*pratītyasamutpāda, pā. paṭiccasamuppāda*). The origin of the groups of being follows this law of conditioned origin, also called the conditional nexus (see table 5).

Table 5	Dependent Arising (*pratityasamutpāda*)	
Number	Members (skt./pā.)	Image
1	Ignorance (*avidyā/avijjā*)	Blind old woman
2	Formations (*saṃskāra/saṅkhārā*)	Potter
3	Consciousness, awareness (*vijñāna/viññāṇa*)	Ape eating fruit in a tree
4	Name and form (*nāmarūpa*)	Boat with rowers
5	Six fields of awareness, sense organs (*ṣaḍāyatana/saḷāyatana*)	House with five windows and a door
6	Contact (*sparśa/phassa*)	Pair of lovers
7	Sensation (*vedanā*)	Arrow in the eye
8	Thirst, desire, sensibility (*tṛṣṇā/taṇhā*)	Wine drinker
9	Appropriation (of earthly life) (*upādāna*)	Fruit picker
10	Becoming, coming to be, begetting (*bhava*)	Pregnant woman
11	(Re-)birth (*jāti*)	Birth
12	Aging and death (*jarāmaraṇa*)	Corpse

This chain of causality is thought to have been taught by the Buddha himself, even though not in this classic form, which is probably the work of monks. The Buddha himself recognized that the teaching was profound and difficult, and it has remained one of the most contentious texts of Buddhism, due not least to the peculiar terminology. The series of concepts is to be read in such a way that the previous component always causes the one that follows. The power to give form arises out of unknowing, and so on. It can also be read both forward and backward: upward to beginning, downward to destruction. The first three components have to do with the previous life, while numbers four through nine are about the present, and the remainder have to do with the future:

1. All suffering begins from the fact that there was unknowing (*avidyā*) in a previous life, that is, lack of knowledge of the Four Noble Truths. Had this knowledge (*vidyā*) been achieved, there would have been no rebirth and so no suffering. Knowledge, then, is salvation, and unknowing is, as it is later called in *Mahāyāna,* almost a "mystical original sin,"[4] because it keeps the karmic

cycle in motion. In *Mahāyānist* depictions, a blind old woman is the image for the "wheel of existences," the Bhavacakra, which is literally a fatal cycle.

2. Out of unknowing arise the powers that enable the giving of forms (*saṃslāra*), the karmic drives that led to rebirth. Unknowing causes the emergence of everything that is formed, that has become (*saṃ-s-kṛ*), and thus all that is transitory. As something is shaped from a lump of clay on a potter's turning wheel, so everything that is formed emerges once unknowing sets the cycle in motion. But what is still more crucial is that the lump, once it has begun to turn, wants to be formed. Thus, unknowing gives rise to the drives that lead to rebirth.

3. And so comes consciousness (*vijñāna*), which is essentially the knowledge of the names and physicality of objects and oneself, including rebirth and individuality. We are looking here at a radically subjective theory of knowledge: no object of knowledge without a subject, but also no subject of knowledge without knowledge as object (or substance). It follows that knowing is itself already the ground of new life, or better, knowing causes new life to come to be, since it is a spiritual element above earth, water, fire, wind, and space. This element seeks a womb adequate to itself, and it can be more or less good according to the deed intended. Thus, from a certain point of view, human bodies consist only of matter that of itself awakens knowledge or consciousness to life. But beyond this, out of consciousness arises a kind of fine karmic material that outlasts the body and must re-embody itself in the next life—just as an ape that leaps from branch to branch, from fruit to fruit, still remains an ape.

4. Only through this fine karmic material are name and form (*nāmarūpa*) made possible. This is an application of an old conceptual structure, already evident in the *Ṛgveda,* to the unity of language/thought and the world of appearances in the sense of a radical nominalism. In earliest Buddhism, *vijñāna* and *nāmarūpa* are complementarily dependent on one another; there is no absolute existence of name or form independent of consciousness. As neither the rowers nor the boat can cross the river alone, so there is no form independent of consciousness and no consciousness without form. It also follows that spiritual consciousness *is* not, but *makes* body-soul individuality (*ātman*). But if there is no substantiality to things (with some reservations, the world of appearances), then there is also no self enduring beyond rebirth as something substantial. The real world depends on knowing; it appears in a sense as will and idea, but knowing itself belongs not to the self, but to the real

world. In this contradiction, which causes *vijñāna nāmarūpa* and vice versa, lies a basis for later scholastic disputes over the reality of the external world. The *Sautrāntikas* take the position of realists, the *Vijñānavādins* are idealists (only *vijñāna* counts), and the *Śūnyavādins* are "negativists" (everything is empty).

5. After consciousness has brought about individuality and spirit and body, or *vijñāna* and *nāmarūpa* have come together, there arise the six regions of the subject (*ṣaḍāyatana*), that is, the organs of the eye, ear, nose, tongue, body (organ for sensations of touch), and the organ of thought. Over against these are the six regions of the objective world: shape, sound, smell, etc. The organ of thought is the door to a house with five windows, symbolizing the other sense organs.

6. The result of this union is contact with the world of objects (*sparśa*). The human being makes use of the organs of sense, touching and understanding objects in the way a pair of lovers touch one another.

7. Thus arise feelings and sensitivities (*vedanā*), impressions that penetrate the memory like an arrow in the eye.

8. These impressions cause thirst (*tṛṣṇā*), the lust for more. In scholasticism (*SN* II.3.17–19), this thirst is again divided into six: thirst for physical forms, sounds, smells, tastes, touches, ideas. It is the real source of suffering and rebirth. Thirst thus leads directly to the next life; it is the thirst for life, imaged by a man drinking wine. When one allows desire to arise from feeling, one plants the seed of new life. And in the opposite case, if one conquers this desire, then salvation is possible because the conditional nexus is interrupted.

9. What a person desires, he or she wants to hold on to; we collect fruits in our basket. So it is with our fateful clinging to earthly existence (*upādāna*), which causes the next steps.

10. Begetting and becoming (*bhava*) are symbolized by a pregnant woman.

11. The (re-)birth (*jāti*) of a child, that

12. again is subjected to aging and death (*jarāmaraṇa*), until as a corpse it is brought to be burned.

The conditional nexus is still more obvious if we read the chain of concepts backward: aging and death (12) presuppose birth (11), and birth presumes becoming (10), which was caused in the previous life by clinging (9) to the sensible world, and this in turn goes back to thirst for life (8). Thirst—one could call it addiction—again comes about because of (pleasant) feelings (7), which are caused by contact (6) between the sense and things, but only because there are the six regions of consciousness (5), namely, the five senses and the organ of thought, which in turn belong to a given person with name and form (4), constituted by a consciousness (3), which has constructed itself through the powers of shaping (2) that were formed in a previous life, only because it had not developed a redemptive knowing (1).

To compare this with Christianity, we should note the following points of the teaching: The explanation of suffering is brought within a philosophical system, but it is not conceived as a theodicy. It is not God or God's opponent who causes suffering to happen in order to bring the human being onto the right path. Rather, the human being is the cause of his or her own suffering. It is also significant that there is one exit, through knowledge, but no entry into the cycle, that is, no inherited guilt or original sin. With knowledge, the alleviation of suffering follows automatically, without reservation or remainder. This alleviation is (to begin with) related only to an individual, not to the community, the neighbor, or the world. In *Mahāyāna* the idea of compassion (instead of suffering/passion) comes more strongly to the fore.[5]

Suffering and Transitoriness

Are we justified in translating *duḥka* as "suffering," when ultimately it is about explaining reincarnation? And does the system not collapse if one does not experience life and thus rebirth as fundamentally painful, as early Buddhism does? In fact, the early Buddhist concept of suffering mixes psychophysical elements with others that are purely mental and metaphysical. The First Noble Truth is itself to be understood in this twofold sense: Soul and body experience painful feelings such as illness, aging, death, but in addition to these, all feelings, even pleasant ones, are declared to constitute suffering (*SN* IV.216.14–18).

Here, then, suffering as pain is coupled with suffering as transitoriness itself. Translating *duḥka* as "suffering" is therefore not quite accurate. "All feeling is suffering" (*SN* IV.216.17–18), including happiness, love, or the rule of God. Tilman Vetter[6] and others have pointed out that in the summary formulation of the First Truth in the *Mahāvagga* of *Vinayapiṭaka,* where the five groups of graspings (*pā. upādānakhandā*) are again named, (*pā.*) *dukkha* is to be read as an adjective: "causing to suffer." The Buddha was not saying by this that everything worldly is painful, but only that it is unsatisfying, not really helpful for salvation.

Thus, basically there are three stages of suffering, as Buddhist dogma also asserts:[7] (1) the "suffering of pain" (*duḥkhaduḥkhatā*), or unpleasant sensations; (2) "suffering from change (or decay)" (*vipariṇāmaduḥkhatā*), the fading of pleasant sensations; and (3) "suffering from transitoriness (of the caused factors of being as such)" (*saṃskāraduḥkhatā*), that is, metaphysical suffering.

The metaphysical concept of suffering rests on knowledge, not pain. It is associated with endurance and with the fact that even a happy life is happy only as long as it lasts. The *Mahāsaṅghikas* even asserted that there are no pleasant sensations or feelings at all, but only ameliorations of pain. According to this, even the way of salvation is painful. This assertion was rejected as an exaggeration. But in a metaphysical sense all the schools considered that everything formed (*saṃskāra*) is suffering, because everything is dependent and transitory. Thus, the metaphysical concept of suffering is associated above all with transitoriness: "The primary characteristics of the absolute are eternity, constancy, and unity; the world of contingency is necessarily characterized by inconstancy, changeableness, and multiplicity."[8] Early Buddhism has no bridge between the worlds such as Jesus represents.

This teaching about the suffering nature of being has, among other things, important consequences for the self: "What is inconstant is suffering; what is suffering is non-self; what is non-self is not mine, it is not I, it is not myself" (*SN* IV.1.13–15). If the human being is transitory, he or she cannot be identified with the absolute, because then even that would be transitory, that is, suffering. The self cannot belong to what is happening and becoming; it cannot manifest itself as individual soul in the world of becoming and passing away, as in the doctrine of the identity of Brahman and *Ātman:*

> There are five things that no being in this world can accomplish, neither monk nor brahman, nor God nor demon [*Māra*]—not even Brahman. They are: that being subject to aging, one avoids becoming older; that being subject to infirmity, one prevents sickness; that being subject to death, one avoids dying; that being subject to decline, one prevents deterioration; that being subject to disappearing, one prevents disappearance. (*AN* III.60.3–11)[9]

Inconstancy and subjection to suffering are therefore nearly identical and likewise are not the self. This is the meaning also of the teaching about the three characteristics of what is caused (*trilakṣaṇa*), according to which all caused beings are inconstant, suffering, and not the self. In contrast, invariance in time is a goal of salvation. This idea led to a special teaching about momentariness, in which there is no possibility of reality enduring over time.[10] Time is understood to consist only in infinitesimal units in a succession of moments of equal length. But each of these moments is caused. Beyond them is nothing enduring, not even God. If something is, it is mutually caused: "Things 'are' only to the extent that they are produced and conditioned by other things, and no more."[11]

Is Buddhism Pessimistic?

The rationality typical of the early Buddhist concept of suffering does not allow for pessimism, as it is often accused of doing. Early Buddhist suffering is not world-weariness, compassion, *memoria passionis* (the memory of suffering), abandonment by God, fear of sin and punishment. This suffering is not brought about by theodicy, the consequence of penance, the cursing of an evil deed, the loss of a paradise without suffering as a consequence of original sin. Early Buddhist suffering does not make way for martyrdom, for representative, self-sacrificing suffering. Early Buddhist suffering is knowledge of transitoriness that is thought through to its logical consequence with the utmost stringency.

Christianity assigns suffering to a place that is at least equal, if not even higher. Unlike Buddhism, in Christianity the founder himself suffered. God did not spare his own Son the deepest suffering, and the response to this God-willed suffering is, for the most part, what makes Christianity. It is no accident that the symbol of the cross and the Crucified, together with the Bible, identify Christianity. This suffering is interpreted in Christianity as, among other things, love, self-sacrifice for humanity, the overcoming of a self-created distance from God—an idea and a belief that would have been utterly foreign to early Buddhism.

Buddhism also aims to conquer suffering. But it does not exclude the possibility of achieving salvation during one's lifetime, whereas Christianity accepts the inevitability of suffering as a fundamental fact that, in faith, is transformed into love and will be rewarded in another life according to the grace of God. Buddhism wants to eliminate suffering, while Christianity wants to overcome it.

There are other distinctions. Buddhist suffering has nothing to do with guilt or punishment (rebirth is a consequence, not a punishment). Death, too, is not "the wages of sin" (Rom 6:23) in Buddhism, so it is not the end of suffering.[12] Buddhism has no Job and knows representative suffering only through its ethics of compassion.

Of course, these differences raise questions. It is always incomprehensible to non-Christians why a suffering, crucified man is worshiped. In Buddhism, too, as we have seen, the concept of suffering is central, but the image of the emaciated Buddha is an exception. The rule, rather, is the image of a smiling Buddha. How does it happen that Buddhism, despite a much more extensive doctrine of suffering—in which even happiness, paradise, and nearness to God are declared to constitute suffering—is seen by many as a less "painful" religion? It seems to me that there are two basic reasons for this. First, in Buddhism one need not accomplish everything in a single life; one can comfortably put off the way of the Buddha to one's next life without thereby being subjected to damnation. Second, suffering is not considered punishment, so it is much less threatening. One may ask, then, from the point of view of Buddhism: Is the theology of Christ's crucifixion really necessary?

Response / *Ulrich Luz*
Why the Cross?

If I am looking for Western parallels to the Buddhist concept of the Four Noble Truths and suffering, I will not find them primarily in orthodox Christianity, but rather in Christian and non-Christian Gnosis. The Valentinian *Gospel of Truth* contains a cosmogony that is very similar to the *pratītyasamutpāda*. The world, and thus suffering as well, has arisen out of unknowing:

> The totality was inside of him, the incomprehensible, inconceivable
> one who is superior to every thought—ignorance of the Father brought
> about anguish and terror; and the anguish grew solid like a fog, so that
> no one was able to see. For this reason error became powerful; it worked
> on its own matter foolishly, not having known the truth. (*Evangelium
> Veritatis* = NHC II.17.5ff.)[13]

In Buddhist terms, the powers of creation arise out of unknowing. The "Gospel" then describes how Error produced Forgetting and Distress. Suffering arose out of unknowing, that is, forgetting the Father. It consists in the fact that people are bound within the world of appearances, the world of sense perception and matter. It is overcome by true knowledge, that is, enlightenment through the hidden mystery of Jesus Christ. In Buddhist terms, knowledge, then, is salvation.

How is redemption brought about in Christian Gnosis? It is by people's recognizing where they come from and where they are going. Once they recognize their heavenly origin, they know that their being enmeshed in the history of becoming and passing away, in matter, is only apparently real; then all appearance vanishes. In the Gnostic *Gospel of Mary* a disciple asks, "'Will matter then be [destroyed] or not?' The Savior said, 'All natures, all formations, all creatures exist in and with one another, and they will be resolved again into their own roots'" (*Gos. Mary* = Cod. Berol. 8502.7.1–6).[14] In Buddhist terms: For a human being to cling to bodiliness is to depend on what is inconstant, that is, filled with suffering. But when one knows that one has no self, the *skandhas* become mere factors of being that are reduced to their own roots. How does this happen? The non-Christian Gnostic tractate "Poimandres" describes how the soul lays aside all the constituents of its being and returns to its purely spiritual origin. The Revealer clothes this in the language of the myth of the ascent of the soul through the hostile planetary spheres. It remains uncertain whether this ascent occurs only after death, or whether it happens now, at the moment of enlightenment:

> To this Poimandres said: When the material body is to be dissolved, first thou surrenderest the body by itself unto the work of change, and thus the form thou hadst doth vanish, and thou surrenderest thy way of life, void of its energy, unto the Daimon. The body's senses next pass back into their sources, becoming separate, and resurrect as energies; and passion and desire withdraw unto that nature which is void of reason. And thus it is that [the inner human being] doth speed his way thereafter upwards through the Harmony. To the first zone he gives the Energy of Growth and Waning; unto the second [zone], Device of Evils [now] de-energized; unto the third, the Guile of the Desires de-energized; unto the fourth, his Domineering Arrogance, [also] de-energized; unto the fifth, unholy Daring and the Rashness of Audacity, de-energized; unto the sixth, Striving for Wealth by evil means, deprived of its aggrandizement; and to the seventh zone, Ensnaring Falsehood, de-energized. And then, with all the energizings of the harmony stript from him, clothed in his proper Power, he cometh to that Nature which belongs unto the Eighth, and there with those-that-are hymneth the Father. (Poimandres = *CH* I.24–26)[15]

This text reads almost like the elimination of becoming in dependency (*pratītyasamutpāda*) in reverse order.

Here we have a pretty close counterpart to Buddhism: suffering is a consequence of dependencies, of being enmeshed in the context of becoming and passing away; the Gnostic would say it is a consequence of being trapped in matter. Suffering is only superficially pain caused by, for example, illness, war, poverty, loneliness, death. Ultimately, in Gnosis as in Buddhism, life itself is suffering. Becoming and passing away, the desire to have and to dominate, feelings, the desire to live—that is, thirst—all is suffering. Even what appears to be good and beautiful in life is suffering, because it is involvement in appearances, in what has emerged from the "fog"[16] of unknowing. Redemption comes through knowledge in that the human being sees through these connections and, with the aid of knowledge, dissolves them. All this links Buddhism and Gnosis; the latter is the closest Western equivalent to Buddhism. The difference between the two is only that Gnosis ultimately thinks theistically and dualistically. The world of appearances and its creator, who brought them into being through unknowing, are opposed to the true God, the Father. Into him the soul, which according to Poimandres ascends through the Harmony, ultimately enters, and its powers become God's powers (Poimandres = *CH* 1.26).

For Gnostics as for early Buddhists, it appears that similar basic but contingent life experiences preceded the intellectual concepts. These experiences can be questioned only conditionally, but they can be accepted only conditionally as well. For Buddhists the experience is that the endless cycle of becoming and of passing away, of desiring to live and of dying, is empty and is nothing but suffering. For Gnostics it is the fundamental experience that the visible world is evil and meaningless.

We may well share these basic experiences. But we may have others as well. For example, we may find that life is good, full of joy, full of love, full of beauty. One can receive it as a gift, as a miracle. One can give thanks for it: "What do I have, that I have not received?" (1 Cor 4:7). One may experience the world as God's good world. In that case one will judge differently than does a Gnostic or a Buddhist. One will not be insensible to suffering in the world and will not foolishly deny it in some kind of romantic religious optimism. Rather, one will protest against it. Suffering in the world, illness, poverty, hunger, tears, bad death, war, exploitation, injustice—all that is contrary to the good world and the gift of life. All that is contrary to the will of God, who created this world and life, and willed them into being. It is not life, then, that is suffering, but the repression of life, the theft of life, injustice, the destruction of the bases of life. Then one will hope, love, and struggle against suffering and against the powers that cause it. One will associate God, the creator of the world and giver of life, with life itself; only paradoxically, indirectly, and always in the context of life will one associate God with suffering. This is where I see the place for Christian faith. It, too, rests on basic experiences that ultimately are contingent, neither refutable nor provable.

If we understand Christianity in this way, the question Axel Michaels posed at the end of this chapter is all the more urgent: Why, then, especially in Christianity, the theology of the cross? Gnostics do not need one, because they were given the knowledge that all suffering belongs to a world to which they themselves—in their true selves—do not belong. Buddhists do not need one because for them there is no escaping the fact that they themselves must gain the knowledge that they do not belong to the world of inconstancy, conditionality, and time. So why is it that in Christianity the cross of Jesus Christ has become such a central symbol? Must that be?

My first answer is: It is so. Christianity is a religion that has grown through history, that lives on the basis of its origins and cannot, without losing its own identity, simply distance itself from those origins arbitrarily or as it sees fit. At the beginning of Christianity, there was a crucifixion. From the beginning it has proved itself, in its Christian interpretation, to be a thing of power and to that extent indispensable.

This is connected to the fact that the beginning of Christianity fell in a period when suffering had become so massive that no one could continue to make light of it. The time when Christianity began—and Gnosis as well—was the era of apocalyptic pessimism about the world. The reality of suffering was so urgent and so great that it was no longer possible simply to believe, easily and as a matter of course, in the goodness of life and the goodness of the world's creator. A great many people experienced the reality of suffering, the enmity of the powerful in this world, and the darkness of death as so overpowering that they were ready to welcome the message that God is especially *in* this darkness and that it is precisely *this* suffering that is the way to life. At that time many people experienced the reality of sin and their alienation from God, the power of evil in which they themselves were enmeshed, as so oppressive that they were unable to remove it by themselves. Christianity and Buddhism agree in the knowledge that human beings and their behavior are probably the most important causes of suffering. Buddhists call it desire or thirst; Christians call it sin. Christians of all times have experienced the power and inescapability of evil as so oppressive, and suffering as so deep and concrete, that a mere insight into the causes of evil and suffering was not sufficient to overcome them. It is not Buddhism that—as regards human beings—is pessimistic; it is Christianity. That is the reason for the central significance of the cross. I presume, of course, that the cross is a symbol of life and not a symbol of suffering or death.

Is the theology of the cross indispensable even today? I would love to live in a world in which the model of the suffering and risen Christ would prove superfluous. That would be a world that was not ruled by suffering caused by human beings. But in the world in which I do live, where rich people oppress the poor, in which past catastrophes shape the present, in which bombs fall on innocent people and billions are suffering, I find that this suffering cannot be overcome by any insight into the true origins of suffering in transitoriness. Therefore I am grateful for the paradigm of the Crucified, which shows me that the power of life—which is the power of God—extends into the uttermost depths of irremovable suffering.

8

Jesus' Passion and the Christian Idea of Suffering

Ulrich Luz

Worlds seem to stretch between the smiling Buddha and the suffering Crucified One. An Asian visitor to Europe would be astonished to find that crucifixes could be the most important religious symbols throughout whole countrysides. Christianity appears to him or her to be a religion in which suffering has central value.

But Christianity is by no means simply a religion of suffering. When our Asian visitor gets better acquainted with the European continent, traveling through many countries and visiting lots of churches and museums, he or she will be astonished to see the variety of ways in which the Crucified One can be depicted. In the ancient church, the early Middle Ages, and especially in portrayals in the Eastern churches, he appears as the victor over death. With extended arms, open eyes, and straight legs, he seems rather to stand upon the cross than to hang there. For the ancient church and the Orthodox churches of the East even today, the Crucified One is above all the one triumphant at Easter over suffering and death. In contrast, in the Western crucifixion scenes of the late Middle Ages and the Baroque, the crucified Christ is depicted as the Man of Sorrows, hanging on the cross with battered or closed eyes, blood streaming over his body, his legs bent, an image of misery and wretchedness. In these images Christ is the scourged, martyred man who appears to combine in his passion everything that suffering can mean for a human being. But then, if our visitor enters Protestant regions, she or he will be amazed to find that representations of the crucifixion are relatively rare, even in the churches, although it is above all in Protestantism that the cross is the center of piety. However, here it is not a question of gazing on and sinking down into the suffering of Christ, but of the good that has come to humanity through Christ's suffering: forgiveness of sin and reconciliation with God. What is in the foreground is not the image of the Suffering One; rather, it is the word of proclamation of the Crucified. In Protestantism the word has triumphed over the image.

Thus, in the course of history the Crucified One has acquired multiple dimensions of meaning. In this chapter I will attempt to trace this multiplicity back to its biblical origins.

Biblical Views of Suffering

The Bible has no general concept of suffering; instead, it highlights concrete forms of experience of suffering. I am thinking of the figure of Job. His miseries include poverty, sickness, loss of his family, loneliness, and ridicule. Suffering is also concrete in the answer Jesus gave when he was asked by the Baptizer's disciples whether he was the one who was to come: "Go and tell John what you hear and see: the blind receive their sight, the lame walk, the lepers are cleansed, the deaf hear, the dead are raised, and the poor have good news brought to them" (Matt 11:5). Thus suffering is illness, death, and poverty. According to the Beatitudes suffering is poverty, hunger, tears, sorrow, persecution (cf. Luke 6:20–21; Matt 5:3–12). Unlike Buddhist tradition, here socially caused suffering is taken very seriously. In the two Jesus texts the perspective of the lower class, which is so characteristic of Jesus, is very clearly expressed. For underprivileged people, suffering is not simply the fruit of their own greed and thirst. Hunger, sickness, war, etc. have an external dimension, and the sufferer cannot eliminate them on his or her own initiative.

Where does suffering come from? The Bible makes a number of attempts to explain it. For Job, as for Jesus, the figure of Satan plays a part. For Jesus, it is the demons, the agents of Satan, that "possess" people, that is, alienate them from themselves. Behind this is the experience that suffering has superior strength. For Paul, death in particular is a power at enmity with God, the "last enemy" to be subjected to Christ as world ruler (1 Cor 15:26). The sufferer is therefore handed over to foreign mastery and cannot escape it.

It is striking that God is almost never seen as the cause of suffering. God wills neither suffering nor sicknesses nor death nor injustice and violence. The Bible is extraordinarily reticent about connecting God with evil. God is, rather, the one who "rescues... from the evil one" (Matt 6:13).

Instead, the Bible repeatedly and in many ways regards the human being as the originator of suffering. This is expressed mythologically in the story of the first parents being driven out of paradise (Gen 3). In the Old Testament the experience of the so-called cause-and-effect relationship plays a major role. The evil that people have done falls back on them and goes on working to the third and fourth generation.[1] Even the broadly attested Old Testament idea that God punishes Israel for its unrighteousness belongs within this cause-and-effect schema: from evil comes suffering. An impressive New Testament text is Romans 8:18–27, where Paul speaks in apocalyptic style of how the whole creation "was subjected to futility, not of its own will but by the will of the one who subjected it" (Rom 8:20). The "one who subjected it" is Adam, who in the apocalyptic view brought suffering and death not only on humanity, but on the whole world. But in Hebrew, Adam means simply "human being." "The sin of Adam" means that the human being, not God, is the cause of the evil and suffering that inevitably afflicts the world. Suffering as God's punishment means, quite unmythologically, that people have to pay for what they do.

To that extent one also can say that, according to broad biblical consensus, sin is the cause of suffering. Every human deed contrary to God's will brings suffering on other people and ultimately—in this life or, since the rise of apocalypticism, certainly at the Last Judgment—on the perpetrators themselves. Here there are points of contact with the Buddhist conviction that "thirst" or "desire" is the cause of suffering.[2]

The beginning of the reign of God, which Jesus brings, includes driving out demons and healing the sick. The messengers of the reign of God are to bring *shalom,* the peace of God, into houses and villages (Luke 10:5). Jesus calls the poor, the hungry, and the weeping blessed because God, whose reign is coming, will quiet their hunger and console them (Luke 6:20–21). The reign of God is not, like *Nirvāṇa,* the elimination of all the factors of becoming and passing away, nor is it the elimination of the thirst that leads to suffering; rather, it is God's gift of life, peace, justice, wholeness, joy for all those who are now living on the shadow side of life. Jesus is their servant.

Jesus' Passion

Jesus also put his life on the line for the reign of God. According to the ancient passion accounts, which essentially presume the same course of events in the last days of Jesus' life,[3] Jesus was arrested in Jerusalem shortly before the feast of the Passover, that is, at a time when the situation in the city was always tense because of the great masses of pilgrims. The reason for Jesus' arrest is not entirely clear, but it is highly probable that Jesus had behaved provocatively in Jerusalem. In the opinion of most scholars, the episode of his driving the money changers and merchants from the Temple courtyard (Mark 11:15–17) rests on a historical event. Jesus' proclamation of the coming destruction of the Temple (Mark 13:2; 14:58; John 2:19) is among his best-attested sayings. Jesus was probably seen as a security risk by the Jerusalem aristocracy—the high priests and the city nobility whom the Roman occupation forces had made responsible for maintaining peace and order in the city[4]—much like the Temple prophet Jesus ben Ananias about thirty years later. He also proclaimed the destruction of the Temple and was arraigned by the Jewish leaders and handed over to the Roman prefect (Josephus *B.J.* 6:300–306). It is historically very probable that one of Jesus' disciples had revealed where he was staying and so made it possible for Jesus to be arrested without attracting public attention,[5] and also that, when Jesus was arrested, his disciples fled for their own safety's sake (Mark 14:50).

The Romans were responsible for Jesus' crucifixion. At that time in the province of Judea, they alone were able to sentence someone to death;[6] besides, crucifixion was a Roman punishment. Therefore, the fact of a trial before Pilate is historical. It is more difficult to say whether there was also a hearing before Jewish authorities, since the gospel accounts of the trial before the so-called Sanhedrin are strongly shaped by Christian creedal traditions.[7] However, the fate of Jesus ben Ananias, which is so similar to that of Jesus of Nazareth, makes this probable. Jesus was then executed in the usual gruesome fashion and was probably buried in the tomb of a respected Jew known to us by name. The grounds for execution were political: Jesus was called "king of the Jews" (Mark 15:26); that is, he was regarded as a messianic revolutionary. In such cases mere suspicion was sufficient for a death sentence.[8]

Much more difficult is the question whether we can say anything at all about the meaning Jesus himself may have seen in his death. In my view we can exclude the possibility that he died by accident and for no purpose. That is scarcely imaginable: Executions on political grounds were rather common in Israel at that time. According to Luke 13:32–33, Jesus responded with these words to reports that he was in danger from the tetrarch Herod Antipas:

> Go and tell that fox for me,
> > "Listen, I am casting out demons and performing cures today
> > and tomorrow, and on the third day I finish my work.

> Yet today, tomorrow, and the next day I must be on my way,
> because it is impossible for a prophet to be killed outside of
> Jerusalem.

Also, the saying about taking up one's cross, which makes readiness for martyrdom a condition of discipleship (Matt 10:38; cf. Mark 8:34), probably goes back to Jesus himself. Besides, he had before his eyes the fate of his teacher, John the Baptizer, and he had been forewarned.

So Jesus went to Jerusalem, the city of the prophets. There he taught and performed a fairly dangerous prophetic action in the Temple, driving the money changers and those who were selling animals out of the Temple courtyard (Mark 11:15–16). If he had wanted to avoid death, he would have had to leave Jerusalem after that action, at the latest. He did not do so. Therefore, we can say with good reason that he accepted at least the possibility of his death. And that means he must have seen a meaning in it.

But what meaning? Here we are feeling about in the dark. The obscurity is especially great because early Christianity had an unusually strong interest in interpreting the death of Jesus contrafactually, against the evidence, not as an end and a catastrophe, but as willed by God and the basis of salvation. This makes it especially difficult to separate genuine Jesus traditions in this area from later interpretations by the community.

Let me first name some non-christological possibilities for interpretation, which have a strong claim to plausibility for the very reason that they were *not* of fundamental dogmatic significance for the later church:

• Jesus died just as he taught. To his last breath, he maintained the idea of nonviolence, love of enemies, and fidelity to God. To that extent he understood his own death as martyrdom, as faithfulness to his own message.

• In his saying against Herod Antipas (Luke 13:32–33), it is clear that Jesus understood his death as that of a prophet. This corresponds to a popular conviction of the day. According to legend, many prophets became martyrs, most of them in Jerusalem, where people pointed out their tombs.[9]

• The last of the sayings remembered in connection with Jesus' farewell meal almost certainly comes from Jesus himself. After blessing the cup, Jesus formulated a kind of vow of renunciation, very archaic in its language and not in accord with the interests of the community, because it indirectly points out that Jesus' hope for the coming reign of God was not fulfilled. He said, "Truly I tell you, I will never again drink of the fruit of the vine until that day when I drink it new in the kingdom of God" (Mark 14:25). These words express

Jesus' knowledge that he must die. At the same time they show that before his death he had not abandoned his assurance that the reign of God would come. They do not establish any direct connection between his death and the reign of God.

Such a connection is, however, possibly present in a puzzling statement that is transmitted only in Luke 12:49–50 but probably goes back to Jesus, since the post-Easter community thought quite differently both about Jesus' mission and also about "going under":

> I came to bring fire to the earth,
>   and how I wish it were already kindled!
> I have a going-under [*baptisma*] with which I must be sent down,
>   and what stress I am under until it is completed!

The metaphor of fire was probably applied by most hearers at the time to the judgment. Here Jesus is probably speaking about the fire of judgment that he must kindle, perhaps as the Son of Man, the judge of the world, who is now working incognito in the world. In the parallel verse he speaks of a "going under." This word—the same Greek word, *baptisma,* that later became the word for "baptism" in Christianity—was, in biblical tradition, an image of extreme suffering. It is perfectly possible that Jesus is referring here to his own death, which is pressing upon him and which he fears.[10] The two verses are parallel; their content refers to related things. Jesus' death is thus somehow connected with the coming of the great fire, the judgment of the world. But unfortunately the saying does not tell us how.

Albert Schweitzer once thought that Jesus might have gone to Jerusalem to take upon himself the last times of distress, the so-called messianic birth pangs, which Jews expected must precede the end of the world and the coming of the reign of God. In this way he wanted to spare his disciples, suffer as their representative and in their place, and thus by himself bring about the coming of the reign of God.[11] Schweitzer's interpretation is one of the few hypotheses that could really explain Jesus' move to Jerusalem and his strange behavior there. I think that even today we need to follow Schweitzer's direction in our search for an answer.

Schweitzer's hypothesis comes close to an interpretation of the death of Jesus as representative substitution or atonement, which became the most important stance in early post-Easter Christianity. There are a great many passages, especially in the New Testament letters, that attest to its significance, but it retreats in the gospels. Only one such passage can go back to Jesus himself, namely, the words of interpretation at the breaking of bread and blessing of the cup at Jesus' last meal, handed on to us in slightly different versions by the gospels and Paul. I will quote Paul's version, which may be the oldest:

> The Lord Jesus on the night when he was betrayed took a loaf of bread, and when he had given thanks, he broke it and said, "This is my body that is for you." ... In the same way he took the cup also, after supper, saying, "This cup is the new covenant in my blood" (1 Cor 11:23–25).

With these words Jesus did not interpret the elements "bread" and "wine," but the ritual of breaking bread and sharing the cup.[12] The ritual with the cup is very unusual in Jewish practice, because at this farewell meal it seems that Jesus passed only one cup to all those present. Consequently, the ritual was especially in need of interpretation, and atonement and representative substitution are possible readings of it.

Early Christianity's Understanding of Jesus' Death

In the light of their Easter vision of the exalted Christ, Jesus' disciples looked back at his death with new eyes. For them "Jesus' resurrection" meant that God had acknowledged Jesus and had responded to his death by raising him from the dead. His death was by no means a catastrophe, and it did not mean victory for the Romans or the leaders of Israel who answered to them. Rather, it meant the victory of God, who triumphed over his enemies. Jesus' death itself was—in light of the resurrection—a victory of life over death and suffering. It was, as the letter to the Colossians later formulated it in traditional words, a triumph over hostile powers (Col 2:15) But it did not represent a direct affirmation of Jesus' own hope for the coming of the reign of God. The latter did include, of course, the hope that God would raise the dead (cf. Matt 11:5; Mark 12:18–27), but for the present only a single person, Jesus, had been raised (cf. Col 1:18; Rev 1:5). God's victory in Jesus' resurrection thus remained hidden and visible only to the eyes of faith.

In early Christianity there began to be a veritable explosion of interpretations of Jesus' death. On one side—to the extent that our hypothesis is correct—they took their initiative from Jesus' own interpretation of his death. But on the other side they were based on a new reading of the Bible, the church's later "Old Testament." With its aid Jesus' adherents gave a new interpretation, after Easter, to Jesus' horrible death. An ancient creed, perhaps formulated in Jerusalem only a few years after Jesus' death, stated, "Christ died for our sins in accordance with the scriptures and was buried" (1 Cor 15:3–4).

The Bible made possible a variety of interpretations of Jesus' death. Even before Paul it was seen as a new and final Day of Atonement, replacing the Jerusalem cult: "God put forward [Christ Jesus] as a cover of atonement[13] by his blood, effective through faith. He did this to show his righteousness, because in his divine forbearance he had passed over the sins previously committed" (Rom 3:25). In an early text preserved in Romans 8:3–4, the death of Jesus is interpreted as a renewal of the biblical sacrifice for sin; in a tradition found in Romans 8:32, it is read in terms of Genesis 22 as a new sacrifice of Isaac. Biblical cultic categories were all the more important for interpreting the death of Jesus as the distance of believers in Jesus from the Temple cult in Jerusalem increased. Besides the cultic interpretations of the salvific meaning of the death of Jesus, there appeared other readings, often also shaped by biblical tradition, e.g., the atoning death of the martyr or an analogy to the redemption of slaves. Paul himself interpreted Jesus' death as representative substitution and as an expression of God's love (Rom 5:5–8; 2 Cor 5:14–15). None of these attempts at interpretation is exclusive and exhaustive; all only approach the reality. All of them have a metaphoric dimension and cannot be advanced to the status of dogma. In all of them we can recognize easily the root of what became so important for Reformation theology: the death of Jesus "for us."

But even late medieval Passion piety had its New Testament roots. It is important for Paul that Jesus' dying became an enduring model for Christian living. He sees his own suffering as an apostle as shaped by the suffering of Christ. In Galatians 2:19–20, the fundamental text that comes so close to *Mahāyāna* Buddhism, where Paul says Christ lives in him as a new self, he can say in the same breath, "I have been crucified with Christ." This being-crucified-with is not something that happened once for all in the past—for example, at his baptism—but it is an enduring condition of his life.[14] Paul can also say that he is "always carrying in the body the death of Jesus, so that the life of Jesus may also be made visible in *your* bodies" (2 Cor 4:10). Here Paul is thinking of his own suffering, his weakness, the persecutions he has undergone, his shipwrecks and imprisonments, perhaps also his illness, from which God did not deliver him (2 Cor 12:7–9). He interprets all these mystically[15] as Jesus' experience of death, which he shares. And he also interprets them as he does the death of Christ: As mere experiences of pain they are not in themselves positive and valuable. Rather, they are positive because they are at the same time the reverse side of the new life that comes to be through Christ: "For while we live, we are always being given up to death for Jesus' sake, so that the life of Jesus may be made visible in our mortal flesh. So death is at work in us, but life in you" (2 Cor 4:11–12). Thus, for Paul, suffering is the verso of love and life and is in their service. Therefore suffering is always a foretaste of Easter and so of hope: "Who will separate us from the love of Christ? Will hardship, or distress, or persecution, or famine, or nakedness, or peril, or sword? . . . In all these things we are more than conquerors through him who loved us" (Rom 8:35, 37).

A similarly existential interpretation of Jesus' death appears also in the post-Easter Jesus traditions; its roots go back to Jesus himself. We have what is probably an authentic saying of his that urged his disciples to be ready for martyrdom: "Whoever does not carry the cross and follow me cannot be my disciple" (Luke 14:27; cf. Mark 8:34). In another saying of Jesus, the subject is surrendering one's own life for the sake of a new one: "Those who try to make their life secure will lose it, but those who lose their life will keep it" (Luke 17:33; cf. Mark 8:35). The second part of Matthew's mission discourse (Matt 10:24–39) made this especially clear: Life in Jesus' service means being conformed to Christ, and that includes Jesus' suffering.[16] In regard to suffering also, the disciple cannot be greater than the teacher, and the servant cannot be different from the master (Matt 10:24).

Such experiences were important in the late Middle Ages, when life was increasingly experienced as suffering, affected by famine, plague, sicknesses, war, and death. These sufferings the faithful interpreted in terms of the sufferings of Christ. In this way the suffering of Christ and hope for the resurrection and a new life helped the faithful to bear their own suffering.

Suffering in Christianity and Buddhism: Critical and Self-Critical Questions

In spite of all the crucifixes that mark many regions of Europe, Christianity is not a religion of suffering; it is a religion of victory over suffering. In this it resembles Buddhism. It differs from Buddhism in that the social aspects of suffering—hunger, poverty, exploitation, war, sickness, possession—are more clearly in the foreground. In particular, the hope that *God's action* will bring an end to the power of evil that causes suffering is specifically Christian, with nothing corresponding to it in Buddhism. For Jesus, this was the hope for the coming of the reign of God.

After the resurrection, the passion of Christ became the crucial point of reference for faith. Its most important "fruit" in the New Testament texts is the forgiveness of sins, atonement, and reconciliation with God. But even in the New Testament texts, a new line of thought also is already in evidence: in light of the passion of Jesus, suffering can become the enduring "signature" of a life with Christ. For Paul, it is the verso of life and love. Both lines of thought are alien to Buddhism.

I would like to close this chapter with two questions. The first is a self-critical challenge to Christian faith. However Jesus himself may have linked his death with his hope for the coming of the reign of God, post-Easter belief in his resurrection meant a transformation of that hope: Jesus' resurrection is a further mysterious sign of God's presence in the world of suffering, but it is not a fulfillment of Jesus' hope for the reign of God. Christians are filled with faith in Jesus' resurrection, and in that light they understand Jesus' death as the cause of reconciliation with God. But all the same, the poor continue to be poor, the hungry are still hungry, the sick are still sick, and the outsiders are, at the very best, integrated within Christian communities. Faith in Jesus' resurrection, which replaced his hope for the coming of the reign of God, meant an inward displacement of Jesus' great hope. It was the first step in transforming Jesus' legacy into a religion, which makes it possible to live with suffering and to delay hope for an end of suffering, injustice, and exclusion to a distant future where awaits the final compensation for the poor and those who suffer. This transformation was necessary because the reign of God, which Jesus hoped for, did not come, but it also meant—not only—saying good-bye to Jesus and domesticating him into a religion. My question then is this: Does Jesus' hope convey anything enduring and valid that, despite the resurrection-inspired transformation of his legacy into a religion within history, must shape Christian faith?

In light of Jesus' hope for the coming of God's ultimate rule, I also want to pose a critical question to the Buddha. For him, the problem of suffering was a question of right knowledge. Overcoming suffering is, for him, above all a question of right consciousness, and the question of an end to suffering is essentially reduced to the question of a change in one's own attitude toward it.[17] Does this do justice to the depth of suffering? Does it do justice to the millions of people who are sick, hungry, beaten or tortured, victims of war, and all the countless ones who are treated as second-class beings? Does it do justice to all the people who cannot free themselves from suffering because they do not suffer from desire or thirst, but have simply fallen under life's wheels? Here I am helped more by the—perhaps utterly unrealistic—hope of Jesus for a coming reign of God, because that hope makes it possible to cry out against the immeasurable flood of human suffering, to call its human causes what they are in the eyes of God (namely, sinners turned against God), and at least to set up signs of hope and protest, as Jesus did.

Response / *Axel Michaels*
Jesus' Karma

Everyone who causes other people to suffer, for example by torturing, enslaving, or killing them, says Ulrich Luz, is "in the eyes of God" a "sinner turned against God." Under the eyes of the Buddha (for example, at the *Svayambhūnātha Stūpa* in Kathmandu), I am glad to reaffirm that. But—one might have to join the Buddha in asking—is everyone who does not help soften the suffering of others, who perhaps does not take notice of it, equally a sinner? It seems as if Gautama Buddha and Jesus Christ would have talked past one another on the subject of suffering, and the reason is probably, in fact, based on their very different experiences of suffering: here the crucified Jesus, there the meditative Buddha, for whom the world was also filled with suffering, but perhaps not governed overall by sin and injustice.

Nevertheless, Christianity, in its undoubtedly admirable efforts to soften the suffering of the world and of human beings, visible above all in its many charitable institutions, has also developed a kind of love of suffering and cultivated it over the centuries. Is this attitude, which for me culminates in the worship of the Crucified One, not also a cause of suffering in the sense that the encounter with Christianity too often leads people to experience bad conscience about their own sinfulness and to fear God's punishment? So I will ask a provocative question: Would not a little less attention to suffering ultimately be good for Christians, too?

In Buddhism, desire (for life) is the beginning of suffering; in Christianity it is desire as sin. For Jesus there is a beginning of suffering (original sin), and there is also an end to it, whenever it comes (the reign of God). For the Buddha there is also a beginning (desire or unknowing); for him also, the human being is the cause of suffering, because through unknowing he or she sets the conditional nexus in motion, over and over again. Because of this karmic link between past, present, and future in the conditional nexus, and despite the denial of the transmigration of souls, the nonredeemed human being is the cause not only of suffering in general but also of his or her own suffering, even if that suffering was imposed on him or her by another. But he or she cannot expect an end to suffering that is not already available in the present. If we were to apply this point of view to Christianity, there might well be an original sin but no future reign of God; should original sin be eliminated, the reign of God would also be impossible or, rather, already present.

The consequence of this attitude is that hope disappears as a means to alleviate suffering, or at least it is much weakened. The Buddha would say, "Hope for what?" For something that is coming to be? That would be something conditioned, something subject to suffering. Therefore the reign of God itself, if it is still to come (no matter how understandable this is from the point of view of the historical Jesus and his circumstances), can only be filled with suffering. It would be different if the reign of God were seen as having already begun. But in that case I am back to what I said in chapter 3 about salvation, i.e., the reign of God as salvation here and now.

But Jesus' suffering is impossible to understand for another reason, and not only from an early Buddhist perspective. This has to do with Jesus' "karma." Jesus' suffering and his passion acquire meaning only through the resurrection. Jesus' suffering is comprehensible only posthumously. Cross and resurrection go together. But this suffering did not come from fate; it was either self-chosen or imposed by God, that is, in either case (as a Buddhist would say) determined by karma. If it was self-chosen, why did Jesus create suffering that could have been avoided? Why did he go willingly to his death? In doing so he imposed unspeakable suffering on himself, but also imposed bad karma on others, including those who crucified him. If the suffering was willed for him by God, why did God cause his Son to die? Does God kill in order to give life? From the Buddha's point of view this answer represents a much-too-violent action, God's bad karma! For this would be an attitude that created Jesus' suffering.

Of course, one may ask with Ulrich Luz whether the Buddha is basically incapable of suffering because he pays too little attention to those who suffer, those marked by pain, sickness, and brokenness, and instead regards suffering more as an intellectual matter. Ulrich Luz asks, "Is a right consciousness alone adequate to the depth of suffering?" It is true that the early Buddhist monks (but not Buddhism as a whole) were less interested in the suffering of others than in their own salvation. They were—from that point of view—in fact incapable of or unwilling to undergo (com)passion. Their concept of suffering was not so much sickness, torture, hunger, war, poverty, etc., as it was a problem of epistemology.

But one could object, from the perspective of early Buddhism, that not all suffering comes from human beings, from sinners opposed to God; some suffering comes from God (or in Buddhist terms, from time). To put it another way, life would be filled with suffering even if there were no more sinners. The question of theodicy has always been a challenge to a supposedly all-powerful, all-knowing, all-loving, just God. Sinless, undeserved suffering, unjust suffering that cries out to heaven—from the death of children to the Holocaust—has caused many people to doubt or despair of God. Even Jesus himself?

And about three o'clock Jesus cried with a loud voice, "Eli, Eli, lema sabachthani?" that is, "My God, my God, why have you forsaken me?" (Matt 27:46).

Part Five
Christology

9

Jesus and Christology

Ulrich Luz

What most impresses me about Buddhism is its tolerance. Once, when I was visiting a temple, a master of the Zen Buddhist Soto school said to me, "You are a Christian; that is good. If you live here and meditate, I may be able to help you become a better Christian, and you can help me become a better Buddhist."[1] This tolerance for other religions, which I find so unusual, is rooted in the Buddhist idea of transcendence and its understanding of the meaning of language. The center of Buddhism is not a God conceived as personal, but *Nirvāṇa*, in which gods and human beings become nothing and in which faith and atheism touch. Higher than language, which in theological arguments also defines and excludes, is silence. This lays the groundwork for a genuine tolerance, since no religion, not even Buddhism, can be more than a way of approaching the Unutterable.

But when a religion centers on a single God of the entire world, it would appear that the seed of an intolerant absolutist claim has been sown from the outset.[2] In the book of a prophet from the time of the Babylonian exile, so-called Deutero-Isaiah, who at the time of Israel's most profound misery proclaimed a programmatic universalistic monotheism, YHWH says, "I am the LORD, and there is no other; besides me there is no God" (Isa 45:5). God extends a missionary claim to the whole earth: "Turn to me and be saved, all the ends of the earth! For I am God, and there is no other" (Isa 45:22). As for the representatives of the other religions that appear to have conquered Israel and its God, the prophet pours scorn on them: "They have no knowledge—those who carry about their wooden idols, and keep on praying to a god that cannot save" (Isa 45:20).

The monotheism of the Abrahamic religions almost inevitably involves some kind of intolerance, even though it may express itself in very different ways: It can result in holy wars such as the Islamic wars of conquest or the Crusades. It can also express itself as a claim to theological inclusivity, as in the Lukan Paul's speech on the Areopagus when he claims to be speaking about a God whom all people worship without knowing him (Acts 17:23). Or it can be expressed as a universal claim to salvation, as is characteristic of Christian missions. Such a salvation claim may take the form of love and service and categorically reject every form of violence and imposition, but that does not change the fact that it has something sublimely intolerant about it.

New Testament Christological Monotheism

In using the phrase *universal claim to salvation*, I have touched the real center of early Christianity, which developed its own form of monotheism marked by two special characteristics:[3] First, Jesus Christ, as the Savior-figure, is so closely associated with God that he himself becomes God, and God in turn takes on the face of Christ. While outsiders, both Jews and Muslims, have always seen here a danger to strict monotheism, it remains astonishing how confidently and as a matter of course early Christians were able to place Jesus at the right hand of God without seeing this as in any way calling monotheism into question.

Second, through Jesus Christ the God of Israel was definitively universalized and made the saving God for the whole world. This universal line, hints of which were found in Judaism as early as Deutero-Isaiah but always in tension with other tendencies that emphasized the particularity and uniqueness of Israel and its God, triumphed in early Christianity. In a certain sense primitive Christianity is nothing but a radically universalized and radically soteriological new form of Judaism.

The universalizing was closely aligned with the divinization of Jesus. Very soon after 50 c.e., Paul wrote, "Indeed, even though there may be so-called gods in heaven or on earth…yet for us"—and here he quotes a traditional confessional text—"there is *one* God, the Father, from whom are all things and for whom we exist, and *one* Lord, Jesus Christ, through whom are all things and through whom we exist" (1 Cor 8:5–6 [emphasis added]). "Lord"

(Greek *kyrios*) is an expression with religious connotations that reminds the Corinthians on the one hand of the various *Kyrios* divinities in their own environment,[4] and on the other of the biblical God.[5] Jesus Christ constituted the antithesis to the former, while the boundary between him and the latter has become permeable.

Other ancient confessional texts also see in Jesus a divine figure: He surrendered his divine dignity and became human (Phil 2:6–11). He is pre-existent and, as mediator of creation, calls the world to life (Col 1:15–20; John 1:1–18). Prayers to Jesus came into being very early (2 Cor 12:8–9; 1 Thess 3:11–13). Not only Hellenistic, but even Jewish Christian texts speak of Jesus in divine categories. For example, the book of Revelation assigns divine attributes to Jesus (e.g., Rev 1:14–16; 19:16), and the Gospel of Matthew speaks of Jesus as "Emmanuel," that is, God present with his people (Matt 1:23). In the Gospel of John (also shaped by Jewish Christianity), this development reached its initial climax: at the beginning (1:1; 1:18)[6] and at the end (20:28), Jesus is confessed as God.

How did this swift and decisive development occur? Why was Jesus not "partially" elevated—for example, to an angelic figure[7] or as a righteous man taken up to God, like the ancients of the Bible (Wis 5)? I think that this has to do on the one hand with Jesus' own self-understanding and on the other with the interpretation of Easter by the earliest community.

Jesus' Self-Concept

The nineteenth-century search for the historical Jesus attempted to discover the true man Jesus behind the Christ of faith and the divine Son of church doctrine. The history-of-religions school of the early twentieth century posited that New Testament Christology was almost completely a secondary application to Jesus of Jewish or Hellenistic ideas about God and hopes for salvation. Since William Wrede,[8] the thesis that Jesus did not in any way regard himself as a messiah or Christ has become increasingly dominant. According to Rudolf Bultmann, Easter (that is, the resurrection) was the prime datum of Christianity.[9] For him, Easter was a nonvisual linguistic event, almost impossible to relate to historical time, not provable; it was a contingent in-breaking of God, descending from above into history, much as the ancient Orthodox described the incarnation of the Son of God.

Historically, this was probably not the case. We have already seen, again and again, that Jesus had a serious self-awareness, though it was not expressed in precise concepts. Recall, for example, his ethical demands, based on his immediate, direct authority, and above all his antitheses, in which he set his own authority against that of the Torah (Matt 5:21–22, 27–28). He regarded his own words and his own person as the crucial factor by which good and evil, the standing or falling of the house would be determined at the judgment (Matt 7:24–27). The certainly genuine saying in Luke 12:8–9 presumes that one's relationship to Jesus would be decisive when the Son of Man comes to judge. Jesus regarded his own works, his exorcisms and healings, as the beginning of the reign of God (Luke 11:20). He interprets them that way in a number of parables, including that of the mustard seed (Luke 13:18–19; Mark 4:30–32). For him, the coming of the reign of God in his own work meant the beginning of a new era; the time of the Torah and the prophets was only until John the Baptizer (Q 16:16). According to Luke 12:49–50, Jesus is the one who is to bring the fire of judgment on the earth. The unique sayings of Jesus that begin with "Amen, amen, I tell you" (e.g., Mark 9:1; 11:23; 13:30; 14:25; Matt 5:26; 10:15; 11:11, etc.) are striking, because there is scarcely any precedent in Jewish tradition for prefixing a saying with "Amen" to give force to one's own authority. Instead, "amen" is always used as an affirming and reinforcing response. Not all, but at least some of these sayings go back to Jesus. In short, the evidence that Jesus claimed for himself a very special authority far beyond that customary for charismatics is so abundant that it is impossible to call this authority claim into question historically.

Jesus does not, in any of these sayings, use any common messianic category to define his authority. He does not have extraordinary authority because he is the Messiah, the Son of Man, or the Son of God; he simply has and claims it. It is connected to the coming of the reign of God and the judgment, with which Jesus associates his work. Here Jesus research has spoken of "implicit" or "indirect" Christology.[10]

But Jesus probably had an "explicit Christology" as well. It is true that Jesus apparently did not consider himself the Messiah (Greek *christos*); there was a great variety of messianic hopes in the Judaism of his time. The most important were the longings for a messianic king from the house of David who would deliver Israel from its enemies and become ruler of the world.[11] This hope was sometimes associated with the expression *Son of God*, because the king enthroned in Jerusalem was proclaimed "Son of God" by the priest at his enthronement (Ps 2:7; cf. 2 Sam 7:13–14; 4QFlor = 4Q174 III). In the gospels this royal title appears often, but almost never in Jesus' own words.[12] Most often it is the content of a heavenly revelation (e.g., Mark 1:11; 9:7) or a confessional title (e.g., Mark 15:39; Matt 14:33; 16:16–17). These texts are post-Easter compositions by the community. At most it is conceivable that Jesus, who spoke so often of the "royal reign of God" or "kingdom of God," awakened messianic hopes and was even confronted by them. Thus, for example, behind the account of Jesus' entry into Jerusalem (Mark 11:1–10) there might be a smaller messianic ovation by Galilean pilgrims. But we do not know how Jesus reacted to it.[13]

The case with regard to the mysterious expression "Son of Man" is quite different. It appears almost exclusively in words of Jesus, more than thirty times in the Synoptic Gospels. The post-Easter communities no longer understood the expression; nowhere is it used as a confessional title. This speaks clearly in favor of the idea that Jesus used the expression. It appears, essentially, in three contexts: The first group of Son of Man sayings speaks about Jesus' future role as heavenly judge of the world. This includes, for example, the saying in Luke 12:8–9: "Everyone who acknowledges me before others, the Son of Man also will acknowledge before the angels of God; but whoever denies me before others will be denied before the angels of God." The second group includes sayings about the suffering and death of the Son of Man. These usually speak also of his rising after three days (e.g., Mark 8:31; 9:31). The third group, finally—and this group contains the most variety—speaks about the current work of the Son of Man. It includes, for example, Luke 7:33–34: "John the Baptist has come eating no bread and drinking no wine, and you say, 'He has a demon'; the Son of Man has come eating and drinking, and you say, 'Look, a glutton and a drunkard, a friend of tax collectors and sinners!'"

The Son of Man sayings present many puzzles to scholars. First, it is unclear how their language is to be understood. The expression *Son of Man* in Hebrew or Aramaic means nothing more than "an individual human being," and usually denotes "anyone." The sayings about the current activity of the Son of Man continually raise the question whether Jesus is not simply speaking about just anybody. But most of the sayings about the work of the Son of Man in the present do not make statements applicable to just anyone; rather, they tend to be about just those things that distinguish Jesus from other people.[14] The determinate expression "the Son of Man" cannot be a mere circumscribing of "I" without any generalizing nuance.

In contrast, the sayings about the future Son of Man as judge of the world make us think of the vision in Daniel 7:13–14, where "one like a Son of Man/human being" comes with the clouds of heaven, approaches God, and receives from God power and world dominion. In this vision, the book of Daniel is probably referring to the archangel Michael, the angel of the people

Israel, the "holy one of the Most High" (Dan 7:27). This text was later interpreted messianically: the visionary image of this "one like a human being" took on an independent life as the figure of a heavenly world judge who sits on God's throne and judges God's enemies. The imagery in the narratives of *1 Enoch* (37–69) attests to this. Two additions depict how the patriarch Enoch is not only taken away into heaven, as in the Bible (Gen 5:24), but is there enthroned as the heavenly Son of Man/world judge (*1 Enoch* 70–71). Certain apocalyptic groups also expected that Enoch, who was taken away before the ages, would be the judge of the world at the end of days.[15] There is also much in favor of the idea that the "one who is to come," of whom John the Baptizer speaks, the one who will baptize with "fire and the Holy Spirit" (Luke 3:16), is none other than the coming Son of Man.[16] In that case Jesus would have shared the hope of his teacher, John.

There is also much to favor the supposition that some of the sayings about the coming Son of Man go back to Jesus. It is disputed whether Jesus expected someone else as the Son of Man[17] or whether he identified himself with that role. Two of Jesus' sayings distinguish explicitly between Jesus and the Son of Man: Luke 12:8–9 and Matthew 19:28. Likewise, the impressive judgment saying that compares the days of Noah and Lot with the coming of the Son of Man (Luke 17:26–30) contains no direct reference to Jesus. All the other Son of Man sayings presuppose that Jesus is speaking about himself. The distinction between Jesus and the Son of Man can also be explained as a stylistic usage.

Add to this that the authenticity even of some of the sayings about the current activity of the Son of Man can scarcely be disputed. This is true especially of Luke 9:58, the saying about the homelessness of the Son of Man, and of Luke 7:33–34, the contrasting of the ascetic John with Jesus, the glutton and wine drinker. These do not speak of Jesus as a human being, but paradoxically of Jesus as the one who in the future will be enthroned as the Son of Man and world judge. They thus acquire an unheard-of edge: "Foxes have holes, and birds of the air have nests; but the Son of Man"—that is, of all people, the one who one day will judge everyone—"has nowhere to lay his head" (Luke 9:58).

If all this is correct, then Jesus accepted that he was the one who one day would be installed by God as the heavenly Son of Man and world judge.[18] He considered himself the designated world judge, now dwelling among human beings incognito, in the most extreme poverty, ridiculed and threatened with death. In the context of the Judaism of the time, this is easy to understand: The closest analogy is the exaltation of Enoch as Son of Man; the difference between the two is only that Jesus was a person living at that time who himself expected to be made the future judge of the world. This fits excellently with other sayings of Jesus such as Luke 12:49, Matthew 7:24–27, and Luke 11:20. Above all, this makes it easiest to understand the role that Jesus played for the post-Easter communities after his death.

It all fits together historically—but for us this immense and, humanly speaking, exaggerated claim remains very off-putting. Among later Jews, the ones who occur to me as the closest analogies to Jesus are Shabtai Zwi and the Lubavitcher rabbi.[19]

The Easter Events and the Uniqueness of Jesus

Jesus was divinized very quickly and almost everywhere in earliest Christianity. To explain this, it is not enough to seek religious-historical analogies that might have been transferred or used as models for interpretation. The religious-historical school in particular has adduced a lot of material here: the Iranian-Indian primeval man, divine Wisdom, Jewish angelic figures such as Metathron, the imperial cult, the dying and rising gods of the mystery religions, the heavenly high priest Melchizedek, the Shekinah, and so on. Most of these analogies, however, cannot explain why early Christianity insisted with such amazing consistency on the absolute uniqueness of Jesus. In the words of Paul, there are many gods and "lords," but Christians know only *one* God and only *one Kyrios* (1 Cor 8:6).

Can the Easter experiences of Jesus' disciples make this comprehensible? These include, above all, various kinds of visions of Christ. Here I am not concerned with what happened historically, but with the question of how Christians interpreted their experiences. Visions are experiences subject to a wide variety of interpretations. Jesus' disciples, however, interpreted their visions of Christ in a very special way: on the basis of their visions, they said, "Jesus is risen." In doing this, they consistently distinguished their interpretation from the mere resuscitation of a corpse; they never thought that Jesus had in any way returned to an earthly life, only to die again one day.[20] Rather, they connected Jesus' resurrection with the general resurrection of the dead that was expected at the beginning of the new age, and saw him as "firstborn from the dead" (Col 1:18; Rev 1:5; cf. 1 Cor 15:20–28). But most of the statements do not even do that; they are simple confessions: "God raised him from the dead" (Rom 10:9), and "He was raised on the third day in accordance with the scriptures" (1 Cor 15:4). The "third day" is a symbolic statement and points to God's saving intervention.[21] That was enough to say, because for Jewish faith God is *the one* who "kills and brings to life," who "brings down to Sheol and raises up" (1 Sam 2:6; cf. Deut 32:39). The second blessing in the Eighteen Benedictions contains a confessional formula: "Blessed are you, Yhwh, who makes the dead to live." The statement that "God raised Jesus from the dead" thus meant for early Christians that God had taken his side, linked the divine Name to Jesus, and at the same time made him God's central agent of revelation.

Another interpretation of the Easter experiences that goes back to earliest times is that of exaltation. Jesus has been "exalted" to God. This, again, does not mean the same thing as what Jews expected for all the righteous (cf. Wis 5:5). Rather, it means that he has been established as ruler over the entire world:

> Therefore God also highly exalted him
> > and gave him the name
> > that is above every name,
> so that at the name of Jesus
> > every knee should bend,
> > in heaven and on earth and under the earth,
> and every tongue should confess
> > that Jesus Christ is Lord,
> > to the glory of God the Father. (Phil 2:9–11)

By his resurrection Christ was installed as the ruler of the world, who is "at the right hand of God" (Rom 8:34), the heavenly Lord for whose return people pray (1 Cor 16:22) and whom they worship. By his resurrection Jesus achieved a place unique in Judaism at the time. The earliest disciples' interpretations of Easter therefore gave an enormous push to the development of Christology that very rapidly led to Jesus' divinization and that, while it was given greater precision in later centuries and defined in new categories—for example, through the doctrine of the Trinity—nevertheless was complete in its essentials in the first decades after Jesus' death.

Such interpretations of the Easter visions are constructions of reality, as are all other statements about reality. But the texts are in agreement that these interpretations have a special character: A person cannot simply "conclude" such a truth on the basis of a vision or the discovery of an empty tomb. Such conclusions are by no means "logical" or probable. Rather, they are as unprovable as Jesus' own claim to be bringing God's rule to earth. Therefore the texts repeatedly say, for example, that an angel opened the eyes of the frightened women, or that the Risen One himself interpreted for the disciples what they were seeing.

If we ask historically why the disciples came to interpret their Easter experiences in just this way and to found their faith in the divinity and irreplaceable uniqueness of Jesus on them, we are pointed back to Jesus himself. The disciples' Easter faith is just as off-putting and exaggerated to absoluteness as Jesus' self-concept: Jesus, who expected to be installed by God as the coming Son of Man and judge of the world—this very one God raised and thus affirmed. So we can say that Jesus' enormous claims about himself prepared for his disciples' interpretations of Easter, and were absorbed into those interpretations, while in turn the Easter experiences affirmed for the disciples Jesus' message and his own claim. Hence there is a direct line from Jesus' self-concept through his disciples' interpretations of Easter to Jesus' divinization and Christology's affirmation of his uniqueness. Therefore it is not incomprehensible that Jesus became the *one* Lord in early Christianity, the "way, the truth, and the life" without which no one comes to the Father (John 14:6).

The Uniqueness of Jesus and Buddhism

Now let me return to Buddhism. Are there convergences here? After what has been said, the question is almost absurd. I can only summarize the clear divergences.

First, New Testament Christology sees Jesus as an incomparable and irreplaceable instrument of God, as *the* Son of God—indeed, as God in person. "Buddha," in contrast, is not a title, but describes the condition of being awake, which is the goal of every person's path. A Buddha is one who has experienced himself or herself as nonself. Such a one is therefore *not* important in himself or herself, and certainly not unique.

Second, the christological monotheism of early Christianity, directed to universal salvation, presupposes that God's holiness and transcendence are infinite. Between the one, holy, and almighty God and the human world ruled by sin and injustice yawns a chasm. Christological monotheism offered early Christianity a possibility for bridging the chasm and located reconciliation within God's own self. Faith in Christ, which God himself offers and makes possible, is the only chance for overcoming the division. The "Buddha," the Enlightened One, by contrast embodies the fundamental goal of human existence, the ultimate meaning of every life. Here there is no chasm to be overcome, but a path to follow. There simply cannot be a need for anything like a Christology in Buddhism.

Finally, New Testament Christology is the root of the later absolutist claims of Christianity. That Christ is Lord of the world—that is, that God, according to Paul, reveals God's righteousness through him—means that salvation is offered to all. God will "justify the circumcised [Jews] on the ground of faith and the uncircumcised [non-Jews] through that same faith" (Rom 3:30). But this salvation has its reverse side as well, and that reverse side is the experience of those who could not make the decision to confess the Son of Man before all—the Jews, for example. Not only does the church proclaim to them that they will be denied before the angels of God when the world is judged (Luke 12:8–9), but they have already had quite enough experience of judgment coming from the church, the possessor of truth. The way of the Buddha is quite different. It ultimately concludes that even Buddhism itself, as the way to *Nirvāṇa*, will vanish in *Nirvāṇa*. Buddhism can make no claim to absoluteness, whereas Christianity today is struggling with its own definitive claims, which it has advanced throughout its history.

Rays of Hope in the New Testament

In this chapter I have taken it as a given that the christologically grounded claim to absoluteness that Christianity links to its universal offer of salvation has become a major problem for Christianity itself. It was a heavy burden at first and is still today for Jews, and especially since the Middle Ages and the colonial era, more and more for the non-Christian so-called pagans. Today it has even become a handicap for Christianity itself, which bears the burden of history and recognizes its own entanglement even in those dark events of history against which it has itself struggled with all its might.

Therefore, in closing I want to point, by way of example, to two New Testament initiatives that challenged the christological claim to absoluteness in a different and very self-critical manner. "Self-critical" means in this case that they addressed it in such a way that *God's* christologically interpreted absolute claim could not give rise to *any* such claims on the part of human beings or the church.

The first of these is Paul's theology of the cross, especially 1 Corinthians 1:18–25 and 3:1–4, 18–23. The "foolishness of the cross" confronts every kind of human wisdom, in this case precisely *not* any kind of non-Christian philosophical wisdom, but rather the Christian "wisdom" of the Corinthians, who thought that they had become "enriched...in speech and knowledge of every kind" (1 Cor 1:5). It is, in fact, Christian claims to truth and Christian possession of truth that are shattered by the fact that "God's foolishness is wiser than human wisdom, and God's weakness is stronger than human strength" (1 Cor 1:25).

The second instance is in the Gospel of John. The christological statement in John 14:6 has become the epitome both of the depth of the Christian religion and of its absolute claim: "I am the way, and the truth, and the life. No one comes to the Father except through me." After these words, the disciple Philip makes a truly stupid statement: "Lord, show us the Father, and we will be satisfied." Jesus answers: "Have I been with you all this time, Philip, and you still do not know me?" So it often goes in the Gospel of John: alongside the high christological statements of the Jesus sent from heaven stand, over and over again, the disciples with their stupid questions. They never get beyond the beginner stage, as shown by the story of Thomas at the end of the gospel (John 20:24–29). Beside the absoluteness of the Revealer stands the ongoing amateurishness of his disciples. This is an enduring biblical warning signal to a church that makes absolutist claims in theology and in practice.

Response / *Axel Michaels*
Buddhology and Atheism

There are no parallels in Buddhism to the Son of Man as world judge, or to the Last Judgment itself. There are, however, some messianic ideas that may be found there—for example, in the *Maitreya* cult (referenced in the *Pāli* canon, but associated with eschatological expectation only from the second century C.E. onward). A doctrine of the different "natures" or bodies of the Buddha may even offer something like a "Christology" of Buddhism. In the first chapter, I pointed out that there cannot be a historical-critical search for the historical Buddha analogous to the search for the historical Jesus. Gautama research is always already "Buddhology" in the sense of Christology, but this exaltation of the Buddha is really not possible in terms of Gautama himself. The historical Gautama and his life are not very significant for Buddhism. The Buddha is not unique; there were a number of Buddhas before him (six are mentioned in the *Pāli* canon). There are Buddhas after him; everyone can—in principle—become a Buddha. And, of course, no absolute claims can be derived from any of this.

Nevertheless, a divinizing exaltation of the Buddha did take place. Gautama was a human being, a holy man, a god, or all those things together. How could this happen? In many of the general accounts of Buddhism, one most often finds the thesis that the teachings of the Buddha were for the broad masses of people so esoteric, monastic, impractical, or incapable of touching the heart that soon after Buddha's death there arose a divinization of the founder that then in turn became the Great Vehicle. It is said that this idea was introduced in the *Mahāvastu* (from the second century C.E.); there the Buddha appears as a superman, and the school of the *Lokottaravādins* is said to speak of Gautama as an otherworldly, transcendent (*lokottara*) being, while that of the *Mahāsaṅghikas* presented the existence of the Buddha as only an appearance. At the latest in the *Lalitavistara* (ca. fourth century C.E.), it is said, the deification was fully developed. A god who "has been dead since his *Nirvāṇa*," as Hendrik Kern once said, was perhaps sufficient for the monks, but not for the masses. The people longed for gods, myths, and personal forms of veneration. While in early Buddhism the Buddha was regarded as a holy man, after his death he was exalted, in *Mahāyāna*, into a superman. In short, the divinization of the Buddha is said to be a concession to human weakness.

This point of view rests primarily on the assumption that the Buddha's teaching cannot be rightly understood. I consider this view understandable in terms of the history of religions, but not really verifiable and, in fact, implausible. It is understandable because religious founders are not, in fact, often recognized in their full greatness by other people in their own lifetime. The thesis is not verifiable because, as we have said, there are scarcely any sources for the life of the Buddha. It is implausible because from the very beginning— perhaps even in Gautama's own lifetime or soon after his death—there was a Buddha cult and an exaltation of the Buddha. *Mahāyāna* only seized upon this and mythicized it. As regards the image of the Buddha, *Hīnayāna* and *Mahāyāna* are not necessarily in succession; they are two forms of Buddhism that have existed simultaneously from the beginnings of Buddhism. However, I have only arguments of plausibility with which to support this thesis:[22]

The Buddha saw himself as a superman (*lokottara*), an unusual being. This, and not only the content of his teaching, was the reason why so many followed him. A completely atheistic teaching could scarcely have succeeded as a religion. People came to Buddhism because they already believed in the Buddha as an otherworldly being. Because the Buddha regarded himself as the truth of the ("eternal") teaching, from very early on there was the fundamental dilemma of how an apparently mortal man, one who has even died, could be immortal: The answers to this dilemma, which is the same for all founders, follow the pattern of recognizing plural natures. This is no different for Jesus than for Buddha. Thus, from a very early period, a super-earthly and an earthly body were attributed to the Buddha. At the latest in the fourth century C.E., such ideas were harmonized in the so-called Three-Body Teaching (*trikāya*) of the *Vijñānavādins* (with reference to the *Laṅkāvatārasūtra*) and then (with the *Sarvāstivādins*) reduced to the following three levels:

1. *Dharmakāya* ("dharma body"): the immaterial, ultimate body of the Absolute or the Buddha principle. This "dharma body" is common to all Buddhas. In it they are identical and one. It is the "personification" of the Absolute and the teaching.

2. *Sambhogakāya* ("enjoyment body"): the body of the heavenly Buddha appearances. These can be experienced only spiritually, not with the organs of sense. Only the bodhisattvas, who have developed advanced spiritual abilities, can see them. These Buddhas are marked by wisdom (*prajñā*) and compassion. They have an enjoyment body because it is only from this level that it is possible to enter into the enjoyment (*sambhoga*) of salvation.

3. *Nirmāṇakāya* ("body of gross material manifestation"): These Buddhas have flesh and blood and therefore are exposed to aging, but spiritually they are superior to human beings. This is their last earthly manifestation before salvation.

As we can see, Buddha here appears as a human being, an otherworldly-transcendent Buddha, and the philosophical idea of absolute Buddhahood. The Christian Trinity presents a similar model:[23] *Logos* or the Holy Spirit, God the Father (usually understood personally, but able to be seen or "experienced" only by believers), and Jesus as the (somewhat deficient) earthly manifestation. But basically there is a still clearer parallel to the Christology of the early church. The *Logos* (as Christ) would correspond to the *Dharmakāya*; the Exalted One who is present with the faithful, that is, the Holy Spirit, to the *Sambhogakāya;* and Jesus to the *Nirmāṇakāya*. The earthly and at the same time divine situation of a religious founder must almost necessarily resort to such models. How else can the founder's mortality be explained?

The incarnation of a god is really a paradox, because the conditions of mortality and immortality are mutually exclusive. The immortality of a god can in a human being only become mortality. In turn, a human being can only be divinized by surrendering the human husk. Neither Jesus nor the Buddha had a really convincing answer; they could not offer more, because they were human beings and only became gods after death.

Certainly, despite the divinization of the Buddha and despite the Three-Body Teaching, talk about God and divinization makes no sense in early Buddhism, or at least it must be understood in a fundamentally different sense than in Christianity.[24] In other Indian systems (and also in the modern West), Buddhism has from the beginning been called *nirīśvaravāda*, "the teaching [that does] without God or a ruler of the world," that is, as atheistic. Nowhere is anything said about God or a single numinous power; at most it speaks of the god (as one among many) or the gods. The various heavenly beings that are certainly known to early Buddhism are part of the world of sense (*kāmaloka*), but not the highest, bodiless world (*arūpaloka*) where there is neither awareness nor unawareness. The gods could be dispensed with in Buddhist doctrine without any fundamental change. They, too, are subject to change and are therefore in need of redemption:

> O monks, even those gods, the long-lived, majestically beautiful,
> dwelling in the fullness of their happiness in noble, heavenly palaces for
> an unimaginable time, even these are sometimes subject to fear, anxiety,
> and shivering when they hear the teaching of *Tathāgata*. "Woe," they
> lament, "that we are transitory, for we thought we were eternal! That we are
> unenduring, for we thought we were enduring! That we are mutable, for we
> thought we were immutable! So we are transitory, unenduring, mutable,
> subject to the cycles of rebirth (*sakkāya-pariyāpannā*). (*AN* II.33.22–30)

Therefore, we maintain with Raimundo Panikkar[25] that early Buddhism is neither atheistic (it acknowledges the world of the gods to a certain degree) nor theistic (it does not acknowledge divine omnipotence). At most it is paratheistic (transcending theism) or supratheistic (setting itself above the gods: a Buddha is master of gods and human beings). But in early Buddhism there is no God (apart from *Brahmā*) who is creator of the world, an almighty being with an independent (nonconditioned) existence. The unconditionedness of God and God's rule, which Ulrich Luz has emphasized in Jesus' teaching, is truly lacking in Buddhism. Even if God could be accommodated in early Buddhism as the most exalted being (which may be important for Christians who practice Buddhist meditation), God is not—as in Christianity and for Jesus—all-sufficient, but is conditioned and thus, fundamentally, subject to suffering.

Part Six
Meditation

10

The Buddha and Meditation

Axel Michaels

The early Buddhist path of salvation is a series of meditative steps through which one prepares for *Nirvāṇa* by means of various exercises and concentrations. The goal of all the exercises is to strengthen one's spiritual powers and abilities in such a way as to achieve a calmness of mood and spirit (*śamatha*) and thus insight, clarity, or bright vision (*vipaśyanā*), resulting in *Nirvāṇa*. In most cases this involves controlling all the activities of the senses in a complex way, making them aware, reducing them through concentration, and ultimately extinguishing them.

This offer of inner calm, this pragmatic application of Buddhist teaching, has always impressed the West, especially in times of unrest. So also, those who introduced Buddhism to the West were highly developed in meditative practice.

The Buddha's Path to Enlightenment

It is true that the Buddha is not central to Buddhist meditation. Nevertheless, the Buddha's own path to enlightenment provides the guiding principle for Buddhist contemplation.

There is in the *Mahāsaccakasutta* (*MN* I.237.5–251.11) a probably authentic account of the Buddha's first meditation,[1] which brought him to enlightenment. Even if the discourse is laden with Docetism, a genuine experience echoes within it. First it tells of the ascetic exercises to which the Buddha subjected himself for years in order to achieve enlightenment. Then it recounts how, after he had rejected those paths, he entered into four (later dogmatized) stages of meditation (*dhyāna, pā. jhānā*). He associates the first level with a recollection of his youth:

> I thought: "I recall once, when my father the Sakyan was working, and I was sitting in the cool shade of a rose-apple tree, then—quite withdrawn from sensuality, withdrawn from unskillful mental qualities—I entered and remained in the first jhana: rapture and pleasure born from withdrawal, accompanied by directed thought and evaluation. Could that be the path to Awakening?" Then, following on that memory, came the realization: "That is the path to Awakening." I thought: "So why am I afraid of that pleasure that has nothing to do with sensuality, nothing to do with unskillful mental qualities?" I thought: "I am no longer afraid of that pleasure that has nothing to do with sensuality, nothing to do with unskillful mental qualities, but it is not easy to achieve that pleasure with a body so extremely emaciated. Suppose I were to take some solid food: some rice and porridge." So I took some solid food: some rice and porridge. (*MN* I.246.31–247.10)[2]

This recollection, this simple experience may have lasted only seconds, but it must have been so overwhelming for the Buddha that he sought thereafter to rediscover and hold fast to the moment. It may have been decisive for the Buddha's later path that the state of happiness arrived unannounced, without any particular effort on his part. This key experience led him to meditation. Abandoned by the disciples who did not approve of his abandoning the strict ascetic path, he allowed himself (though this part of the account may not be authentic) to fall into three further stages of contemplation.

In that night Gautama, at the age of about thirty-five, became Buddha, for he achieved enlightenment (*bodhi*). According to tradition, this happened at the full moon of the month of *Vaiśākha* (April/May) at Uruvelā (present-day Bodhgayā) under an asattha or pipal or poplar fig tree *(Ficus religiosa)*, a supposedly surviving shoot of which is still venerated. It has been shown that the tree was uprooted by a storm in 1876 at the latest, but many believe that this is the original Bodhi tree that was placed under special protection by Aśoka himself.

In the Buddha legends the enlightenment comes at the end of the search for salvation. The Buddha is supposed to have remained in meditation for seven days, and we owe it only to the god *Brahmā* or, in another version, the temptation of the adversary Māra, that he handed on his experiences in his first sermon, for the good of humanity, and did not keep them to himself. In this teaching, the path to the goal of salvation, which is enlightenment, is represented as a process, the Noble Eightfold Path.

But even at the Buddha's complete departure, *Parinirvāṇa,* according to the legends, he entered again into the stages of contemplation. His adversary Māra challenged the Buddha finally to enter into *Nirvāṇa* by reminding him that the Buddha had promised him he would pass away when he had proclaimed his teaching and established a community. In fact, the Buddha kept his promise and said that he would enter into *Nirvāṇa* after three months. In deep meditation, he surrendered his bodily will to extend his life. Then the earth quaked, and Buddha arose from his contemplation and announced his decision to depart. There followed one final sermon in Vaiśālī, in which he spoke again of the mutability of forms; once again he urged the assembled monks to take the key concepts to heart and preach them. In Kuśinagara he took a meal with a blacksmith—spoiled pork or boar or a mushroom dish (*sūkaramaddava*), no one is sure. The Buddha became ill, perhaps with dysentery, but got slightly better. He had his deathbed set up between two *Śāla* trees. The whole scene has been elaborated: miracles occur, the trees bloom although it is the wrong time of year, heavenly music sounds. In an insertion, Ānanda begs for final instructions. The Buddha names four holy places that are to become pilgrim centers: the cities of his birth, enlightenment, first sermon, and death. Ānanda asks how one should deal with females; the Buddha advises looking away, not speaking with them, and practicing awareness. Ānanda is sad; the Buddha comforts him and exhorts him not to moan. There are more insertions about *Stūpas* and directions for the burial, etc., until finally the Buddha speaks his last words: "Well now, you monks, I tell you: all forms are subject to mutability. Never falter in your striving!" (*DN* II.156.1–2). Then the Buddha passes into the different levels of contemplation until he reaches the level of not-anything-ness, the level of neither thinking nor not-thinking, and the level where thinking and feeling are removed, then onward to the first and again to the fourth level of contemplation. After this the Buddha arises and goes immediately into *Nirvāṇa*. At that moment there is a great, fearful earthquake, and the drums of the gods thunder.

Did the Buddha's enlightenment rest on the recollection of an almost instantaneous "aha!" experience in his youth, or on a discovery of truth for which he had prepared through a long process of inquiry? The discussion of the concept of *Nirvāṇa* (see chapter 4) has shown that we cannot achieve absolute certainty even in this regard, but such certainty is not worth seeking. The legends show only the way, not the result, not the internal situation of the Buddha. But they make it clear that meditation and *Nirvāṇa* are closely linked together.

The Steps of Salvation

In the *Pāli* canon many of the Buddha's discourses end with the Buddha describing the path of salvation to his hearers.[3] The wording is always very similar, and most scholars of Buddhism agree that these texts are among the oldest parts of the Buddhist tradition.

In descriptions of this path of salvation there first appears someone, that is, the Buddha, who teaches the hearers and enables them to enter on the path of monasticism and meditation:

> Then the perfected one (*tathāgata*) appears in the world, the holy (*arhat*), fully enlightened one (*samyaksambuddha*), gifted with knowledge and experience of life, the tested one, knowing the world, the incomparable educator, teacher of gods and humans, the Lord (*bhagavat*), the Buddha. He instructs this world, including all the heavenly gods, gods of the dead, and Brahma-gods, he instructs all beings, including ascetics and Brahmans, gods and people, out of his own knowledge and observation. He proclaims the teaching that is beautiful at the beginning, beautiful in the middle, and beautiful at the end, perfect in content and form. He preaches the perfect, purely holy way of life (*brahmacarya*).[4]

Hearing the teaching means thoroughly changing one's behavior and thought, but it presupposes belief and trust (*śraddhā*) in the Perfected One. When this is accomplished, the hearer of the teaching may leave the house: "Life in a house, a dirty little corner, is narrow; freedom comes in leaving the house (*pravrajyā*). It is not easy for someone who dwells in a house to lead the utterly perfect, completely pure life, holy as mother-of-pearl."[5] Then what usually follows is a listing of moral commandments for the monk, such as those in the Noble Eight-Part Path. Of the eight parts, the last three—right effort, thought, and contemplation—belong to the realm of meditation (*samādhi*), but even the ethical parts three and four (*śīla*)—right speech, deeds, and way of life— are considered preparatory to meditation. The texts of the way of salvation now and then introduce further prescriptions for the monks' behavior.

Preparatory exercises also include sloughing off all ties that bind. According to a (later) dogmatic series of ten (*AN* X.17.6–16), these include: (1) false belief in the personhood or bodiliness of the self (*pā. sakkāyadiṭṭhi*); (2) addiction to doubt (*vicikicchā*); (3) attachment to rituals and vows (*sīlabbataparamāsa*); (4) lusts of the flesh (*kāmarāga*); (5) wishing harm or ill (*paṭogaha*); (6) desire for existence in the world of forms (*rūparāga*); (7) desire for existence in the world of non-forms (*arūparāga*); (8) darkness (*māna*); (9) inner unrest, excitement (*uddhacca*); and (10) ignorance (*avijjā*). The first five bonds, if one does not surrender them, lead to a lower rebirth, while the second five bonds lead to a higher rebirth.

The moral exercises are followed by exercises to observe the sense organs (*indriyasaṃvara*). These are techniques for concentration:

> When one sees a form with one's eyes, hears a tone or noise with the ears, detects a smell with the nose, tastes a flavor with the tongue, feels something palpable with the body, or recognizes a matter (*dharma*) with the mind (*manas*), one takes note neither of the whole nor of the details.... By practicing this way of watching over the organs of sense one experiences inner happiness without distraction.[6]

This is followed by the practice of alertness and recollection (*smṛtiprajanya*), which is also about concentration on what is being done in the present:

> In going and coming one acts with awareness, in seeing and looking around one acts with awareness, in bowing and stretching the limbs one acts with awareness, in wearing one's clothes and holding the alms bowl one acts with awareness, in eating and drinking one acts with awareness, in the processes of elimination one acts deliberately, in walking, standing, and sitting, in sleeping and waking, in speaking and being silent one acts with awareness.[7]

Only then comes meditation itself, which ends with the Buddha's four stages of contemplation (*rūpadhyāna*). This so-called Four-Dhyāna Path (Path of the Four Meditations), which possibly corresponds to or augments the cosmic spheres,[8] is as follows:

> When he [the monk] thus keeps the group of moral commandments, carefully observes the organs of sense, and practices alertness and awareness, he seeks a remote place to abide, a wood, the foot of a tree, a

mountain, a gorge, a cave, a tomb, a wilderness, a place under the open sky, or a heap of straw. There he sits down after his meal, after returning from gathering alms, with his legs crossed, his body erect, making recollection (*smṛtiḥ, pā. sati*) present (*MN* I.181.9–15).[9]

Now it is a matter of abandoning sensual desire and unhealthful excitements, so that well-being will be established. For this, five obstacles (*nīvaraṇa*) must first be eliminated: (1) greed, (2) malice and anger, (3) inflexibility and sleepiness, (4) agitation and regret, and (5) doubt. This leads, step by step, to knowledge of the disturbances (*upakleśa*) that weaken the senses, and to the abandonment of desires and unhealthful things (*akuśalā dharmāḥ*). From this, with reflection (*vitarka*) and consideration (*vicāra*), come satisfaction (*prīti*) and a feeling of well-being (*sukha*). This is the first stage of contemplation, in which one can no longer be seen by Māra, the personification of death (*MN* I.159.10–15).

When reflection and consideration have come to rest, the seeker of salvation achieves an inner calm (*adhyātma-samprasāda*) and a concentration of the spirit (*cetasa ekotībhāva*) that again lead to satisfaction and a feeling of well-being. This is the second stage of contemplation. One calmly, alertly, and deliberately pursues a renunciation of satisfaction and feels in one's body a sense of well-being. This is the third level of contemplation. When one has removed both well-being and discontent (*duḥka*) from the body, one again achieves a pervasive, pure calm and alertness (*upekṣāsmṛtipariśuddhi*) and persists in it. This is the fourth level of contemplation.

Now the disciple is ready for saving knowledge. To this end, one first directs one's spirit to the memory of previous rebirths, then to knowledge of the death and reconstitution of the being, and finally to knowledge of the disappearance of defilements. Thus one knows the Four Noble Truths. The knowledge of being saved arises in the one who is thus saved: "Rebirth is destroyed, the holy way of life is perfected, obligation is fulfilled, there is no more return to this world. So he knows!"[10] Erich Frauwallner rightly points to similarities between early Buddhist meditation practices and yoga: trust in the teacher, the association with morality, presumption of a monastic life, removal of internal obstacles, concentration in the form of shutting off discursive thought, and finally the redemption from rebirth.

Certainly there are unique features as well: The stages of contemplation do not lead to an immediate *experience* of salvation, but to a meditative knowledge that is salvation in the highest consciousness. In early Buddhism meditation is not so much a mystical practice; it is primarily an intellectual matter, although it is prepared for through numerous exercises and is meant to be surpassed by a higher, non-intellectual knowledge. This practice comes close to the original meaning of the word *meditatio* (from Latin *meditari*), but differs through its concentration on a particular object of meditation. Perhaps most important to keep in mind when making a comparison with Christianity is that all meditation is a preparation for *Nirvāṇa*. This occurs, it comes to the person, but no technique can force it.

The "System" of Meditation

The Four-Dhyāna-Path is only one, though perhaps the oldest and most important, of many exercises in meditation, all of which can be classified typologically into three groups:

1. Exercises for body and breath

2. Exercises in concentration of the senses on present action, an object, pictorial images (e.g., *maṇḍala, yantra*), symbols, the Buddha, the teaching, etc.

3. Exercises in intuitive knowledge that lead to a special clarity of insight

In simplified terms, all exercises are about calmness—of body, of mind, or of spirit, but beyond that also about the development of a higher consciousness or even of "magical" supernatural powers (*siddhi*).

The conceptual system of the monastic *Theravāda* tradition distinguishes, first of all, two forms of meditation exercise. First come exercises in concentration that serve to educate one in alertness. These exercises are generally spoken of as training in higher thought (*adhicitta*). This leads to internal calm (*śamatha*), which can, but need not, be a precondition for the second category. Second are exercises in perception and awareness, called training in higher wisdom (*adhiprajñā*), which lead to a distinguishing insight (*vipaśyanā*) into the Four Noble Truths. At the end, then, comes letting-go (*vimukti*) or salvation (*nirvāṇa*).

The exercises as a whole are called meditation. In Buddhist texts the predominant expression is *samādhi* ("collectedness"), but other favorite terms are *bhāvanā* ("generation" of a quiet mind, *śamatha*, or clarity of sight, *vipaśyanā*), *dhyāna* (pā. *jhāna*, Chinese *ch'an*, Japanese *zenna* or *zen*;

"contemplation"), or *samāpatti* ("regard"). Three degrees of intensity of meditation are distinguished:

1. In a preliminary (*pā. parikamma*) or preparatory meditation, full attention is given to some object.

2. With the appearance of a spirit-like counter-image of the object, one arrives at an adjacent (*upacāra*) meditation.

3. The designation of full (*pā. appanā*) meditation applies to the spiritual condition during contemplation.

With complete concentration it is possible to enter into the four stages of contemplation in certain exercises; in others—such as the *Kasina* exercises, described later in this section—only a preliminary or adjacent focus is reached. In the process certain supernatural abilities and knowledge are achieved, but not the distinguishing insight.

The supernatural powers (*siddhi*) include, for example, miracle working, the ability to produce manifestations of the divine, and the ability at will to multiply oneself or to pass through walls. The supernatural knowledge (*abhijñā*) includes, for example, the ability to read thoughts, recollection of previous births, and the heavenly eye.

The various Buddhist schools have reduced the exercises to numerous systems and series. One of these is the four awakenings of attentiveness (*smṛtyupasthāna, pā. satipaṭṭhāna*),[11] in which attention is gradually directed to the body (*kāya*), the feelings (*vedanā*), spirit (*citta*), and reality (*dharma*). Another system is the four right endeavors (*samyakprahāṇa, pā. sammappadhāna*), through which future unhealthful realities will be avoided and removed beforehand, while future healthful realities will be evoked, and present healthful realities will be promoted.

A canonical number of forty exercises has developed for training in higher thought. They include the following concentrations:
• Ten exercises in which one concentrates entirely on a visible object or its field of consciousness (*pā. kasina*), until one sees a reflection with closed or open eyes. With further concentration comes the adjacent meditation. Appropriate for this are four element-*kasiṇas* (earth, water, fire, and wind), four color-*kasiṇas* (blue-black, yellow, red, and white), one light-*kasiṇa,* and one limited spatial-*kasiṇa.*
• Ten disagreeable exercises (*pā. aśubha,* literally "not beautiful"), or medita-

tions on the state of corruption of a corpse, comparable to a *memento mori* (meditation on death), which lead to liberation from sexual desire and are appropriate for people who are inclined to excitement. The corpse can be (1) bloated (rotting), (2) blue-black (with lividity), (3) festering, (4) distended, (5) gnawed by various animals, (6) cut up, (7) hacked to pieces and scattered, (8) bloody, (9) maggoty, or (10) skeletized.

• Ten visualizings (*pā. anussati,* "recollection"): contemplations of (1) the Buddha, (2) the dharma or the teaching, (3) the *Saṅgha* or the community, (4) morality, (5) generosity (*dāna*), (6) divinities (*deva*), (7) death, (8) the body, (9) breathing in and out, and (10) peace.

• Four divine points of rest (*brahmavihāra,* also *apramāṇa*): (1) kindness, (2) compassion, (3) sharing joy, and (4) equanimity.

• Four disembodiednesses (*arūpa*), through which the adept must pass: (1) the realm of infinite space, (2) the realm of infinity of knowledge, (3) the realm of nothingness, and (4) the realm beyond consciousness and unconsciousness.

• One apprehension of the disgustingness of food.

• One analysis of the four elements (*dhātu*).

Although the various meditation exercises as a group are devoid of any strict system—Ernst Frauwallner calls this "a characteristic of the oldest Buddhist teaching"[12]—it can be said that the Buddha offered a new teaching on some points. First, ascetic and meditative exercises should not be painful; they should be carried out in a healthy bodily state. The Buddha rejected self-scourging and self-castration as bad means, preaching instead the Middle Way. A second point is that all the exercises have knowledge as their goal; from this comes salvation. Finally, the exercises serve the purpose of self-salvation; the vision of God may be a result of them, but it is not a condition required for salvation.

Meditation and Prayer

Nothing in Jesus' life and teaching corresponds to the Buddha's contemplations. Nor is much in Christianity comparable to the various forms of Buddhist meditation. At most there might be some correspondence if one equates meditation with "contemplation," for in that respect it resembles prayer.[13] Gustav Mensching rightly observed that the Buddha meditated in what were probably the most important phases of his life, while Jesus prayed.[14] And Friedrich Heiler saw in this some clear differences in the character of the two founders:[15] the Buddha seems to have been rather silent, while Jesus shouted aloud and called on God audibly. The Buddha sought slowly, moving upward according to plan to a higher awareness, while Jesus pressed passionately toward God. The Buddha sank gradually into a calmness of mind and spirit, while Jesus longed for the reign of God. The Buddha rested in equanimity and impersonal being; Jesus sought conversation with God. In the Buddha we see a dying to all impulses; in Jesus, powerful feelings of happiness and despair.[16] The Buddha recommended, for the path to salvation, that one should leave one's house and withdraw into solitude; Jesus also wanted a complete change of life, but no ascetic seeking of self. What was important for the Buddha was his teaching; what was important for Jesus was God:

> Buddha: "Whoever sees me, sees the teaching" (*SN* III.120.28–31).
> Jesus: "Whoever sees me, sees the Father." (John 14:9)

No wonder these essential characteristics shaped a difference between Buddhist meditation and Christian prayer: Meditation is empty, at least as regards external objects, the *materia metandi,* the body or doctrines; prayer, by contrast, is directed to God. Meditation is silent, wordless sinking down; prayer is a dialogue or address, often audible, sometimes loud, and requires words. Meditation is devoid of passions or emotions; prayer, in contrast, is urgent even to the point of passion. Certainly, these are ideal extremes, and counterexamples are easy to cite. Not every Christian prayer is loud and passionate, and not every Buddhist meditation is wordless and empty.

The sharpest contrast, however, results from the goal of salvation: redemption from the self in contrast to grace. The Buddhist path of salvation is a technique; the Christian path is a search for encounter. Buddhism is about accepting oneself; Christianity is about being accepted by God. Asking (petitionary prayer), thanking (prayer of thanksgiving), hoping, worshiping, praising (prayer of praise)—all these are possible only if there is a personal opposite number: "Thus prayer is a living interaction of the devotee with God, thought of as personal and experienced as present, an interaction that reflects the forms of human social relationships.... Praying means talking and interacting with God."[17] Thus, in early Buddhism prayer is impossible, even though in every age of Buddhism there has been belief in gods and demons, and consequently prayer as well.

Are the contradictions irreconcilable? Or are there, after all, possibilities for joining meditation to a Christianity linked to Jesus and the New Testament? One such possibility lies in Herbert Braun's analysis of prayer.[18] He emphasizes that salvation in New Testament prayer (as distinguished from the religious environment of the New Testament) is not petitioned for, but instead comes to the one who prays. "Differently from ancient prayer, there is no intent on the part of the people of the New Testament to affect the divinity through prayer. 'Your Father knows what you need.'"[19]

This is how he explains the brevity of words (for example, in the Lord's Prayer) and the separation of prayer from the act of praying, with the consequence that one can pray always, in the strict sense only as thanksgiving, because salvation is already present. In the raising of Lazarus (John 11:42), Jesus speaks aloud only for the sake of the people what he already knows within himself, because God always hears him. This means the concrete act of praying is ultimately a superfluous addition. Finally, Braun points out that in the Pauline texts, the "you" of prayer address is practically the same as the "he" of the devout wish that someone may be blessed: "So for example, 'may God protect you,' or 'may he lead our steps to you'; that can be expressed either as prayer or in this meditative form in the third person."[20] In other words, what is new about New Testament prayer is that the one praying is not the one giving, but the one receiving. If the certainly daring construction of an approximation between the reign of God and *Nirvāṇa* has any validity,[21] there should also be possibilities of approach here between prayer and meditation. Of course, Braun also says, "Prayer is not a private matter between people and the deity, but its reflection inevitably includes also what is most essential, the neighbor."[22] In most forms of Christian contemplation and mysticism, there is indeed a distinct similarity to Buddhist meditation. Here again, what is primary is the setting aside of distracting sense impressions, passions, and thoughts, preparatory emptying, for the sake of the resting unity of the *unio mystica* (mystical union). Perhaps in the end it does not matter what happens in this state. In any case, it cannot be named.

Response / Ulrich Luz
Buddhist Meditation Is Not Prayer

Early Buddhist meditation is not only one exercise among many; it is the fundamental exercise in which the Buddhist's attitude toward the world and relationship to the self is concentrated. Something similar is true of prayer in early Christianity. Here the whole relationship to God and at the same time the relationship to one's fellow human beings and the world around one is both concentrated and tied together. I will take as my starting point the

Our Father, which in all probability goes back to Jesus himself.[23] It has been handed down in three versions; Jesus' original prayer was probably closest to the shortest version, which is found in Luke 11:2–4:

> (Our) Father (in the heavens),
> hallowed be Thy Name,
> Thy kingdom come,
>   (Thy will be done,
>   on earth as in heaven).
> Our bread for tomorrow
>   give us today;
> and forgive us our debts,
>   as we also have forgiven our debtors;
> and lead us not into temptation,
> (but deliver us from the Evil One).
>   (Matt 11:9–13; cf. Luke 11:2–4)[24]

First, some basic information about the meaning of the text:

• The address is simple. "Father" (without "in the heavens") translates the Aramaic *abba*, a word that early Christianity accepted as a special feature of Jesus' own way of speaking. The closeness between God and the one praying is thus clear from the outset. It corresponds to Jesus' unconditional and absolute certainty that his prayer was heard. "Ask, and it will be given you; search, and you will find; knock, and the door will be opened for you" (Matt 7:7). No father would give a stone to a child who asked for bread (Matt 7:9). In Matthew 6:7–8, Jesus advises, "When you are praying, do not heap up empty phrases as the Gentiles do; for they think that they will be heard because of their many words. Do not be like them, for your Father knows what you need before you ask him." This prayer is sustained from the beginning by the experience of God's nearness. Therefore—even as early as Paul's letters—the most fundamental form of Christian prayer is that of thanksgiving.

• The Our Father is extraordinarily brief, even terse. God doesn't need a lot of words. The prayer's formulation is very loose. From a literary-critical point of view, one can regard it as a collection of "open spaces," permitting those praying to bring themselves into the text. Thus it is a prayer for everyone. It contains nothing about the special needs or concerns of Jesus' disciples. It is no accident that, even today, it is one of the Christian texts that have an influence far beyond Christianity.

• The Our Father is a community prayer, although not a disciples' prayer. The third, fourth, and fifth petitions are formulated with "we."

• Like parallel Jewish prayers, it begins with two petitions addressed to God (referring to "your name" and "your kingdom"). God, who is addressed as "Father" by those praying, also is an object of the prayer.

• The Our Father is altogether related to daily life. Its original language was probably Aramaic, the tongue of everyday speech, not Hebrew, the liturgical language. The content of the third, fourth, and fifth petitions—bread for the next day, forgiveness of sins, and preservation from temptation—has nothing to do with special religious perfection or higher knowledge; these are everyday needs.

• In the Our Father, God's action is extraordinarily close to human action. Except for the petition for the coming of the kingdom, nothing is asked for that lies outside the scope of human action. "Hallow your Name" includes *our* hallowing the Name of God. "Give us our bread for tomorrow" is also a prayer for a job. "Lead us not into temptation" supposes human consciousness and human self-determination. And with its formulation "as we have forgiven our debtors," the petition for forgiveness makes human action an explicit precondition of the prayer. Prayer and action, prayer and ethics thus go hand in hand. The Our Father is not a prayer for those who would lay their hands in their laps and expect everything from God while they remain passive.

The Our Father, like most early Christian prayers, is far removed from Buddhist meditation. Like Axel Michaels, I see the core of the difference in the fact that prayer is addressed to a counterpart, to God, while meditation is "empty." Other differences are connected to this fundamental divide:

• Prayer is a speech-act. In a religion of prayer, language is a fundamental dimension of humanity. (The same is true for Judaism and Islam.) If God "hears" prayers, our part is not to enter into silence.

• The community context relates to this also. Language brings people together. Spoken prayer unites people not only with God, but also with one another. Vertical transcendence toward God, which is characteristic of Christian prayer, is tied to horizontal transcendence toward fellow human beings. It is no accident that prayers of petition were of high importance even as early as Paul.

• Early Christian prayer is the central form of expression of a religion that tends toward "democracy." It is a way for all to express themselves, whereas early Buddhist meditation appears rather to be a technique for a few. This is connected to the fact that prayer that comes from Jesus has, from the very beginning, already reached its goal: namely, God the Father.

• Prayer sets the one praying in the midst of the world; it does not lead away from it. The concrete, worldly, suffering human being stands before God and knows that she or he is taken seriously and heard by God. Prayer is about gaining strength and courage and help in the world and for the world, not about distancing oneself from it.

In spite of these great differences, there are also points of contact between prayer and meditation. Axel Michaels, following Herbert Braun, has pointed out that prayer shaped by Jesus is not intended primarily to affect God; instead, the beginning of a prayer inspired by Jesus starts with the experience of the presence of God and thus the assurance that prayer will be heard. Of course, it is not really true that therefore "the concrete act of praying is ultimately a superfluous addition" (see the section titled "Meditation and Prayer"). Instead, it serves above all to give assurance and make one conscious of this presence of God.

Two further points of contact seem important. The first is that *Nirvāṇa* comes to pass, but no technique can force it. This corresponds to the fact that in New Testament prayer the experience of the presence of God is accompanied by a contrasting truth: Although God is always present with the one praying, one can never have control over God. Therefore one must pray, one must seek for God—that is, for God's reign and God's presence. God is always present to those praying in the mode of the now *and* the yet to come, the one present *and* the uncontrollable. Therefore faith is never a possession.

Second, in prayer, the boundaries of the self are open. The praying self is not in control of himself or herself. Prayer is a fundamental attitude corresponding to the "I-exchange" that I associated with the Buddhist teaching about the non-self. In the Our Father, those praying ask God for their own actions, which they do not control. In prayer, the "I" of the human being is open; the praying person is not an autonomous subject, but one who is held by God and open to others.

Until now I have attempted to indicate points of contact that appear when one interprets meditation as a fundamental "exercise" of early Buddhism and prayer as a fundamental religious expression of early Christianity. More and deeper contacts appear when, today, Christians introduce Buddhist forms of meditation into their own Christian context in life and no longer interpret them "from outside," but link them to their own Christian faith and "fill" them with their own person. Since this occurs very often nowadays, I would like to say something about it, even though in doing so I will be breaching the boundaries stated for this book: limiting ourselves to early Buddhism and early Christianity.

I see two fundamental ways in which Christians can understand and practice Buddhist meditation. First, one can see meditation as an opportunity to distance oneself from the self or to achieve a new relationship to oneself and to life. It is then a good and healthful exercise, parallel to much that happens in prayer, but not—or not directly—aimed at a relationship with God. In that case it is not prayer. Its religious significance for Christians can be described only indirectly, if at all.

Another way is to see meditation as a form of prayer to God, either as silent prayer or as a path of mystical contemplation that leads to a deeper experience of God. The religious significance of meditation is then direct; experience of God takes the place of enlightenment, and God replaces *Nirvāṇa*. "The aim...in this kind of meditation must always be Godself, God in the divine essence."[25]

In this second understanding, Buddhist meditation is instrumentalized by Christians. Enlightenment is removed from its Buddhist context in an atheistic experience of transcendence and relabeled as a type of experience of the Christian God. My respect for the differentness of Buddhism forbids me to do this. Buddhists do not understand meditation as prayer, and they do not regard enlightenment as an encounter with God. Christians should not reinterpret them, but rather take Buddhists' own self-understanding seriously. "God" can then never be the "aim" of meditation or the content of enlightenment, but is only one of various possibilities for naming and interpreting religious experiences that may be similar or even identical for Buddhists and Christians. The names, the interpretations, the constructions of reality remain different. This again corresponds to the experience of the Our Father prayer: that those who know themselves sustained by the presence of the Father do not possess it, but only pray for it.

Part Seven
Community and Church

11

Monks and Laity
in Early Buddhism

Axel Michaels

The Buddha himself was an ascetic, and early Buddhism is, from its own point of view, monastic—so much so that one can say, radically, that it is no more possible for Buddhist laity to be a *basis* for Buddhism than for there to be what Richard Gombrich calls a "low-caste tradition of brahmanism." In his history, Gombrich explains, "Were it a lay tradition it would not be *Theravāda*, 'the doctrine of the elders,' i.e. of the fully-trained members of the Sangha."[1] Therefore, the significance of the monastic order (*saṅgha*) for early Buddhism cannot be overestimated.

The core of every Buddhist movement is monasticism, not the laity, even though the number of monks in Buddhist countries is shrinking. At one time a third of the population of Tibet lived in monasteries, and even now every Buddhist in Myanmar spends a period of days or months as a monastic.

The Founding of the Order

Did the Buddha himself found an order? This is another question for which the sources yield no really secure answer. According to the legends he apparently was undecided. When Ānanda was afraid that the Buddha would depart without naming a successor for the monastic order already established, he only said, "All those who, after my departure, remain as those who take themselves for their light, serve as their own refuge, and have none other, who take the teaching as their light and their shelter, and have no other shelter, these monks of mine will therefore be at the head of these; they, the monks, will desire instruction" (*DN* II.101.1–4).

In spite of these hesitant words, in which the Buddha appears to endanger the cohesion of the order, it was probably founded by the Buddha himself. Several observations favor this interpretation. He is supposed to have consecrated five disciples himself, in Sārnāth, and he probably ordained other monks by telling the candidates, "Come (be a monk)!" (*pā. ehi bhikkhu: Vin* I.12.23–24) and letting them follow him. Also, it is said that a monastery was founded for him in Magadha by King Bimbisāra. The Vinayapiṭaka, the "basket of disciplines," with "rules for monks and nuns" (*bhikṣu(ṇī)vibhaṅga*) contains the oldest texts of the *Pāli* canon, namely the so-called *prātimokṣa* rules. At least some of these instructions seem to come from the Buddha himself. In the *Vinayapiṭaka*, this list of faults is embedded in an often extensive commentary, yet the list has also been transmitted separately, as the (*pā.*) *Pātimokkhasutta*. It is true that the list does not have canonical status, but it is highly authoritative because the text is recited twice a month before the assembled monastic community.

Organized monastic life as foreseen by the Buddha was something relatively new, but ascetic shunning of the world as a form of life was common in Buddha's time. It existed as an anti-Brahmanic reaction against sacrificial ritualism and a resulting internalization of the principle of sacrifice (of the type *tapasvin*), as a form of life for non-Vedic seekers after salvation who employed "magical" shamanistic practices (of the type *vrātya*) and later also as an ethicized philosophical form of ascesis (of the type *yogin*). We find these three forms of ascesis repeated in Buddhism; similarly, celibacy, lack of possessions, mobility, and the begging life were not invented by the Buddha. Yet the Buddha created something new in his environment: a form of asceticism that did not break off contact with the laity and the general population.

According to the *Dīghanikāya* (II.76.11–77.26), the Buddha preached seven conditions for the development of the *Saṅgha*. According to this text, the *Saṅgha* cannot cease to be, so long as (1) there are assemblies, (2) at which harmony reigns; (3) no novelties are introduced or valid things abolished, but the monks live according to the rule of discipline; (4) the older monks, the fathers of the order are respected; (5) the monks do not submit to the desire that leads to rebirth; (6) they prefer to dwell in the forests; and (7) they prefer that fellow monks of like mind come to them from afar and those already here in residence feel content.

Each of these prescriptions leads to a principle or commandment that is constitutive of the Buddhist order: (1) the commandment that the monks assemble regularly, (2) the principle of consensus in all questions affecting the order, (3) a principle of preservation, or conservatism, (4) a principle of preference for the aged as leaders of the order, (5) an indirect commandment of poverty and begging, (6) a certain separation of the monks from the world of ordinary people, and (7) a principle of brotherhood. We can see from these principles that the Buddhist order did break a radical path but did not sever all ties to society. Let me make this clear with a few examples.

Monastic Life

Not everyone could become a monk. Soldiers on active service were excluded, as were criminals, men who had been branded, debtors, and slaves (*Vin* I.73.21–76.27). In other places, the sick (lepers, those with tuberculosis, epilepsy, and elephantiasis), eunuchs, the lame, the blind, the physically handicapped, those afflicted with dwarfism, the deaf, those infirm with age, and others also are listed. Thus, in the liturgy for ordaining a monk (*upasampadā*), a monk asks the candidate:

> Do you have any of these illnesses:
> Leprosy? — No, my Lord.
> Boils? — No, my Lord.
> Rash? — No, my Lord.
> Epilepsy? — No, my Lord.
> Are you a human being? — Certainly, my Lord.
> Are you male? — Certainly, my Lord.
> Are you a free man? — Certainly, my Lord.
> Are you no mercenary of the king? — Certainly, my Lord.
> Do you have your parents' consent?
> — Certainly, my Lord. (*Kammavāca* II.1)[2]

The order was not to be a charitable institution or home for the sick; it was not to take in the people on the margins of society, for it was dependent on the goodwill of the community. But it remained unusual in the climate of the time that casteless men and even women could be ordained.

Thus, Buddha—unlike Jesus—did very little to oppose the existing social systems of dominance. However, he did—like Jesus—demand a radical break with family, even though no one could be received without parental consent (*Vin* I.83.12–14) and women required spousal permission (*Vin* II.271.27–28).

Once, when the wife of the monk Saṅgāmaji came running after her former husband, bringing their son with her, to try to move him to turn back, Saṅgāmaji remained hard and unmoved. "Feed me, monk, and our little son," said she, but the monk remained firm. "At least feed our son," she said, and laid him at the monk's feet, but again Saṅgāmaji did not react. So the woman took up the boy and went away (*Ud* 5.10–6.11).

The Buddha was also rather moderate regarding the age of acceptance. In particular, he scarcely ever received any child ascetics. It is true that the minimum age for reception as a novice was seven or eight—"when he is old enough to hunt crows" (*Vin* I.79.19–20), but only after fifteen years (from the time of reception) could one receive the lower order, and full ordination could happen only after twenty years.

Reception took place, and still takes place, in two stages. First is the novitiate (*parivrājaka, pā. pabbajā*), that is, entry into a state of homelessness and reception into the group of monks in the status of novice (*sāmaṇera*). The second stage is full ordination (*upasampadā,* literally "entry") as completely a monk (*bhikṣu, pā. bhikkhu*), with rights and duties. The novitiate was precondition for full ordination; between the two, according to the rule for the order, at least three months must elapse. Departure from the order was and is possible at any time, as is reentry.

The process for accepting someone into the community as a lay associate was and is as simple as can be: One must simply—once in a while, this is done three times—repeat the threefold formula of hope in the Buddha, the teaching, and the order (*triratna*); that is, a kind of confession of faith. In some schools there were additional instructions in five commandments (against killing, stealing, adultery, lying, and drinking alcohol). There are no sanctions for laypersons.

At the lower ordination, normally the hair of the head and the beard were shaved, a saffron-colored monastic robe was donned, and sometimes the consent of the parents was presented. If there were no objections or rejoinders, the candidate was received; silence signified consent.

Full ordination required a quorum of ten monks (*thera,* "elders," after twenty years *mahāthera*), and the novice chose a personal instructor and teacher from among them. There was a test of personal behavior and health. The four "bases" of the monastic life (*nissaya:* obtaining food only from alms, dwelling at the foot of a tree, wearing ragged clothes, cow urine as medicine) were explained.

The candidate swore an "oath" against the modes of behavior that would lead to expulsion (sexual intercourse, theft, killing, and praising oneself).

Monastic life was a largely regulated daily routine with many rules for care of the body (especially shaving the hair of the head), eating, and what not to touch (women, gold, silver, other things of value, weapons, musical instruments, etc.). Within the order, there was a principle of respect for elders, reckoned according to their age within the order, not their calendar age. The eldest presided at the monastic assembly. Nuns, who required a double ordination before nuns and before monks, were subordinate to monks and arhats, even the youngest.

There was a rule of poverty. Only a few things were permitted as personal property: pieces of cloth (hip scarf, shoulder scarf, coat scarf); nuns could have two more pieces. Clothing (pā. cīvara) was the monk's most valuable possession, and its renewal is even today often liturgized in the so-called kaṭhina (vesting) ceremony. Additional items permitted were an alms basin of iron or clay, but not of valuable metal (Vin II.122.18–27), for the purposes of begging for food, which was to be received silently, no matter what was offered; a razor for shaving the head (hair was not plucked out, as the Jains did); needle (and thread); a belt; possibly also a cloth as a water filter, so that one might not accidentally kill tiny creatures; and sometimes also sandals (Vin I.188.7–8) or umbrellas (Vin II.131.13–14).

Originally, individuals were not allowed to receive money. Consequently, trade and business were impossible for individuals, though they were permissible for the order, which in that way could acquire land or monasteries and so have a solid basis for expansion. There was, in fact, a serious debate over these questions after the death of the Buddha, and repeated accusations were made against monks who were surrounded by a certain sumptuousness.

At the beginning the monasteries were probably only temporary gathering places for the rainy season or monastery groves that had been donated or placed at the monks' disposal. The order thought of itself as a congregation of those monks who lived within an area inside the boundaries of a community (sīma) that in the beginning was certainly established by prominent features of the landscape and could not be more extensive than three journeys with an ox (about thirty kilometers). Later, the monasteries added fixed monastic buildings (vihāra), where the monks stayed even beyond the rainy season.

The command to beg, coupled with a prohibition of working (monks did not even participate in caring for the monastic gardens), headed off the danger of isolation because it necessitated steady contact between the monks and the laity. It also prevented pride, since beggars were often exposed to humiliations. One must not avoid any house, must not pick out the raisins for oneself, and must not refuse any gift, because that would endanger the religious service of the giver. In Theragāthā (1054–1056), it is reported that the monk Mahākassapa even ate the thumb of a leper when he found it in his alms bowl, and unlike the story of Francis of Assisi, as recounted in Thomas of Celano's *Lives of St. Francis of Assisi,* the bitter mixture was not transformed into sweet food. One was allowed to accept only prepared food, since cooking was a duty of the man (or woman) of the house. The food need not necessarily be vegetarian, but the animal could not be killed especially for the monk. The process of begging was part of self-discipline and led to the monks' exposure to constant mobility and homelessness, interrupted only by the rainy season.

In the monastic establishments each monastery was headed by an abbot, but decisions were made by consensus. A set of rules had to be kept. Every two weeks a monastic chapter assembled, and the eldest spoke the two hundred fifty rules of the *prātimokṣa,* the confessional formula from the *Vinayapiṭaka,* and asked the monks whether they were pure. Later an explicit confession was added. These obligatory confessional services (*pā. uposatha*), which the Buddha himself is supposed to have instituted, became a sign of the purity and existence of the *Saṅgha,* a constitutive ritual of solidarity of the community, and thus, in Emile Durkheim's terminology, of its "church." In a certain sense the institution of the confessional service was what really created the community of the order, because when monks of the same place held a separate confessional service it served to split them off from the rest of the people. At least four monks were needed to celebrate the confessional service, and laity could not be present. These rules called for a minimum of solidarity and organization without establishing hierarchical structures and monastic disciplines that might have hindered the monks too severely in their individual pursuit of salvation.

Monasticism and the Lay State

The Buddha placed great value on maintaining contact between monks and laity, though it should not be too intense. This was part of his Middle Way and developed two factors of the *Saṅgha*: the command to preach and the command to beg.

The command to preach required the monks to convert others. Buddhism is therefore in principle a missionizing religion:

You monks, go and travel about for the sake of the blessing and happiness of the people, out of sympathy for the world, for the service of blessing and the happiness of gods and humans. No two of you should follow the same path. You monks, teach the Dhamma…and proclaim a pure, holy life. There are beings that by their nature have but little passion (*kāma*) and [therefore] are desirous of hearing the teaching; they will understand it. (*Vin* I.20.37–21.8)

The Buddha also taught that one should never reject an invitation to preach. Such an open attitude was fairly unusual. After all, Brahmanism and the other ascetic movements were elitist religions. Vedic Brahmans did not preach to just anyone who desired to be taught.

The command to beg, along with the command not to work, which was indirectly connected with it, prevented the monasteries from becoming autarchies, as happened in the Christian Middle Ages, when some monasteries thereby shut themselves off from the world. Buddhist monks retained their ability to function only as long as they were connected to the people. The relationships between laity and monks therefore rested on mutuality, as the Buddha himself is supposed to have said:

O monks, of great service to you are the Brahmans and citizens who support you with what you have need of: monastic robes, food, your camp and place to sit, medicine when you are sick. And you in turn, O monks, are of great service to the Brahmans and citizens when you teach them. …So, O monks, both parts of holy living rest mutually on one another, so that we may come across the floods and bring an end to all suffering. (*It* 111.9–18)[3]

The lay adherents supported the monks through gifts of food and material goods, by founding monasteries, and through other gifts (*dāna*). Generosity was always demanded of them. Nevertheless, the texts speak of how the Buddha came to a village with two hundred fifty or five hundred monks. But the lay adherents were to give their gifts only to those monks who were of the right— that is, selfless—mentality, because only then could they expect an adequate gift in return. In this way they exercised a certain degree of control over the monks.[4] Essentially, the monks gave the laity *dharma* (that is, teaching) and thus performed a religious service by giving them hope for a better rebirth or a life in the heavenly world, the world of the gods (*devaloka*):

> In five ways the son of (good) family...shall serve the monks
> (*samaṇabrāhmaṇa*): by serving them with kindness (*metta*) in thought,
> word, and deed, by not keeping doors closed, (and) by providing them
> with food. Through these five forms...the monks show their compassion
> toward the son from (good) family in six forms: they keep free from evil
> (*pāpā*), admonish for good, teaching what has not been heard before,
> show compassion with a friendly spirit, purify what has been heard, and
> declare the way to heaven. (*DN* III.191.13–21)

The commands to preach and beg cause the monks also to be dependent on
political support; otherwise they could scarcely have pursued their lives as
monks. To that end, it was helpful that soldiers could not become monks, so
there was no danger that they would corrupt the defense forces. Likewise, the
demand that thieves, debtors, or slaves not be ordained made the powerful
more favorable toward the monks. All the same, they admitted that the *Saṅgha*
retained its own system of laws.

But what real use were the monks to the laity, if what they essentially
preached was only the abandonment of their current lives? An intense
discussion of this question is in progress. Martin G. Wiltshire offers a view
that is exaggerated, or at least not well supported.[5] He asserts that there
was a pre-Buddhist tradition of ascetic individuals (which is true), whose
enlightenment was nonverbal and therefore could not be conveyed to others
(which is only partly true), so there was no sense in teaching, preaching, or
mission. According to Wiltshire, the Buddha was one of these (which cannot
be proven), who created a cult around himself and became a prisoner of his
own creation as it developed (which is true of all founders).

Much earlier, Max Weber gave a more realistic assessment of the situation.[6]
Weber saw early Buddhism as really a doctrine of salvation for religious
virtuosi, which, however (unlike Protestantism), could not create an economic
drive.[7] Weber saw early Buddhism (before Aśoka) as a rejection of the world
by elite groups. He thought early monks were individuals without any great
interest in the laity. The monks, according to Weber, were apolitical and even
antipolitical; the Buddha himself did not found a monastic order, and early
Buddhism was therefore without structure, sustained solely by the principle
of deference to the eldest and by teacher-student ties. Hence, he thought,
early Buddhism was unable to make any universal claims: why should a monk
be concerned about the health of someone else's soul? Weber also thought
Buddhism was really opposed to work, so there was no proof of worth in one's

life out of which a positive ethic for laypersons, with a religious premium on particular economic behavior and a rational economic ethics, could have developed. Instead, there was an ethics of non-action. In short, "Knowledge of one's own, final salvation [is] not sought by proving oneself in any kind of—this-worldly or other-worldly—action, in 'works' of any kind, but, on the contrary, in a competence to which activity is foreign."[8]

According to Stanley Tambiah, Weber falsely shifts the type of the individual monk in search of salvation to the center.[9] This so-called *paccekabuddha* (skt. *pratyekabuddha,* probably "the one awake to himself")[10] is a solitary ascetic who goes his own way and does not pass the teaching on to others, whereas the *samyaksambuddha* ("the perfectly awakened") hands on the teaching and his own experiences. Tambiah objects that the individual ascetic who withdrew totally from society was always rare and was given exaggerated importance in the secondary literature, especially since there is a good deal of uncertainty about the expansion and even the existence of such a practice.

This is certainly true, yet the tension between various ascetic ideals in early Buddhism cannot be denied. On the one side is the ideal of the search for salvation, which can best be realized through the greatest possible withdrawal and in meditation, and on the other side are the commandments to pray and to beg, which are indispensable for maintaining *Sangha.* This fixing of the structure of the order to the disadvantage of the individual path is connected with what Max Weber called the objectification (or institutionalization) and accommodation to the ordinary of a religious founder's charisma. This was as true for Gautama Buddha as for Jesus Christ. Nevertheless, the ancient ideal of the founder—who at first was, after all, an individual without followers—remained alive. So we find, even in the *Pāli* canon, passages in which, for example, preaching is called "idle chatter" (*pā. biḷibiḷikā*), as when Ānanda is advised to meditate instead of teaching lay disciples (*SN* I.199.24–200.4). This tension continued to a great extent in Buddhism, but even early Buddhism offered the spiritual path of salvation to lay followers as well.

Tambiah is, however, right in rejecting Max Weber's view that early Buddhism contained no worldliness, and hence none of its resulting economic drives. Thus, for example, models of tribal federation (instead of hierarchical royal empires) favored democratic structures in monasticism. Also, the anti-Brahmanic attitude gained great sympathy among the rising class of merchants and traders, courtiers, ordinary city folk, and large-scale farmers, as well as literate officials, for whom Buddhism was an aid to gaining respect and identity. In addition, even early Buddhism produced many social-political initiatives: compassion, help for the poor and the sick, preaching against the squandering of wealth.

I agree with this point of view. Moreover, the Buddha abolished constraining strictures regarding purity, which were at the apex of Brahmanism. Anyone who makes a thorough study of the traditional legal writings of ancient India will soon discover extensive rules for social contact, food prescriptions and prohibitions, rules for marriage, and restrictions on jobs and professions. There is little trace of any of that in the *Pāli* canon. In principle, the Buddha proposed an egalitarian, casteless, and classless order at least for monastic structures. That was in itself revolutionary, and in the framework of an economy that produced a surplus of food, it indirectly influenced economic behavior as well.

Buddhist and Christian Asceticism

If we compare early Buddhist asceticism with that of Christians (not only early Christians), major differences are apparent. In Christianity, *ora et labora* ("pray and work") is probably the tersest formula for asceticism; in Buddhist ascesis the aspect of work is absent. Christian asceticism—at least since the dawn of modernity—has had to defend and justify itself against the world, so it has been closely linked to the idea of *caritas* and to the therapeutic uses of work. Add to this the difference in the hierarchical structures of the monastic orders. In Christianity these tend to be centralizing and hierarchical, with a strong emphasis on obedience, while in Buddhism they are more decentralizing and egalitarian.

Of course, Gautama Buddha and Jesus Christ were themselves ascetics. We have regularly pointed to their similarities and differences. Following Gananath Obeyesekere,[11] I would like to contrast Jesus and Buddha once again under the aspect of their relationship to the world and to rejection of the world.

Jesus was a prophetic ascetic, the mediator of a transcendent, ethical God, sustained by revelation and the intensive, emotionally laden, prophetic message of a God. The church that resulted was shaped by commandments, authority, obedience, little willingness to compromise, and a high potential for conflict with the world order. On the whole, however, Jesus and "his" church were turned toward the world. That is the strength of Christianity. Or is it its weakness?

The Buddha was an ethical ascetic, practiced in the schooling of the spirit and the mind, in contemplative meditation. He got his knowledge not from someone else, especially not from a god. His teaching (not a message, but a guiding thread) was directed to the individual, and more inwardly than toward the world. The Buddha's community, his "church," was therefore extraordinarily vulnerable to compromise and revision. The development of the newer forms of Buddhism, Mahāyāna, Vajrayāna, and Tantrayāna, of Zen and Amida Buddhism, on the whole reveals more differences than common features. That is a weakness of Buddhism. Or is it its strength?

Response / *Ulrich Luz*
Jesus, Asceticism, and Relationship to the World

Are Jesus and Buddha really such opposites? I see a close resemblance between the two in the group of disciples Jesus gathered around himself. The Buddha also called individuals to the wandering life of the monk. It is true that Jesus did not organize his disciples into an order, but simply gave them a share in his task of preaching the reign of God in Israel. Thus, the institutional basis is indeed different, but still there are surprising parallels, especially in Jesus' special commands to his disciples.

For Jesus' disciples, too, there was a command of poverty and one of "homelessness." According to Luke, Jesus' disciples were to renounce all possessions, whatever they had (Luke 14:33; cf. Luke 5:11; 12:33). There is the familiar story of the rich young man who had kept all the commandments from his youth but was not ready to sell his possessions and give the proceeds to the poor, and as a result could not follow Jesus (Mark 10:17–22). Of course, it is disputed whether Jesus really made a fundamental demand that his followers give away all their possessions, as Luke depicts. Peter, for example, seems still to have owned a house where his mother-in-law (and his wife!) lived, and the fishery belonging to the sons of Zebedee, James and John, was not simply sold. The uncertainty is connected to the fact that Jesus worked for only a very short time and expected the rapid arrival of the reign of God. Under those conditions no one could establish solid institutions and institutional rules. But it is clear that a demonstrative poverty was part of the preaching of the reign of God in Israel. As they went about the land, the disciples were to carry neither bag nor purse; they were not even supposed to wear shoes (Luke 10:4). They were also not supposed to accept money, but only food (cf. Matt 10:9–10). They were traveling with Jesus, so they naturally renounced the exercise of their trades; this is clear in the well-known stories of the call of Peter, Andrew, the sons of Zebedee, and Levi (Mark 1:16–20; 2:14). The preachers' poverty had symbolic character: the reign of God has come especially for the poor, not the rich (Luke 6:20; Mark 10:25). The disciples share their poverty and homelessness with Jesus, who also has no place to lay his head (Luke 9:58).

The differences in this regard are relatively small. The earliest Buddhist monks had monasteries, but they were not yet fixed abodes for the monks. Moving about was more essential for the disciples of Jesus than for the early Buddhist monks because missionary preaching was the disciples' central task. For the post-Easter itinerant radicals, the centers of support and temporary places to stay were not monasteries but the resident communities. Early Buddhism placed a clear emphasis on the command to beg. The early Christian itinerant preachers, in contrast, lived by claiming the hospitality that was a matter of course in the Near East. Begging was scorned, because religious begging was a rather common phenomenon at that time and they had to distinguish themselves from those who practiced it.[12] In early Christianity the command not to work was not articulated as a prohibition; it simply arose as a matter of course from the task of preaching the message about the reign of God everywhere. In most cases it was impossible to take along one's work, for example a fishery or a toll booth. Paul is the first one we know of who earned most of his livelihood while traveling, through his own craft work. He could do it because he was a leatherworker, and he wanted to do it because he did not want to be dependent on the communities in which he worked (cf. 2 Cor 11:7–11; 12:16–17). It was seen as very unusual that he took nothing for his preaching from the communities, and his opponents even made it an accusation against him (cf. 2 Cor 12:14–17).

There are still more agreements. The renunciation of family life also links the disciples of Jesus with the early Buddhist monks. Drastic illustrations include Jesus' sayings about not burying one's father (Luke 9:59–60) and about hating one's family (Luke 14:26). On the surface this renunciation of family ties is easy to understand, because it is connected to the abandonment of a fixed abode. It could also have symbolic significance and, like Jesus' celibacy for the sake of the reign of God (Matt 19:12), represent the end of all family relationships in God's kingdom. By doing without a staff as a means of protection (Luke 9:3; Matt 10:10)—that is, through their absolute defenselessness—the disciples are also similar to the earliest Buddhist monks. They probably symbolize the fact that the coming of the reign of God is associated with an end to all violence (cf. Matt 5:38–42). On the whole, these apparently ascetic features of Jesus' circle of disciples are more radical than the corresponding rules for the *Sangha*, because they are signs that symbolize the coming reign of God.

Much like the Buddhist *Sangha*, or perhaps even more strongly, the group of Jesus' disciples is characterized by an egalitarian trend. There is no priestly dominance within it. Purity regulations were not very important, just as they were not for Jesus' interpretation of Torah. When traveling, one must eat what one received (cf. Luke 10:7) and could not ask questions about the cleanness or uncleanness of the food. The Jesus movement was probably more egalitarian than the Buddhist order in that women were equal members of the group of Jesus' disciples. It is also clearly said that the world's power relationships are not to hold among Jesus' followers: "Whoever wishes to become great among you must be your servant, and whoever wishes to be first among you must be slave of all" (Mark 10:43–44). This, too, corresponds to the coming reign of God, with its reversal of all relationships of dominance.

Axel Michaels has characterized early Buddhism as a "form of asceticism" that could not break contact with the laity and the population in general; he sees early Buddhism as, in principle, a missionizing religion. For the group of Jesus' disciples, whose duty was to proclaim the reign of God, and for early Christianity overall as it set out to missionize the world, this is true to a still greater degree.

The agreements are so many that we might ask ourselves why the developments after Jesus and after the Buddha were so different: The Buddha founded an order of monks, but there was never a solid institutionalization of a "lay church" in early Buddhism. In contrast, no monastic order arose from the circle of Jesus' disciples or the early Christian itinerant radicalism that replaced it, although the creation of Christian monasticism within the church of laity and priests in late antiquity had roots that can be traced back into primitive Christian itinerant radicalism. Even so, monasticism was something new within the church's history and can only be understood as a reaction to the secularization of the church. The relationship of the orders of monks and nuns to the church was almost always one of clear subjection and inclusion: the Christian orders were part of the church, integrated and domesticated within it. The danger that monasticism would get out of the church's control, which threatened at times in the late Middle Ages, was on the whole successfully averted by the church. The primacy of the church over the orders is, from the point of view of religious sociology, the major difference between Christianity and Buddhism.[13]

The view of Christianity stated by Axel Michaels, which I regard as too one-sided, needs to be refined. It is very questionable that, or to what degree, the church shaped by "commandments, authority, obedience, little willingness to compromise, and a high potential for conflict with the world order" really developed out of the proclamation of the "prophetic ascetic" Jesus (see the preceding section). The earliest Jesus communities were egalitarian and not hierarchically structured;[14] the hierarchical structure of the church shaped by commandments, authority, and obedience developed successively, and certainly not under the influence of Jesus. At the church's beginning there was a high potential for conflict with the world order on only one point: Christians were inclined to martyrdom because they would not let themselves be integrated into the religious system of Roman late antiquity. These conflicts should be sharply distinguished from those that were fought against the "world order" by the church that had become a political force and even a world power after Constantine.

In turn, the later Christian monasticism preserved and carried forward many of the features of Jesus' attitude toward the world—namely, on the one hand, a radical difference in lifestyle from that of the world and, on the other hand, a concern for the world, not in the form of conflicts, but in prayer, proclamation, and service. At this point Buddhism and monastic Christianity are not very dissimilar. Their strengths and weaknesses are to a great extent the same. The great question, however, is whether the different forms of institutionalized, patriarchal, and hierarchical church that developed from Jesus' work can in any way be legitimated in terms of Jesus' proclamation and work, or whether, in light of that, they are even bearable.

12

Jesus and the Church

Ulrich Luz

The Buddha founded a monastic order, and a lay movement rose around it; from the Jesus movement came the Christian church, or the different Christian confessions and sects. As regards its social form, Christianity has distanced itself more from its "founder," Jesus, than Buddhism has moved from Gautama Buddha: Jesus proclaimed the nearness of the reign of God, and what came was the church.[1] Jesus' concern was to call Israel to repentance and to God; what came was a new religion separate from Israel, to which almost no one but non-Jews belonged. Jesus' first care was for the poor, the disadvantaged, the women, the sick in Israel; the church that appealed to his leadership was at times the most important political power in the world.

Did Jesus Found the Church?

Unlike the Buddha and the *Saṅgha*, Jesus cannot be said to have founded a religious organization. The word *church* appears only twice in the gospels. The most important passage is Matthew 16:17–18.[2] When Peter has confessed Jesus as the Christ, the Son of God, Jesus responds, "Blessed are you, Simon son of Jonah! For flesh and blood has not revealed this to you, but my Father in heaven. And I tell you, you are Peter, and on this rock I will build my church, and the gates of Hades will not prevail against it." Behind the word *church* is presumably the Hebrew word for "assembly." Jewish texts speak of Israel as "God's assembly"; in Matthew 16:18, Jesus speaks strikingly of "*my* assembly." Superficially, the word appears to clarify the meaning of Simon's nickname, whose Aramaic form is *Kepha*, the Greek *Petros*. This nickname has early attestation (1 Cor 15:5). The saying about the rock plays on the Greek word *petra*, meaning rock. The play on words is more obvious in Greek than in Aramaic.

It is easy to understand, from the history of early Christianity, why Peter is seen as the "rock" on which Jesus built his church, because after Easter Simon Peter became the central figure in a number of ways. According to the Synoptic Gospels, he was the first to be called (Mark 1:16–18; Matt 4:18–20; Luke 5:1–11), so he was with Jesus in the beginning and was therefore something like a guarantor in the early church for the Jesus tradition. According to 1 Corinthians 15:5 and Luke 24:34, he received the first appearance after Easter; he is therefore not only one of the apostles, but the central figure among the apostles. He, the fisherman from Galilee, left Jerusalem very early and apparently worked in the Diaspora in the Gentile mission. We come across traces of him in Antioch (Gal 2:11–14), possibly in Corinth (1 Cor 1:12), and in any case in Rome (1 Pet 5:13;[3] cf. *1 Clem* 5:1–7). Peter is therefore a figure well suited to bind together the several wings of the later church, unlike Paul, who was only the apostle to the Gentiles, or James, the brother of the Lord, who represented only Jewish Christianity. There are, then, a number of reasons why early Christians saw the church as having been built on the "rock," Peter.

But the saying can scarcely have come from Jesus. Not only Protestant, but even Catholic critical exegesis is in general agreement about this.[4] It comes either from the earliest community or a later Hellenistic congregation. It began to be interpreted as a foundation for papal primacy only in the fifth century—and even then very seldom.[5] Thus it seems that Jesus did not found a church.

Jesus and Israel

Jesus knew that he had been sent to the people Israel. He addressed himself to the whole, complete people of God. In his proclamation of the reign of God, he was especially concerned for those on the margins: disadvantaged women, sick people often branded as unclean, the poor, the toll collectors, the whores. For him the Samaritans, who rejected Temple worship, were also part of the people of God; this is evident from texts such as Luke 10:30–37 and Luke 17:11–19, which present Samaritans as models of piety. In his interpretation of the Torah, too, he emphasized not the commandments that distinguished Israel from the nations, such as male circumcision, purity, or Temple worship.

For him, the coming of the reign of God meant a completely new beginning that far exceeds God's earlier love for Israel. Unlike other Jewish movements of renewal, including those of the Essenes or even the Pharisees, Jesus did not define Israel in such a way as to cut it off from the Gentiles.

It is true that Jesus could be very critical of Israel. Like his teacher, John the Baptizer, he was a prophet of judgment. Both men regarded Israel's election as anything but an inevitable given (Matt 3:8–9; 8:11–12). But all the same, he knew that he was sent to Israel with his message about the coming of the reign of God, and only to Israel. God's love was for Israel, and so was God's judgment.

Jesus had nothing against Gentiles. The tradition tells of two very similar incidents in which a Gentile woman and a Gentile man approached Jesus to ask him for healing: the story of the Syro-Phoenician woman (Mark 7:24–30) and the story of the centurion of Capernaum (Matt 8:5–13). It is possible that these stories have a historical kernel. But they show not only that Jesus had basically nothing against Gentiles, but also that encounters with Gentiles were for him notable and memorable exceptions, rather than the rule. Matthew 8:11 shows that he expected the Gentiles to make pilgrimage to Israel in the future reign of God: "Many will come from east and west and will eat with Abraham and Isaac and Jacob in the kingdom of heaven." And above all, the Gentiles will be present in the coming reign of God—but Jesus says not a word about the church.

Jesus seems to have gathered three groups of followers around him. The outer circle consisted of those who reacted positively to him; the gospels normally call them "the people," and recent scholarship, following Gerd Theissen, often refers to them as "sympathizers."[6] The response to Jesus' preaching was probably quite strong in his home country of Galilee.[7] The second, middle circle was made up of those who "followed after" him and shared his itinerant life. Luke speaks retrospectively of the Seventy (Luke 10:1). The innermost circle consisted of the twelve disciples. We need to speak first about them, because they have a direct connection with Israel.

The Group of the Twelve

For a long time the historicity of the group of the Twelve was disputed. Many scholars at an earlier period regarded the Easter appearance to the Twelve (1 Cor 15:5) as the moment when this group of twelve came into existence. But the Judas tradition, according to which a member of Jesus' closest group of followers betrayed him, could scarcely have been invented; after all, that betrayal was more than embarrassing to the post-Easter followers of Jesus. Therefore, it is very probable that the Twelve existed before the resurrection as Jesus' most intimate group of disciples. It appears that they were all men. The Synoptic Gospels and the Acts of the Apostles give us most of their names, but they are not in complete agreement (Mark 3:16–19; Matt 10:2–4; Luke 6:14–16; Acts 1:13).

It seems obvious that the Twelve should be associated with the twelve tribes of Israel, and that is explicitly stated in Jesus' saying about the twelve thrones: "Truly I tell you, at the renewal of all things, when the Son of Man is seated on the throne of his glory, you who have followed me will also sit on twelve thrones, judging the twelve tribes of Israel" (Matt 19:28). The Twelve functioned as representatives of the twelve-tribe nation of Israel.[8] But in what sense? The people of Jesus' time were no longer a nation of twelve tribes; everyone knew that, and they hoped that the scattered nine and a half tribes would someday, in the end-time, return to the land.[9] The Twelve signaled Jesus' eschatological claim, the hope for the end-time restoration of the twelve-tribe nation of Israel. This group signaled the beginning of the new, whole Israel being created by God. It confirmed that Jesus' mission was to Israel.

It is striking that among the members of the Twelve there are two purely Greek names, Andrew and Philip. Of course they were Jews, like the others; the latter may have gotten his name from the ruler of his region, Herod's son, the Tetrarch Philip. But the names may also once again show that Jesus was not particularly interested in setting Israel apart from Hellenism. If the disputed name Iscariot is derived from the Judean village of Kerioth, the group of the Twelve would include not only Galileans, but at least one Judean as well. Thus, some very different Israelites made up the group of the Twelve, but evidently all of them were simple, ordinary people.

After Easter the Twelve played almost no continuing role. Many New Testament authors identify the Twelve with the apostles; this is clearest in Luke's Acts of the Apostles. But the ancient tradition in 1 Corinthians 15:5, 7—which on the one hand speaks of appearances of the Risen One to Peter and the Twelve and on the other hand mentions such appearances to James and all the apostles—shows that the two groups must be distinguished. Thus, we cannot say whether the Twelve still played any part in the earliest church, or whether the group was a link between Jesus and the later church. From the words Jesus spoke at his last meal we can only reservedly conclude that he hoped the Twelve would survive his death and endure until the coming of the reign of God.

Disciples, Male and Female

Unlike the Twelve, the middle circle of disciples awakens no direct associations with Israel. With supreme authority, Jesus called people who were willing to share his itinerant life: "As he was walking along, he saw Levi son of Alphaeus sitting at the tax booth, and he said to him, 'Follow me.' And he got up and followed him" (Mark 2:14). The word *follow* is to be taken literally. Those who followed Jesus gave up their fixed abodes and their crafts or businesses and traveled through the country with Jesus, the Son of Man, who unlike the foxes and birds had no place to lay his head (Luke 9:58). The example of Levi, like the names of the disciples that are recorded in the Gospel of John, shows that the group of Jesus' disciples included members who were not among the Twelve.

In all probability there were also women among the disciples. Apart from the women who went with Jesus from Galilee to Jerusalem and were witnesses to his crucifixion (Mark 15:40-41), the famous saying about the ravens and the lilies of the field gives us the clearest indication of who they were:

> He said to his disciples, "Therefore I tell you, do not worry about your life, what you will eat, or about your body, what you will wear. . . . Consider the lilies, how they grow: they neither toil nor spin; yet I tell you, even Solomon in all his glory was not clothed like one of these. But if God so clothes the grass of the field, which is alive today and tomorrow is thrown into the oven, how much more will he clothe you—you of little faith!" (Luke 12:22, 27–28).

Who could take their model from the lilies of the field, which do not spin and weave—that is, perform the work of the women of the household—except women who no longer do household work because they are following Jesus?

There are no contemporary analogies for Jesus' call to follow him. He had nothing to do with the system of rabbinic students in his time. Rabbis did not call their students; the latter applied to be allowed to study with the rabbi. Moreover, they were as a rule sedentary, in contrast to Jesus. Becoming the student of a rabbi did not mean breaking with one's family; on the contrary, the family considered itself honored when one of their own became a rabbinic student. Likewise, becoming a rabbi's student had nothing to do with abandoning one's trade or craft; the rabbis for the most part exercised an auxiliary trade, craft, or profession. It would be easier to point to related phenomena in Hellenism, such as the Cynic philosophers, who were often itinerant and whose extreme simplicity was similar to that of the Jesus movement.[10] But among the Cynics there are no comparable call stories.

The sole analogy lay many centuries in the past: namely, the call of Elisha by Elijah (1 Kings 19:19–21). The two disciple stories in Luke 9:59–60 and 61–62 play very clearly on this example. In addition, especially in the Synoptic miracle traditions, there are close connections to the Elijah/Elisha tradition.[11] The poverty and itinerancy of Jesus' disciples are also a good fit with Elijah. Mark 6:15 and 8:28 report that Jesus' contemporaries thought he was Elijah returned. It is therefore very possible that he modeled himself directly on the biblical Elijah.

The purpose of Jesus' call to discipleship was to involve selected people in the preaching of the reign of God to Israel.[12] Discipleship is thus a task, not a condition for entry into the reign of God. This point is very clear in the story of the rich young man (Mark 10:17–22): Keeping the commandments is quite enough for attaining life, but discipleship means taking on a task. Jesus concludes the harsh saying to another young man about the dead being left to bury the dead with a command: "But as for you, go and proclaim the kingdom of God" (Luke 9:60). He says to Peter and Andrew, "I will make you fish for people" (Mark 1:17). The Sayings Source Q links the call to discipleship in Luke 9:57–60 with the mission discourse in Luke 10:2–12: for these, the disciples are the "workers in the harvest" (Luke 10:2). They receive the assignment to go into houses and villages, heal the sick, and proclaim that the reign of God is at hand (Luke 10:9). Probably the core sayings in the mission discourse come from Jesus himself.

In the "Response" to the last chapter I already mentioned the special instructions Jesus gave his disciples. These were partly about sharpening things that applied to everyone—for example, in the commandment not to defend oneself (Matt 10:10), the renunciation of wealth (Luke 14:33), and the radical reversal of the world's structures of dominance (Mark 10:42–44). Here it is especially clear that this community was shaped in a particular way by the approaching reign of God. In part the instruction contains entirely different commands, almost the opposite of those Jesus gave other people: for example, the command not to bury one's own father (Luke 9:60) and the renunciation of family (Luke 14:26). Elsewhere Jesus highly valued the Decalogue, and thus also the commandment to honor one's parents (cf. Mark 7:1–13), and he accounted marriage of great worth. Here we may see the appearance of the idea of asceticism, which was otherwise foreign to Jesus. But I regard that as false: The special way of life of those who followed Jesus had at most a symbolic function; we might speak of a "symbolic asceticism" reflecting what Jesus and his disciples were preaching—namely, the coming reign of God, the end of the world, and the approach of the judgment. We should also not speak of the beginnings of a two-level ethics with Jesus; such a thing developed in Christianity only in the High Middle Ages in connection with monasticism.

The circle of disciples was not an institution conceived as something enduring. For example, we do not know whether, if Jesus had lived longer, he would have let his disciples go home again for "family visits." We also do not know whether and how he would have looked after their needs in the middle term. If he had lived longer, and in the face of the delay of the reign of God, would he have made the circle of disciples into a kind of missionary order with a constitution similar to the one the Essene community in Qumran had? All we can be sure of is that the disciples were not some kind of core of the new Israel as people of God; they were preachers of the reign of God for the original people of God. It is true that they were something like a seed of the later church, but that was not Jesus' intention.

Itinerant Radicals after Easter

The proclamation of the reign of God by itinerant disciples of Jesus continued after the death of Jesus. Thanks to Gerd Theissen, this movement arising out of the work of Jesus' disciples has acquired the name of "early Christian itinerant radicalism"[13]—a happy formulation, because the expression *discipleship* was understood differently from an early date. But after Jesus' death the relationships changed very quickly. People could not over a long period of time continue to go from place to place on foot, without shoes, staff, or bag, in utter poverty; even the gospels show how Jesus' commands were relaxed and adapted.[14] The apostles and Jesus missionaries also traveled to the Diaspora and to the Gentiles. The missionary activity of Paul and his coworkers reflected the changed situation. A planned, well-organized mission, sustained by the communities and extending throughout the whole Roman Empire, became the central effort, replacing Palestinian itinerant radicalism.[15]

The itinerant radicals, in fact, were shifted to the margins of the church. It is theologically significant that the word *discipleship* was reinterpreted even as early as the gospels, and was associated with the possibility of having a fixed abode and living in a settled congregation. *Discipleship* and *following* became expressions, even in the gospels, that described an actively engaged

Christianity, oriented to Jesus and his commandments and prepared to undergo martyrdom.[16] "Following Jesus" thereby became a heritage of early Christianity that radicalized the settled and institutionalized church of later times.

The itinerant radicals themselves, in contrast, remained essentially restricted, geographically speaking, to Syria. The document called "The Teaching of the Twelve Apostles," originating in Syria about 120–130, shows they could be a problem for the settled communities (*Didache* 11–13). Apparently they were numerous, and when they entered a community they claimed not only authority but also lodging and maintenance for long periods of time. At the beginning of the third century we encounter their successors in the form of itinerant ascetics who visited one another and the congregations.[17] From the fourth century onward, first the Christian hermits, then monasticism acquired the essence of the thought of the early Christian itinerant radicals. In Christianity, in contrast to Buddhism, it was only later that the monastic orders became settled, and even domesticated, *within* the Christian church of laity and priests. That the domestication was not always free of problems is clear, for example, from the history of the late medieval poor people's movements, including those of the Franciscans and the Waldensians. But on the whole it succeeded. This is evident from the fact that the origins of Christianity in primitive itinerant radicalism were recovered only in the second half of the twentieth century.

Origins of the Settled Church

Previously the historical picture painted by the Acts of the Apostles, augmented by reports in the Pauline letters and other biblical books, dominated the story of early Christianity. On the one hand, at the center was the missionary activity of the church's apostles, at first primarily Peter and then, in the second part of Acts, exclusively Paul. It was important for Luke that the church from the very beginning was a unified and single institution guided by the Holy Spirit and led by the twelve apostles. On the other hand, Luke was interested in the founding of communities in the important metropolitan centers of the Roman Empire and the expansion of the church throughout the whole realm. Clearly, a great deal was sacrificed to this version of history, and it is difficult to distinguish between what Luke did not know and what he did not want to write. For example, in Acts we hear nothing about what happened in Galilee, the homeland of the Jesus movement, after Jesus' death. Nor do we hear anything about early Christian itinerant radicalism, apart from a single Jewish itinerant prophet named Agabus (Acts 11:28; 21:10–11). Luke presupposes that from the very beginning there were settled Christian communities that baptized in the name of Jesus, celebrated the Lord's Supper, and had close communion among themselves (Acts 2:42–47; 4:32–35).

Luke's picture is certainly one-sided, but probably it is not simply false. The beginnings of the church remain obscure, and we must suppose there was a fairly long phase of creation and self-definition.[18] According to every indication, at a very early date settled Jesus communities in Israel celebrated their own liturgies and awaited the coming of the reign of God. In comparison to other Jewish groups, among which they essentially belonged, they quickly developed their own identifying ritual characteristics, if they did not have them from the very beginning: their own initiation ritual of baptism in the name of Jesus and the Lord's Supper, which apparently was never an annual celebration, but was always held weekly—that is, alongside the Passover and not as a Paschal feast. The oldest confessions and acclamations of Jesus transmitted to us by the New Testament also go back to a very early time. Likewise very early, the boundaries of Israel were passed; the universalistic feature of Jesus' preaching would at least have made that step somewhat easier. It is also remarkable that the Jesus communities, even those that were not Jewish, regarded themselves from a very early moment as belonging together. Testimony to this includes the intensive traveling back and forth between communities in early Christianity, the so-called Apostolic Council, and, of course, Paul's collection.[19] Finally, it is striking that the separation from "mother" Israel progressed rapidly. In particular, the Jewish-Christian-based writings in the New Testament, with their embittered polemic against majority Judaism, attest that by about 100 c.e., the separation was largely complete, even though not fully resolved.

Thus, in the first and second generations after Jesus, it was clear that the major result of Jesus' work was the settled Jesus communities. They rapidly developed a common sense of identity and understood themselves not only as "disciples of Jesus," but as a new "assembly of God" (Gal 1:13), the "assembly of Jesus" (cf. Matt 16:18), the "body of Christ" (1 Cor 12:12–27), or the new people of God.[20]

The development of early Christianity thus differed from that of early Buddhism. The Buddha founded a monastic order. The sympathizers and laity associated with the order were only loosely organized. They could support the order, accept its teaching, and take part in its exercises to a certain extent. Although the disciples accompanying Jesus are comparable in many ways to the disciples of the Buddha, they did not develop into an order. Out of their preaching activity arose the communities and the church, and the itinerant radicals existed *within* or *on the margins of* that church without solid institutionalization and for a time only.

Why the Church?

Why did the two develop so differently? Jesus did not want a church and did not found a church. All the same, several "factors and impetuses in Jesus' work...led to the creation of the church":[21]

• *Jesus' preaching of the reign of God*—Jesus spoke of the coming of the reign of God. He proclaimed God's future for the whole world, not a way of salvation for individuals. His concern was with God and what God does for the world and humanity: hence the importance of preaching. While the Buddha, according to legend, first had to be convinced by the god *Brahmā* that it was right to preach the path to enlightenment also to the unredeemed,[22] Jesus' group of disciples existed only for the sake of preaching. However, there were no beginnings of a spiritual praxis in early Christianity comparable to the Buddhist monks' path to enlightenment. When the preaching is so important and the path so unimportant, it is impossible for an order to become the central institution. Instead, the assembly of the "many" (cf. Mark 14:24) who hear this preaching and respond to it must have a weight all its own.

• *The singularity of Jesus*—Because Jesus intertwined his own work so completely with the coming of the reign of God and the judgment of the world, preaching about him took on a crucial importance after his death. It was thus quite natural that the disciples of Jesus quickly came to see themselves as a separate community with its own ritual of initiation. Jesus' claims about himself, confirmed by his resurrection, led almost inevitably to the formation of a separate community that interpreted itself as something other than one of the various competing Jewish "sects" of the time. In my opinion, this primacy of Christ over all the convictions, texts, and institutions that constituted Israel, including faith in the uniqueness of YHWH and the election of Israel, the Torah, and the Temple, was the crucial reason why, sooner or later, the Jesus communities separated from Israel and so made the Jesus movement into a new religion and a separate church.[23] Jesus probably would not have approved of this development, but he participated in bringing it about.

• *Love as central to life*—For Jesus, the love commandment was central to his ethical preaching, which was directed almost exclusively to the community and not to individuals. The same is true of early Christian ethics based on the preaching of Jesus. Almost everywhere in the New Testament, the love commandment is central; New Testament ethics is almost entirely a community ethics. For Jesus, the community of disciples contained features of a "contrast society" because it symbolically embodied, in a special way, the reality of the coming reign of God. Paul developed this idea further on the basis of his christological initiative, seeing the church as "the body of Christ," which for him meant that it was a space created by Christ within which to shape a common life formed by love (cf. 1 Cor 12:12–31). Something similar is true of other New Testament authors, for example, the Gospel of Matthew (Matt 18) and the letter to the Ephesians (Eph 4:1–16). For them the community of the church is fundamental, because in light of Christ, love is fundamental.

• *The delay of the Parousia*—The delay of the return of Christ necessarily strengthened the significance of the church. Of course, the church did not originate only because the reign of God did not arrive, but the already existing church became more and more important as the hope for the coming of the reign of God shifted increasingly to the margins of Christian faith. The coming of the reign of God was replaced by experiences conveyed by the present church: manifestations of the Spirit, preaching, baptism, the Lord's Supper, community, the new way of life, and hope for life eternal. Buddhism, which has no cosmic eschatology, also needs no institution that would take up and compensate for a "blank space" created by the delay of the Parousia.

Buddhism and the Christian Dilemma of Church

When I consider the church in light of Jesus, I find three things that are important. First, Jesus did not found a church, because he knew that he was sent to Israel. Second, the creation of the church and its separation from Israel were the indirect results of Jesus' preaching. And finally, the development of the church, indirectly caused by Jesus' preaching, also meant that the Jesus movement shifted away from Jesus.

Thus, on the one hand, the church is a necessary consequence of Jesus' work, if the experiences of salvation he brought about and the praxis he initiated were to continue in some way. On the other hand, by becoming a church, the followers of Jesus distanced themselves mightily from Jesus. The further history of the Christian churches, their institutionalization, patriarchalization, hierarchization, their development into majority churches with the associated increase of influence, and their progressive accommodation to the world and its power structures have steadily magnified their separation from Jesus. Jesus, who caused the church's creation, was absorbed or dogmatically domesticated, so that even the modern question of who Jesus was became, to a great extent, an implicit or explicit critique of the church.

Can an examination of the *Sangha* be of help to the Christian churches? I find myself on the horns of a dilemma: I am convinced that a church community, as the place for common experience of salvation and common praxis, is a necessary part of Christian faith. Moreover, I am grateful for the churches, because without them a Christian identity probably could not have survived through the centuries. Yet I see that many people are blocked from choosing a Christian identity by today's churches, so distant from Jesus himself. In that situation the idea of something like "Christian *Sanghas*" can be inspiring.

I am not talking about a direct orientation to the Buddhist *Sangha*. Rather, we should live more directly from the heritage of those things in Christianity that correspond to it: primitive Christian itinerant radicalism and monasticism. Concretely, I desire Christian institutions that make possible an authoritatively Christian life and let others experience it, but do not assert any sort of control over other people. These institutions could be Christian monasteries, communities of common life, base communities, or other types of societies of critical minorities that live as heirs of Jesus and early Christianity. But the Christian churches should stop trying to do the splits—really impossible nowadays—by being both the critical minority and the whole people, or by representing both the "contrast society" and the whole society.

Response / *Axel Michaels*
From Founder to Religion

The transmogrifications from religious founder to god, from movement to institution, from internal focus to public activity, from revolution to preservation and tradition, from minority to state church—these are processes in the development of religions that reveal many common features.[24] In what follows, I will concentrate on one of these aspects by discussing the tension between community and individualism.

We have seen how the Buddha was deified; we have also seen, in the Doctrine of the Three Bodies, that, early on, there arose a variety of images of the historical Buddha: human being, superman (bodhisattva), spiritual principle (dharma), "god" (Tathāgata). Various forms of bodiliness (spirit-body, somatic body, etc.) appear as resurrection, as well as in the Trikāya doctrine. I have pointed out parallels to the doctrine of the Trinity and also that every religious founder, and in principle every saint, is subject to these processes of deification, since otherwise they would remain merely ordinary human beings. Exaltation is practically a foregone conclusion. From this point of view every religious founder, everyone who proclaims a religious teaching, is the guarantor of his or her doctrine. To put it another way, one can predict the collapse of a religious movement that arises from a single person if, after that person's death, there is no such exaltation.

However, the exalting is done by other people: the founder's followers. The founders themselves are only individuals who could see themselves as Son of God or Awakened One, but who had to achieve social recognition (that is, from other people) if they were not to be dismissed as fanatics. How does this exaltation take place? In part it is inherent in the teaching itself (it gives "good" answers to current religious questions), but to a significant extent it depends on an institutional anchoring of the teaching. This requires, first of all, opportunities for the symbol system to be reinterpreted by individuals, the possibility for religious revolution on the basis of developed social structures. In modern societies, religious founders like Gautama Buddha or Jesus Christ are scarcely possible any longer, because in modernity the religious system and source of meaning is only one of many, so religious changes can hardly ever lead to social revolutions. If the Buddha and Jesus were to appear today, they could no longer be effectively deified after their death, so their influence would remain very small. For that reason it is possible that there can be no more religious founders.

Of course, almost all the great religious founders, including the Buddha and Jesus, did not intend to found new religions. They were really not the founders of religions, but people who wanted to transform religion, and in this sense they were revolutionaries. They did not want to start new communities; they wanted to influence the existing communities. Their audience and addressees were in their own environment, their own society: Israel or the society shaped by Brahmanism. This is a difference between religious revolutions and mission: whereas missions intend to bring a new religion to other people, a religious revolution makes new people of the members of their own community. This, too, is a difference from the new forms of encounter between Christianity and Buddhism.

Because religious founders, as we have said, do not begin as such, but simply as individuals who want the people of their own community to be different from what they are, their appeal is extended to a type of person who in some sense is already outside the community, a type that in reality does not yet exist: the new people of the reign of God, transcendent selves, non-selves. Thus religious founders' appeal often appears as universalistic, eschatological, even if that is not at all their intention.

The new thing and the new person[25] must be visibly distinguished from the old: A turnaround, a transformation is demanded, one that is outwardly evident and thus documents the new community. Here clear differences between the Christian church and the *Saṅgha* appear. A Christian confession demands more transformation than a confession of Buddhism. For example, there is the question of allowing oneself to be circumcised or baptized, while in Buddhism a formulaic confession of Buddhism as a whole (that is, not a commitment to monastic Buddhism) suffices.

It is true that various Buddhist "churches" have developed, as in Christianity, Buddhist institutions in the form of monastic communities, political organizations, world congresses, and so on. And if we understand "church" in Durkheim's sense—that is, to put it in simplified terms, as a "solidary system of convictions and practices"—then every Buddhist community has such a structure. But there was no Constantinian shift in Buddhism, and no world-encompassing or at least temporarily supra-regional powerful official church with clear hierarchies, central institutions, and structures of control. Why not, even though the historical preconditions were present in the reign of Aśoka? There are two primary reasons.

The first reason is the highly individualistic relationship to salvation. In India the search for salvation was, from a very early time, the particular task of the individual as member of his line of descent; it was thus genealogical and therefore restrictive.[26] In the Brahmanic society of ancient India, the Vedic house fire and domestic sacrifice constituted the dominant symbolic system, so much so that even the gods were less powerful than the priestly sacrificial laws. Offering sacrifice was the privilege of individual clans of priests and their clientele, who were integrated into the genealogical line of the priests by means of ritual series of identifications. With the internalization of the sacrifices in the ascetic movements beginning in about the eighth to sixth centuries B.C.E., this genealogical connection, which had been necessary for sacrifice, was broken; however, the individualistic and ultimately restrictive components were retained. There was such a thing as community religion, but more within the realm of popular religiosity. Public celebrations, temples, shrines, public religious cults—all these were much less common than rituals and sacrifices on behalf of the well-being of an individual as part of a line of descent. This ideal of salvation was thus individualistic from the beginning. Gautama Buddha, like Jesus Christ, overcame the old forms of this genealogical relationship to salvation and the inherited priesthood, but the institutional structures available to him were essentially applicable to the monastic community and not to a church for religious virtuosi and laity.

The second reason for the lack of an official Buddhist "church" involves accommodation: The Buddha wanted to show a path that was separate both from the costly, priest-dependent sacrificial ritual and from strict world-avoiding asceticism—namely, the Middle Way. For that purpose he placed very few tensions between the world and his teaching. He wanted to overcome the world, to leave it behind him, to be freed from it, but not to remake it. Therefore, he also developed no religious syncretism; instead, he associated himself with other forms of religious devotion while leaving them largely intact. Richard Gombrich has called this phenomenon "accommodation." In contrast, with Jesus one constantly senses the tension between the world and his teaching, the dissatisfaction with an existing world. For Ulrich Luz, Jesus, as the point of identification of the Christian church, is always also hope and protest, but in any case directed to the future. For the Buddha, even the future can never be anything but suffering and mutability, which is why there can be neither hope nor faith.

Can Christianity learn from these loose forms of Buddhist institutionalism? Given present reservations about the institutional church, the hierarchy, the solidification of offices and administration, it would almost seem so. Of course, Buddhism's student-teacher relationships and—on a superficial view—

the egalitarian structure of the order have been hastily idealized and stylized into a community of those who are religiously free. One should not overlook the fact that personal student-teacher relationships sometimes imply severe dependency, often characterized by tyranny and caprice.

It seems to me that what we can learn from early Buddhism is not a new form of institutionalization of religion and church, but something else: No matter whether a formal or ritual confession is involved, most people in the West still belong to a community of belief that is in search of the new humanity. New self-development projects and social utopias are being constantly produced. Again and again, what now exists is revolutionized. We can almost speak of a religion of novelty, of faith in the new per se. I see the roots of this "background religion" in Jesus and the tension with the world of which he spoke.

If there is something we can learn from Buddhism, it is less about forms of institutionalization and more about knowledge of the suffering nature of mutability, even toward the new. If this knowledge is translated in Buddhist terms there might be a diminution of the tension still created in us, and between us and the world, by Christian eschatology, which makes even Buddhism appear suddenly to be a new alternative or accommodating religion. It may well be "Buddhist" not to be continually striving for what is new; it is "Buddhist" to remain what one is and to acknowledge that there is no self, not even a new self, and that this knowledge alone leads to an end to suffering, if one—alone or in community—helps in making it the possession of all.

Epilogue

Can Buddhism Heal Christianity?

Buddhism Cannot Heal Christianity!
Ulrich Luz

Is Christianity sick? If we understand health as simply the external condition of a religion, the number of members, the rate of growth, the sum of its activities, one could speak, in the primarily Protestant regions of northern and western Europe, of a "sickness" or, to use a different metaphor, of an "aging" of Christianity. But the same is not true for many of the countries in eastern and southern Europe, for North America, and certainly not for South America, Africa, and many countries in Asia. The best diagnosticians for "sicknesses" of this sort that are subject to objective scholarly investigation are the sociologists of religion, and they would certainly not prescribe Buddhism as the right medicine for Christianity.

Therefore, I would prefer to understand sickness in a different sense—namely, as a deficiency that I, as a Protestant theologian, see in our contemporary western European, ecclesiastical Christianity. A "diagnosis of sickness" understood in this way can by no means be objective, because it presupposes one's own interpretation of Christian faith, one's own view of our contemporary society, and a personal background of experience and location within the church.

189

I am convinced that a historically developed religion like Christianity, located within a particular history, cannot change for the better unless it lives from its own roots. Otherwise, it loses its identity. This does not exclude, but rather includes a very critical and self-critical reflection on those roots. The relationship to the church's own roots and its own understanding of those roots can and should change, but not the roots themselves. I therefore have no use for deliberately chosen syncretism and tinkering with religion. Religions are like mothers: one has them, one owes much to them (in fact, the most crucial thing of all), but one cannot exchange them, and there is not much point in asking whether someone else's mother is better, prettier, kinder, etc., in this or that respect. Mothers are not perfect, not absolute, but they are the givers of life and as such they are, to their own children, irreplaceable. "Healing" Christianity in a fundamental sense can be achieved only if a livelier Christianity can be brought forth from its own roots and its own strengths.

Even though I have little use for tinkering with religion, I do place great value on dialogues, because they make it possible for us to see ourselves mirrored in another. My interest in conversation with Buddhists, and my theological interest in this book, is in the possibility of encountering a reflection of Christian faith from outside. This has been done here in two ways: one way through the Buddha and early Buddhism, and the other through my coauthor and conversation partner, Axel Michaels, and his view of Christianity from outside. But such reflections from outside can bring us further only if the lopsided and burdensome self-images we see in such reflections can at the same time help us see the roots—perhaps atrophied or buried—in our own tradition that need to be rediscovered. Here two things were especially important to me: the Buddhist capacity for tolerance and, closely connected to that, the *Saṅgha* as a form of "church" that embodies the civility of life, its nature as a system of obligations that nevertheless do not infantilize or dominate the individual. In both cases there are also Christian roots that we can rediscover, but we cannot solve the problem simply by resorting to the old Reformation slogan, "back to the Bible," or the motto of nineteenth-century liberal theology, "back to Jesus." Both Jesus and the Bible are ambivalent, so, aided by the reflections from outside, we not only rediscover buried nuggets of gold in our own tradition but also can better recognize and reflect on the problems in that tradition.

Buddha or Jesus? Buddha and Jesus!
Axel Michaels

Can Buddhism heal Christianity? We really tried to avoid this question. Instead, we have emphasized the right of each religion to its own independent existence, without attack from without and without being absorbed by something else. The question is mainly asked by non-Christians who are interested not in "healing" Christianity but in developing a new, syncretistic religiosity (not religion).

However, the question of whether the influence of Buddhism aids or damages Christianity is not only a favorite, but also a justified question; the flood of books on this theme answers an obvious need. Apparently mature, institutionalized religions are no longer satisfying the desire for this new form of religiosity. They have perhaps become too "inhuman," and Buddha Gautama's and Jesus of Nazareth's concern for "the human being," combined with their turning away from official religion, corresponds to the trend.

What desires underlie this trend? My impression is that they are rather diffuse. But I have no basis, certainly no scholarly basis, on which to judge them adequately. So I can only speak for myself, although—strictly speaking—that is not the scholar's task.

For me, mature, institutionalized religions are refuges from questions about death, life, and afterlife. But they are not the only refuges. As I look around me at the offerings of the modern system for providing meaning, to see which blanket I can happily snuggle into and where I prefer to take refuge, the first thing that gratifies me is the opportunity to weigh these possibilities. This was not always available in the history of religions, and religions that one cannot choose for oneself can be torture.

But at the same time I am saddened precisely by this range of choices, because it reveals that I have lost my religious refuge, my religious home. I observe, with a mixture of admiration and mistrust, that people who feel at home in their religion have easier answers for the questions to which I find only optional responses. Two of those options are Gautama Buddha and Jesus Christ.

What convinces me most in what is offered by Jesus and Christianity is the experience of love, the message about fulfillment, and especially the offer of acceptance (by Jesus, by the Father) and thereby the unburdening of the self.

What persuades me most in the Buddha's gift is the epistemological clarity in the doctrine of suffering, the offer of peace in meditation, the attitude toward nature and fellow beings, especially animals, and the unburdening of the self in the doctrine of Anātman.

In both cases I have mentioned the unburdening of the self, even though, as we have tried to explain, that may take very different forms. Liberation of the self really does seem to be one of the great longings of our highly individualized era. Less self-centeredness, less egoism, not needing to put so much emphasis on one's own importance, in order—with great calm—no longer to sense the overburdened, driven, lonely "I," or to be able to open oneself in selfless love to the other or others: that message might be one that the Buddha and Jesus could have united on. In this sense I gladly "confess" both: Buddha *and* Jesus. But I owe my ability to do so, above all, to the Buddha.

Notes

Introduction

1. Richard Garbe, *Indien und das Christentum: Eine Untersuchung der religionsgeschichtlichen Zusammenhänge* [India and Christendom: The Historical Connections between Their Religions] (Tübingen: Mohr, 1914), 12.

2. For the state of phenomenology of religions, see Axel Michaels, Daria Ogliati-Pezzoli, and Fritz Stolz, eds., *Noch eine Chance für die Religionsphänomenologie?* (Bern: Lang, 2001).

3. See, for example, Friedrich Heiler, *Erscheinungsformen und Wesen der Religion,* 2nd ed. (Stuttgart: Kohlhammer, 1961), 16.

4. Gerd Theissen, *Die Religion der ersten Christen* (Gütersloh: Gütersloher Verlagshaus, 2000), 20–28.

5. Ibid., 44, 385.

6. Gustav Mensching, *Vergleichende Religionswissenschaft,* 2nd ed. (Heidelberg: Quelle & Meyer, 1949), 151.

7. Cf. the fascinating "conversation" between the Buddha and Jesus in Carrin Dunne, *Buddha and Jesus: Conversations* (Springfield, Ill.: Templegate, 1975).

1. One and Many Buddhas

1. Étienne Lamotte, *History of Indian Buddhism: From the Origins to the Śaka Era* (Louvain-la-Neuve, Belgium: Université Catholique de Louvain, Institut Orientaliste, 1988), 1:219ff.

2. Cf. especially Heinz Bechert, *The Dating of the Historical Buddha,* 3 vols. (Göttingen: Vandenhoeck & Ruprecht, 1991, 1992, 1997); idem, *Die Lebenszeit des Buddha—das älteste feststehende Datum der indischen Geschichte?* (Göttingen: Vandenhoeck & Ruprecht, 1986), 129–84.

3. For more detail, see Richard Gombrich, *Theravada Buddhism: A Social History from Ancient Benares to Modern Colombo* (New York: Routledge & Kegan Paul, 1988), 49–59.

4. Tilman Vetter, in Andreas Bsteh, ed., *Der Buddhismus als Anfrage an christliche Theologie und Philosophie* (Mödling: Verlag St. Gabriel, 2000), 58.

5. Hermann Oldenberg, *Buddha: Sein Leben, seine Lehre, seine Gemeinde* [Buddha: His Life, His Doctrine, His Order] (1881), 13th ed. (Stuttgart: Cotta, 1959), 114.

6. Dieter Schlingloff, "Die Meditation unter dem Jambu-Baum," *Wiener Zeitschrift für die Kunde Südasiens* 31 (1987): 111–30.

7. According to David L. Snellgrove, *Indo-Tibetan Buddhism. Indian Buddhists and Their Tibetan Successors* (Boston: Shambhala, 1987), 7.

8. Oldenberg, *Buddha*, 93.

9. Edward Conze, *Der Buddhismus: Wesen und Entwicklung* [Buddhism: Its Essence and Development], 8th ed. (Stuttgart: Kohlhammer, 1986), 35–36.

10. Oldenberg, *Buddha*, 106.

11. For the *Mahāyāna* teaching of the three bodies, see chapter 9.

12. Johannes Mehlig, *Weisheit des alten Indien* (Leipzig: Kiepenheuer, 1987), 2:412.

13. On this, see Ernst Steinkellner, "Buddhismus: Religion oder Philosophie? und Vom Wesen des Buddha," in Bsteh, ed., *Der Buddhismus als Anfrage*, 261–62.

14. Dorothee Sölle, *Stellvertretung. Ein Kapitel Theologie nach dem 'Tode Gottes'* (Stuttgart: Kreuz-Verlag, 1965). Translated by David Lewis as *Christ the Representative; An Essay in Theology after the Death of God* (Philadelphia: Fortress Press, 1967).

15. The formula appears frequently in this or a similar form, e.g., with Athanasius, *Or de inc.* = MPG 25, 192B. Cf. Alois Haas, "Jesus Christus—Inbegriff des Heils und verwirklichte Transzendenz im Geist der deutschen Mystik," in *Geistliches Mittelalter*, ed. idem, 291–314 (Fribourg: Universitätsverlag, 1984).

16. Meister Eckhart, *Deutsche Werke* 1:72, 9ff.

2. Jesus: His Life and His World

1. In Syria, the Diatessaron, a harmony of the four canonical gospels completed by Tatian, a Syrian, was the accepted form of the text.

2. For the reconstruction of the account by Josephus, see Gerd Theissen and Annette Merz, *The Historical Jesus: A Comprehensive Guide* (Minneapolis: Fortress Press, 1998), 74–82.

3. Cf., for example, Wolfgang Schrage, *Das Verhältnis des Thomas-Evangeliums zur synoptischen Tradition und zu den koptischen Evangelienübersetzungen* (Berlin: Töpelmann, 1964).

4. Helmut Koester, *Ancient Christian Gospels: Their History and Development* (Philadelphia: Trinity, 1990). For an overview of the questions of genuineness in

the Jesus tradition, the most important book is a work that values the Gospel of Thomas very highly in that regard: Robert W. Funk et al., eds., *The Five Gospels* (New York: Macmillan, 1993). This book summarizes the conclusions of the Jesus Seminar as regards the authentic words of Jesus.

5. Especially fundamental here is John S. Kloppenborg, *The Formation of Q* (Philadelphia: Fortress Press, 1987).

6. For the judgment sayings, this appears especially in the important monographs by Marius Reiser, *Jesus and Judgment* (Minneapolis: Fortress Press, 1997); and Christian Riniker, *Die Gerichtsverkündigung Jesu* (Bern: Lang, 1999).

7. Marcus Borg, *Jesus, a New Vision: Spirit, Culture, and the Life of Discipleship* (San Francisco: HarperSanFrancisco, 1991).

8. John Dominic Crossan, *Jesus: A Revolutionary Biography* (San Francisco: HarperSanFrancisco, 1994).

9. Geza Vermes, *Jesus the Jew: A Historian's Reading of the Gospels* (London: Collins, 1973); Vermes, *The Religion of Jesus the Jew* (London: SCM; Minneapolis: Fortress Press, 1993); E. P. Sanders, *The Historical Figure of Jesus* (New York: Penguin, 1995); John P. Meier, *A Marginal Jew: Rethinking the Historical Jesus,* 3 vols. to date (New York: Doubleday, 1991–); and Dale C. Allison, *Jesus of Nazareth: Millenarian Prophet* (Minneapolis: Fortress Press, 1998).

10. Albert Schweitzer, *Geschichte der Leben-Jesu Forschung* [The Quest of the Historical Jesus] (1906), 9th ed. (Tübingen: Mohr, 1984), 631–42; and Schweitzer, *Reich Gottes und Christentum* [The Kingdom of God and Primitive Christianity], ed. Ulrich Neuenschwander (Tübingen: Mohr, 1967), esp. 94–195.

11. Jürgen Becker, *Jesus von Nazaret* [Jesus of Nazareth] (Berlin: de Gruyter, 1995), 122–233; Theissen and Merz, *Jesus,* 241–50; and Jürgen Roloff, *Jesus* (Munich: Beck, 2000), 72–86.

12. Rudolf Bultmann, *Jesus.* Die Unsterblichen: Die geistigen Heroen der Menschheit in ihrem Leben und Wirken, vol. 1 (Berlin: Deutsche Bibliothek, 1926); Günther Bornkamm, *Jesus von Nazareth* [Jesus of Nazareth], 15th ed. (Stuttgart: Kohlhammer, 1995); and Herbert Braun, *Jesus: Der Mann aus Nazareth und seine Zeit* [Jesus of Nazareth: The Man and His Time], rev. ed. (Gütersloh: Mohn, 1989).

13. The chronological and geographical "frame" of Jesus' story has been seen as secondary to individual traditions since the foundational book by Karl Ludwig Schmidt, *Der Rahmen der Geschichte Jesu* (Berlin: Trowitzsch & Sohn, 1919).

14. On this, see Gerd Theissen, *Soziologie der Jesusbewegung* (Munich: Kaiser, 1977), 34–46, translated by John Bowden as *Sociology of Early Palestinian Christianity* (Philadelphia: Fortress Press, 1978).

15. Cf. Séan Freyne, *Galilee from Alexander the Great to Hadrian, 323 B.C.E. to 135 C.E.: A Study of Second-Temple Judaism* (Wilmington, Del.: Glazier, 1980), 281–87.

16. For details, see Roloff, *Jesus,* 56–60.

17. The Gospel of John, the Synoptics, and Q all report healings, or exorcisms and healings. In addition, the sayings tradition confirms the accounts of Jesus on this point (e.g., Luke 7:22; 11:18–20; Mark 11:23–24). Jesus was regarded as a magician in Jewish tradition.

18. Cf. Oskar von Hinüber, *Der Beginn der Schrift und frühe Schriftlichkeit in Indien* (Stuttgart: Steiner-Verlag Wiesbaden, 1990); and Harry Falk, *Die Schrift im alten Indien: Ein Forschungsbericht mit Anmerkungen* (Tübingen: Narr, 1993).

19. For what follows, see Raimundo Panikkar, *The Silence of God: The Answer of the Buddha* (Maryknoll, N.Y.: Orbis, 1989), 37–52.

20. Claus Oetke, "Die 'unbeantworteten Fragen' und das Schweigen des Buddha," *Wiener Zeitschrift für die Kunde Südasiens* 38 (1994): 85–120.

3. Jesus' Preaching of the Reign of God

1. *Songs of the Sabbath Sacrifice*, 4QShirShabb = 4Q400–407 = Florentíno García Martínez. *The Dead Sea Scrolls Translated. The Qumran Texts in English* (2nd ed. Leiden, New York, and Cologne: Brill; Grand Rapids: Eerdmans, 1996) 419-31.

2. Text in Hermann L. Strack and Paul Billerbeck, *Kommentar zum Neuen Testament aus Talmud und Midrasch* (Munich: Beck, 1928), vol. IV, part 1, 212.

3. Text in C. K. Barrett, ed., *The New Testament Background: Selected Documents*, rev. ed. (London: SPCK, 1987), no. 212.

4. Gershom Scholem, "Die Krise der Tradition im jüdischen Messianismus," in *Judaica*, 3:152–97 (Frankfurt: Suhrkamp, 1981); see also Scholem, "Offenbarung und Tradition als religiöse Kategorien im Judentum," in *Judaica*, 4:81–164 (1984).

5. Cf. Peter Müller, *In der Mitte der Gemeinde: Kinder im Neuen Testament* (Neukirchen-Vluyn: Neukirchener Verlag, 1992), 81–164.

6. Cf. Ulrich Luz, *Das Evangelium nach Matthäus (Mt 8–17)*, 3rd ed. (Neukirchen-Vluyn: Neukirchener Verlag; and Düsseldorf: Benziger Verlag, 1999), 169, translated by James E. Crouch as *Matthew: A Commentary*, vol. 2, Hermeneia (Minneapolis: Fortress Press, 2001).

7. Ernst Waldschmidt, *Die Legende vom Leben des Buddha* (Berlin: Volksverband der Bücherfreunde, Wegweiserverlag, 1929), 199–205.

8. This is the choice of John P. Meier, *A Marginal Jew: Rethinking the Historical*

Jesus, 3 vols. to date (New York: Doubleday, 1991–), 2:483. The (Gnostic or proto-Gnostic) Gospel of Thomas was first to point to the invisible sparks of the divine light within the human being: *Gos. Thom.* logion 113.

9. Cf. 2 Kings 4:42–44.

10. Criterion of context: Sayings are most likely to have come from Jesus if they fit the Jewish context at that time. Criterion of plausibility of effect: Sayings are most likely to have come from Jesus if they had a continuing impact on early Christianity.

11. For Jesus' preaching of judgment, see the two monographs cited in n. 6 of chapter 2.

12. This would match the way he made its fulfillment not dependent on human effort, but left it to God (Mark 4:26–29).

13. Is this also the locus of what we might call Jesus' and his disciples' "symbolic asceticism" in light of the reign of God? The disciples who follow Jesus are without possessions; they surrender the practice of their trades, life in their families, and a fixed abode (cf. Luke 9:58). Jesus, too, lives without family or trade (cf. Luke 9:58). Is this meant to symbolize that the coming of the reign of God or the judgment puts an end to all these things, as the saying about the Son of Man in Luke 17:26–30 so drastically depicts?

14. Of course, the question of whether Jesus saw himself as the coming Son of Man and world judge is important for the interpretation of these proclamations. On this, see chapter 8.

15. The suggestion for this interpretation of the resurrection originates with Wilhelm Thüsing, *Die neutestamentlichen Theologien und Jesus Christus* 1 (Düsseldorf: Patmos, 1981), 125–44. However, I do not find it as easy as he does to combine "Jesus' Gospel of the *basileia*" and the "post-Easter Gospel of Jesus Christ" as a single "unity." Cf. Thüsing, *Die neutestamentlichen Theologien* 3 (Münster: Aschendorff, 1999), 364–69.

16. For the problem of atheism, see also the response in chapter 9.

17. Herbert Braun, *Jesus: Der Mann aus Nazareth und seine Zeit* [Jesus of Nazareth: The Man and His Time], rev. ed. (Gütersloh: Mohn, 1989), 48.

18. Cf. Gerd Theissen and Annette Merz, *The Historical Jesus: A Comprehensive Guide* (Minneapolis: Fortress Press, 1998), chap. 9.

19. Braun, *Jesus,* 48.

20. Cf. also ibid., 47: "We are not serving a genuine and honest understanding of Jesus if we hide from ourselves and others the fact that Jesus' expectation of the imminent end, at home in Jewish apocalyptic, was a mistake."

4. Self, Nonself, and Nirvāṇa

1. I learned of their "extinction" as I was writing the word *Nirvāṇa*.

2. Cf. the most recent overview and references in Peter Harvey, *The Selfless Mind: Personality, Consciousness and Nirvāṇa in Early Buddhism* (Surrey, England: Curzon, 1995), 8, 17ff.; and Steven Collins, *Selfless Persons: Imagery and Thought in Theravāda Buddhism* (London: Cambridge University Press, 1982).

3. Cf. Erich Frauwallner, *Geschichte der indischen Philosophie* [History of Indian Philosophy] (Aachen, Germany: Shaker, 1953), 1:224; Hermann Oldenberg, *Die Lehre der Upanishaden und die Anfänge des Buddhismus* (Göttingen: Vandenhoeck & Ruprecht, 1915), 303ff., translated by Shridhar B. Shrotri as *The Doctrine of the Upanishads and the Early Buddhism* (Delhi: Motilal Banarsidass, 1991).

4. Cf. Lambert Schmithausen in Andreas Bsteh, ed., *Der Buddhismus als Anfrage an christliche Theologie und Philosophie* (Mödling: Verlag St. Gabriel, 2000), 76: "Nowhere in the whole canon is there the assertion either that 'There is a self,' or that 'There is no self.'"

5. The basic discussion of this is in Lambert Schmithausen, *Ālayavijñāna: On the Origin and the Early Development of a Central Concept of Yogacāra Philosophy*, 2 vols. (Tokyo: International Institute for Buddhist Studies, 1987).

6. Tilmann Vetter, *The Ideas and Meditative Practices of Early Buddhism* (Leiden: Brill, 1988), 35ff.; Vetter, "Die Lehre des Buddha," in Bsteh, ed., *Der Buddhismus als Anfrage,* 59–66; and Lambert Schmithausen, "Spirituelle Praxis und philosophische Theorie im Buddhismus," *Zeitschrift für Missions- und Religionswissenschaft* 57 (1973): 161–86.

7. Ernst Steinkellner, "Das Leid im Buddhismus," in *Von der Erkenntnis des Leides* (Vienna: Akademie der Wissenschaften, 1988), 91.

8. Vetter, *Ideas and Meditative Practices,* 40; cf. Frauwallner, *Geschichte,* 1:225.

9. Hermann Oldenberg, trans., *Reden des Buddha: Lehre, Verse, Erzählungen* (Freiburg: Herder, 1993), 277.

10. Ibid., 304.

11. Constantin Regamey, "Der Buddhismus Indiens," in *Christus und die Religionen der Erde* 3, ed. Franz König, 229–317 (Freiburg: Herder, 1956), 275.

12. Paul Tillich, *Christianity and the Encounter of the World Religions*, Bampton Lectures in America 14 (New York: Columbia University Press, 1963), 68. Here quoted from Mensching, *Buddha und Christus—ein Vergleich* (Stuttgart: Deutsche Verlagsanstalt, 1978; abbreviated new ed., Freiburg: Herder, 2001), 118. Tillich's attempts to draw together the reign of God and *Nirvāṇa* were already rejected by Mensching, ibid.

13. Walpola Rahula, *What the Buddha Taught*, 2nd ed. (New York: Grove, 1974), 56.

14. Ibid., 58.

15. John Paul II, *Crossing the Threshold of Hope* (New York: Knopf, 1994), chap. 14, "Buddha?" Accessible at http://www.catholic.net/RCC/POPE/HopeBook/chap14.html.

16. Ibid.

17. Ibid.

18. Gustav Mensching, *Buddha und Christus*, 169.

19. Thus, e.g., Max Weber, *Wirtschaft und Gesellschaft: Grundriß der verstehenden Soziologie*, 4th ed. (Tübingen: Mohr, 1956), 334–35, translated by Ephraim Fischoff as *Economy and Society: An Outline of Interpretive Sociology*, Guenther Roth and Claus Wittich, eds. (Berkeley: University of California Press, 1978). "Thereby was the path to self-divinization and the genuine mystical possession of God closed to [Christianity's] mode of redemption."

20. References in Udo Tworuschka's afterword to the new edition of Mensching, *Buddha und Christus,* 237.

21. Wolfgang Schluchter, "Weltflüchtiges Erlösungsstreben und organische Sozialethik: Überlegungen zu Max Webers Analysen der indischen Kulturreligionen," in *Max Webers Studie über Hinduismus und Buddhismus*, ed. idem (Frankfurt: Suhrkamp, 1984), 30.

22. The Greek word *psyche* should probably be translated in the sense of the Hebrew *nephesh*, as "life." The text is probably about martyrdom.

23. Cf. John 3:3, 5; Titus 3:5 ("washing of rebirth").

24. Cf. Bernhard Neuenschwander, *Mystik im Johannesevangelium: Eine hermeneutische Untersuchung aufgrund der Auseinandersetzung mit Zen-Meister Hisamatsu Shin'ichi* (Leiden: Brill, 1998), 33–42.

25. Seiichi Yagi, "Ego und Selbst im Neuen Testament und im Zen," in *Bibel in Weltkontext*, ed. Walter Dietrich and Ulrich Luz (Zurich: TVZ, 2002).

5. Jesus' Ethics

1. Gustav Mensching, *Buddha und Christus—ein Vergleich*, 151.

2. Hans-Joachim Klimkeit, *Buddha: Leben und Lehre* (Stuttgart: Kohlhammer, 1990), 219–32.

3. Dale C. Allison, in *Jesus of Nazareth: Millenarian Prophet* (Minneapolis: Fortress Press, 1998), is interested only in the ascetical side of Jesus, the prophet of the end-time. For Herbert Braun, in *Jesus: Der Mann aus Nazareth und seine Zeit,* rev. ed. (Gütersloh: Mohn, 1989), 43–49, the eschatology is only about the "horizon of the last things."

4. One example of reinterpretation: For Marcus Borg, in *Jesus, a New Vision: Spirit, Culture, and the Life of Discipleship* (San Francisco: HarperSanFrancisco, 1991), 224–25, the "reign of God" is only a traditional Jewish "linguistic symbol" signifying participation "in the life of the spirit."

5. For Martin Ebner, in *Jesus—ein Weisheitslehrer? Synoptische Weisheitslogien im Traditionsprozess* (Freiburg: Herder, 1998), 421, Jesus is an "(apocalyptic) disciple of the Baptizer" who returns "to his (Wisdom) homeland." Ebner therefore is inclined to regard judgment sayings and Son of Man sayings as ungenuine.

6. Heinz Schürmann, "Das hermeneutische Hauptproblem der Verkündigung Jesu: Eschatologie und Theologie im gegenseitigen Verhältnis," in idem, *Traditionsgeschichtliche Untersuchungen zu den synoptischen Evangelien* (Düsseldorf: Patmos, 1968), 13–35.

7. See chapter 3.

8. Cf. Hans Haas, *Idee und Ideal der Feindesliebe in der außerchristlichen Welt* (Leipzig: Edelmann, 1927); and Joachim Gnilka, *Jesus von Nazaret* [Jesus of Nazareth] (Freiburg: Herder, 1990), 229–30.

9. Gerhard Lohfink, *Wem gilt die Bergpredigt?* (Freiburg: Herder, 1988), esp. 99–160.

10. The episode with the woman taken in adultery (John 7:53–8:11, a later addition), which presumably goes back to Jesus, speaks against this.

11. Max Weber, "Politik als Beruf," in *Gesammelte politische Schriften*, 2nd ed., ed. idem, 505–60 (Tübingen: Mohr, 1958).

12. For my reasoning, see *Matthew 1–7: A Commentary* (Minneapolis: Fortress Press, 1992), 282–86.

13. 11Q19, Florentino García Martínez, *The Dead Sea Scrolls Translated. The Qumran Texts in English,* translated by Wilfred G. E. Watson (Leiden, New York, and Cologne: Brill; Grand Rapids: Eerdmans, 1996) 154–84.

14. Cf. also, e.g., Luke 18:9–14; 14:28–32; Matt 18:23–34; 13:44–46.

15. In the ancient church's interpretation, the enemy to be loved is the pagan, to whom is owed the gospel, that is, mission. Karlmann Beyschlag, "Zur Geschichte der Bergpredigt in der Alten Kirche," *Zeitschrift für Theologie und Kirche* 74 (1977): 314–25.

16. Claude J. G. Montefiore, *The Synoptic Gospels*, 2nd ed. (London: Macmillan, 1927), 2:523.

17. Lambert Schmithausen, "Gleichmut und Mitgefühl: Zu Spiritualität und Heilsziel des älteren Buddhismus," in *Der Buddhismus als Anfrage an christliche Theologie und Philosophie,* ed. Andreas Bsteh (Mödling: Verlag St. Gabriel, 2000), 134.

18. The "immeasurable" (*apramāṇa*); see "Buddhist Love," in chapter 6; and cf. Gal 5:22.

19. Edward Conze, *Der Buddhismus: Wesen und Entwicklung* [Buddhism: Its Essence and Development], 8th ed. (Stuttgart: Kohlhammer, 1986), 61, mentions a few exceptions. For a full discussion, see Lambert Schmithausen, "Buddhismus und Glaubenskriege," in *Glaubenskriege in Vergangenheit und Gegenwart*, ed. Peter Herrmann, 63–92 (Göttingen: Vandenhoeck & Ruprecht, 1996); and idem, "Aspects of Buddhist Attitudes towards War," in *Violence Denied*, ed. Jan E. M. Houben and Karel R. van Kooij, 45–68 (Leiden: Brill, 1999).

20. Glen H. Mullin, "An Interview with the Dalai Lama," *Tibetan Review* 21/9–10 (Sept.–Oct. 1986): 18.

21. Heinz Bechert, "Ethik der Buddhisten," in *Ethik in nichtchristlichen Kulturen*, ed. Peter Antes et al., 114–35 (Stuttgart: Kohlhammer, 1984), 132.

22. *AN* II.95.23–25; cf. Schmithausen, "Gleichmut und Mitgefühl," 125.

6. Ethics in Early Buddhism

1. Richard Gombrich, *Theravada Buddhism: A Social History from Ancient Benares to Modern Colombo* (New York: Routledge & Kegan Paul, 1988), 78–81; and Gombrich, *How Buddhism Began: The Conditioned Genesis of the Early Teachings* (London: Athlone, 1996), 51–52.

2. Cf. chapter 1, "Buddha Śākyamuni and His World."

3. Cf., for example, Hammalava Saddhatissa, *Buddhist Ethics: The Essence of Buddhism* (London: Allen & Unwin, 1970), 87ff.; and Peter Gerlitz, "Die Ethik des Buddha," in *Ethik der Religionen: Ein Handbuch*, ed. Carl Heinz Ratschow, 227–348 (Stuttgart: Kohlhammer, 1980), 291ff.

4. Some parts of this problem are discussed, for example, by Saddhatissa, *Buddhist Ethics*, 131–64; Richard Gombrich, "The Duty of a Buddhist according to the Pali Scriptures," in *The Concept of Duty in South Asia*, ed. Wendy Doniger O'Flaherty and J. Duncan M. Derrett (New Delhi: Vikas, 1977; repr. 1978), 107–18, especially 109ff.; and Gerlitz, "Die Ethik des Buddha," 302ff.

5. On this see, for example, Damien Keown, *Buddhism and Bioethics* (New York: St. Martin's, 1995), as well as Lambert Schmithausen, "Religion und Bioethik: Buddhismus," in *Lexikon der Bioethik* (Gütersloh: Gütersloher Verlagshaus, 1998), 1:185–88.

6. Gustav Mensching, *Buddha und Christus*, 150.

7. Hermann Oldenberg, "Der Buddhismus und die christliche Liebe," in idem, *Aus dem alten Indien* (Berlin: Weidmann, 1910), 22.

8. *DN* III.223.25–224.9; cf. Mudagamuwe Maithrimurthi, *Wohlwollen, Mitleid, Freude und Gleichmut: Eine ideengeschichtliche Untersuchung der vier apramāṇas in der buddhistischen Ethik und Spiritualität von den Anfängen bis hin zum frühen Yogacāra* (Stuttgart: Steiner, 1999).

9. Walpola Rahula, *What the Buddha Taught*, 2nd ed. (New York: Grove, 1974), 157–58.

10. Cf. Hermann Oldenberg, *Buddha: Sein Leben, seine Lehre, seine Gemeinde* [Buddha: His Life, His Doctrine, His Order] (1881), 13th ed. (Stuttgart: Cotta, 1959), 307–8.

11. See Ulrich Luz's objections to this concept below in his response to this chapter.

12. Lambert Schmithausen, "Gleichmut und Mitgefühl," in *Der Buddhismus als Anfrage an christliche Theologie und Philosophie*, ed. Andreas Bsteh (Mödling: Verlag St. Gabriel, 2000), 135.

13. Lambert Schmithausen, "Buddhismus und Natur," in *Die Verantwortung des Menschen für eine bewohnbare Welt im Christentum, Hinduismus und Buddhismus*, ed. Raimundo Panikkar and Walter Strolz (Freiburg: Herder, 1985), 100–33; Schmithausen, *The Problem of the Sentience of Plants in Earliest Buddhism* (Tokyo: International Institute of Buddhist Studies, 1991); Schmithausen with Mudagamuwe Maithrimurthi, "Tier und Mensch im Buddhismus," in *Tiere und Menschen. Geschichte und Aktualität eines prekären Verhältnisses*, ed. Paul Münch with Rainer Walz, 179–224 (Paderborn: Schöningh, 1998); Schmithausen, "The Early Buddhist Tradition and Ecological Ethics," *Journal of Buddhist Ethics* 4 (1997): 1–74; and Schmithausen, "Buddhism and the Ethics of Nature—Some Remarks," *The Eastern Buddhist*, n.s. 32 (2000): 26–78.

14. Schmithausen and Maithrimurthi, *Tiere und Menschen*, 181.

15. Schmithausen, "Buddhismus und Natur," 116.

16. Cf. Schmithausen, "Buddhism and the Ethics of Nature," 56ff.

17. Jesus also desired the rejection of violence; that is clear. But his concern was more for human beings than for animals.

18. Hans Windisch, *Der Sinn der Bergpredigt*, 2nd ed. (Leipzig: Hinrichs, 1937); similarly before him Johannes Weiss, *Die Predigt Jesu vom Reiche Gottes*, 3rd ed. (Göttingen: Vandenhoeck & Ruprecht, 1964), 138.

19. Albert Schweitzer, *Reich Gottes und Christentum* [The Kingdom of God and Primitive Christianity], ed. Ulrich Neuenschwander (Tübingen: Mohr, 1967), 429.

20. Jürgen Becker, *Jesus von Nazaret* [Jesus of Nazareth] (Berlin: de Gruyter, 1995), 290.

21. John Dominic Crossan, *Finding Is the First Act* (Philadelphia: Fortress Press, 1979).

22. What is meant in Leviticus 19:18 is, of course, not the command to love one's neighbor and oneself equally, but the command to love the neighbor in the same way as one loves oneself.

23. Mensching, *Buddha und Christus*, 169. Udo Tworuschka, in his afterword to the new edition of Mensching's book, also remarks, "The historian of religions … [knows] not a single religion that places the acquisition of salvation exclusively within the realm of human achievement" (p. 237). Certainly in early Buddhism, it is not a question of redemption by another, but what is at issue is a "salvation" that is not at human disposition and, in Söderblom's sense (see chapter 4), is a "gift of grace."

24. Lambert Schmithausen, in *Der Buddhismus als Anfrage an christliche Theologie und Philosophie,* ed. Andreas Bsteh (Mödling: Verlag St. Gabriel, 2000), 178.

7. Suffering in Early Buddhism

1. Hermann Oldenberg, *Reden des Buddha: Lehre, Verse, Erzählungen* (Freiburg: Herder, 1993), 72.

2. Ernst Waldschmidt, *Die Legende vom Leben des Buddha* (Berlin: Volksverband der Bücherfreunde, Wegweiserverlag, 1929), 149.

3. Erich Frauwallner, *Geschichte der indischen Philosophie* (Aachen, Germany: Shaker, 1953), 1.183–84.

4. Hermann Oldenberg, *Buddha: Sein Leben, seine Lehre, seine Gemeinde* (1881), 13th ed. (Stuttgart: Cotta, 1959), 251.

5. Ernst Steinkellner, *Das Leid im Buddhismus,* 96ff.

6. Cf. Tilman Vetter, "Explanations of *Dukkha,*" *International Journal of Buddhist Studies* 21/2 (1998): 383–87; cf. also Helmuth von Glasenapp's afterword in Oldenberg, *Buddha,* 474.

7. Cf. Lambert Schmithausen, "Zur buddhistischen Lehre von der 3-fachen Leidhaftigkeit," *Zeitschrift der Deutschen Morgenländischen Gesellschaft,* Suppl. III.2 to 19th German Orientalist Congress (1977), 918.

8. Constantin Regamey, "Der Buddhismus Indiens," in *Christus und die Religionen der Erde* 3, ed. Franz König, 229–317 (Freiburg: Herder, 1956), 270.

9. Raimundo Panikkar, *The Silence of God: The Answer of the Buddha* (Maryknoll, N.Y.: Orbis, 1989), 60.

10. Alexander von Rospatt, *The Buddhist Doctrine of Momentariness: A Survey of the Origins and Early Phase of This Doctrine up to Vasubandhu* (Stuttgart: Steiner, 1995).

11. Panikkar, *The Silence of God*, 57.

12. Gustav Mensching, *Buddha und Christus—ein Vergleich* (Stuttgart: Deutsche Verlagsanstalt, 1978; abbreviated new ed., Freiburg: Herder, 2001), 134.

13. English translation by Harold W. Attridge and George W. MacRae in James M. Robinson, ed., *The Nag Hammadi Library in English*, 3rd ed. (San Francisco: Harper & Row, n.d. [© E. J. Brill, 1988]), 40.

14. Walter Till, *Die gnostischen Schriften des koptischen Papyris Berolinensis 8502* (Berlin: Akademie Verlag, 1955), 63, translated by George W. MacRae and R. McLean Wilson in *The Nag Hammadi Library in English,* 524.

15. *Das Corpus Hermeticum Deutsch I: Die griechischen Traktate und der lateinische 'Asclepius,'* translated by Carsten Colpe and Jens Holzhausen (Stuttgart and Bad Cannstadt: Frommann-Holzboog, 1997), 19–20. English from G. R. S. Mead, trans., *Thrice Great Hermes: Studies in Hellenistic Theosophy and Gnosis.* 3 vols. (London: Theosophical Publishing Society, 1906).

16. *Evangelium Veritatis* = NHC I.17.31–32.

8. Jesus' Passion and the Christian Idea of Suffering

1. Klaus Koch, "Gibt es ein Vergeltungsdogma im Alten Testament?" *Zeitschrift für Theologie und Kirche* 52 (1955): 1–42.

2. According to Paul (cf. Rom 1:24; 7:7–8) and the letter of James (1:15), desire is the beginning of sin. The background of this widespread view is Genesis 3.

3. The passion accounts used by Mark and John in their gospels are independent of each other. It is possible that there was a third ancient passion account that Luke used, alongside the Gospel of Mark, for his own passion story, which contains many special traditions.

4. Peter Egger, *"Crucifixus sub Pontio Pilato": Das "crimen" Jesu von Nazareth im Spannungsfeld römischer und jüdischer Verwaltungs- und Rechtsstrukturen* (Münster: Aschendorff, 1997), 100–47.

5. Cf. Hans-Josef Klauck, *Judas—ein Jünger des Herrn* (Freiburg: Herder, 1986), 137–38.

6. This is the conclusion of a long scholarly discussion; cf. Raymond E. Brown, *The Death of the Messiah* (New York: Doubleday, 1994), 1:363–72. Possible exceptions to this principle, such as the execution of a Gentile who entered the inner court of the Temple, do not affect the case of Jesus of Nazareth.

7. Cf. Ulrich Luz, *Das Evangelium nach Matthäus (Mt 26–28)* (Neukirchen-Vluyn: Neukirchener Verlag; Düsseldorf: Benziger, 2001), 198–99.

8. I think it more likely that Jesus' Roman trial was an administrative emergency process (*coercitio*) rather than a formal trial (*cognitio*). But even

in a *cognitio,* the prefect had almost unlimited discretion when dealing with provincial subjects.

9. Cf. Joachim Jeremias, *Heiligengräber in Jesu Umwelt (Mt 23,30; Lk 11,49): Eine Untersuchung zur Volksreligion der Zeit Jesu* (Göttingen: Vandenhoeck & Ruprecht, 1958). According to the Jewish *Vitae Prophetarum,* Isaiah, Jeremiah, Ezekiel, Amos, Micah, and Zechariah were martyred.

10. Both this fear and the use of the word *baptisma* without reference to Christian baptism speak in favor of the genuineness of the saying.

11. Albert Schweitzer, *Reich Gottes und Christentum* [The Kingdom of God and Primitive Christianity], ed. Ulrich Neuenschwander (Tübingen: Mohr, 1967), 132–41. Originally Jesus would have expected that the Son of Man, the world judge, would come before the return of the disciples from their mission within Israel (Matt 10:23). He was disappointed in this, so he went to Jerusalem. Luke 12:49–50 is probably the strongest support for an interpretation in Schweitzer's sense of Jesus' move to Jerusalem, but he himself overlooked that saying.

12. Cf. Luz, *Matthäus (Mt 26–28),* 112, 116.

13. This apparently refers to the cover of the Ark of the Covenant in the Holy of Holies, onto which, on the Day of Atonement, the blood of the goat was sprinkled (Lev 16).

14. In Greek, the statement is formulated in the perfect tense.

15. Mysticism is here understood in the sense of "Christ mysticism."

16. Luz, *Matthäus (Mt 8–17),* 155.

17. The relationship between early Buddhism and the later Stoa is very close at this point!

9. Jesus and Christology

1. Yamada Koun writes something similar: cf. Michael von Brück and Whalen Lai, *Buddhismus und Christentum* (Munich: Beck, 1997), 529.

2. Cf. Friedrich Heiler, *Erscheinungsformen und Wesen der Religion,* 2nd ed. (Stuttgart: Kohlhammer, 1979), 461, who also associates the appearance of a "theoretical monotheism" with intolerance.

3. For the two fundamental moments in New Testament christological monotheism, see Gerd Theissen, *Die Religion der ersten Christen* (Gütersloh: Gütersloher Verlagshaus, 2000), 36–37.

4. There are examples from numerous cults, including that of Isis. In addition, *kyrios* is an important title in various cults of the ruler, both for the Ptolemies and for the emperors of Rome.

5. The fact that in Greek-speaking Judaism the Tetragrammaton was read as *kyrios* is seen especially in Paul's biblical quotations regarding the "Lord," which Paul then attributes to Jesus, e.g., Joel 2:32 LXX (= Rom 10:13); Isa 40:13 LXX (= 1 Cor 2:16).

6. Differently from most translations of the Bible, in John 1:18 one should read with the best ancient manuscripts "only-begotten God," rather than "only-begotten Son."

7. This is explicitly rejected in Hebrews 1:14.

8. William Wrede, *Das Messiasgeheimnis in den Evangelien*, 2nd ed. (1913; repr., Göttingen: Vandenhoeck & Ruprecht, 1965), especially 213–29.

9. Rudolf Bultmann, *Theologie des Neuen Testaments* (1948), 9th ed. (Tübingen: Mohr, 1984), 2.

10. For example, Hans Conzelmann, *Grundriß der Theologie des Neuen Testaments* (1967), 4th ed. (Tübingen: Mohr, 1987), 85.

11. E.g., *1 Enoch* 90:9–38; 4Q521 fr. 2 II; 1QSa 2, 12; 4QPatr = 4Q252; *Pss. Sol.* 17–18.

12. Only at Matt 11:27//Luke 10:22 (community composition!).

13. The same is true of the High Priest's question whether Jesus was the Son of God (Mark 14:61–62).

14. Mark 2:10; 2:28 could be about anybody. But this is clearly not the case, for example, in Luke 7:34, where Jesus distinguishes himself from John, or in Luke 9:58, where he, the homeless man, separates himself from the foxes and birds.

15. *Jubilees* 4:23 (2nd century B.C.E.) already knows that the Enoch who has been taken up to heaven will rule there as the recorder of judgment, even though the expression *Son of Man* is not present here yet. Unfortunately, the images in the discourses in *1 Enoch* cannot be dated.

16. According to Luke 7:22, John could not have seen Jesus as the "one stronger than he" from the beginning. The anthropomorphic formulation "I am not worthy to untie the thong of his sandals" (Luke 3:16) speaks against seeing God himself as "the one who is to come."

17. According to the classic thesis of Heinz Eduard Tödt, *Der Menschensohn in der synoptischen Überlieferung* (Gütersloh: Mohn, 1959); now, e.g., E. P. Sanders, *The Historical Figure of Jesus* (New York: Penguin, 1995), 245–48; and Jürgen Becker, *Jesus von Nazaret* [Jesus of Nazareth] (Berlin: de Gruyter, 1995), 249–67.

18. Similarly, e.g., Peter Stuhlmacher, *Biblische Theologie des Neuen Testaments* (Göttingen: Vandenhoeck & Ruprecht, 1992), 1:107–25; Jürgen Roloff, *Jesus* (Munich: Beck, 2000), 118–19; and Gerd Theissen and Annette Merz, *Der*

historische Jesus: Ein Lehrbuch [The Historical Jesus: A Comprehensive Guide] (Göttingen: Vandenhoeck & Ruprecht, 1997), 476–80.

19. Shabtai Zwi was called Messiah in Smyrna in 1665. For the Lubavitcher rabbi (d. 1994), whose followers believe in his resurrection, cf. Joel Marcus, "The Once and Future Messiah in Early Christianity and Chabad," *New Testament Studies* 47 (2001): 381–401.

20. Only Luke—who saw Jesus' resurrection and his ascension (Luke 24:50–53) as two different events, separate in space and time, and thus understood Jesus' resurrection as the first stage, still within history, of a broader event—takes a step in this direction.

21. Karl Lehmann, *Auferweckt am dritten Tag nach der Schrift* (Freiburg: Herder, 1968), especially 176–81.

22. Cf. Constantin Regamey, "Der Buddhismus Indiens," in *Christus und die Religionen der Erde* 3, ed. Franz König, 229–317 (Freiburg: Herder, 1956), 261ff.

23. Cf. von Brück and Lai, *Buddhismus und Christentum,* 462–64.

24. The following is according to Raimundo Panikkar, *The Silence of God: The Answer of the Buddha* (Maryknoll, N.Y.: Orbis, 1989), 16–23.

25. Ibid.

10. The Buddha and Meditation

1. Cf. Friedrich Heiler, *Die buddhistische Versenkung* (Munich: Reinhardt, 1989); Paul Horsch, "Buddhas erste Meditation," *Asiatische Studien* 17 (1964): 100–54; Lambert Schmithausen, "Spirituelle Praxis und philosophische Theorie im Buddhismus," *Zeitschrift für Missions- und Religionswissenschaft* 57 (1973): 161–86; Johannes Bronkhorst, *The Two Traditions of Meditation in Ancient India* (Stuttgart: Steiner, 1986); and Tilman Vetter, *The Ideas and Meditative Practices of Early Buddhism* (Leiden: Brill, 1988), 3–34.

2. Translated from the *Pāli* by Thanissaro Bhikkhu. Text at http://www.accesstoinsight.org/canon/sutta/majjhima/mn-036x-tb0.html. Also in Kurt Schmidt, trans., *Buddhas Reden: Majjhimanikaya. Sammlung der mittleren Texte des Pali-Kanons* (Reinbek by Hamburg: Rowohlt, 1961), 122–23.

3. Cf., for example, *MN* I.178.37–184.4, or *MN* I.267.13–270.36. There is a good summary of *DN* 2, 3, and so on in Erich Frauwallner, *Geschichte der indischen Philosophie* (Aachen, Germany: Shaker, 1953), 1:162ff. My description builds on this.

4. Frauwallner, *Geschichte*, 1:162.

5. Ibid., 1:163.

6. Ibid., 1:165.

7. Ibid., 1:166.

8. Cf. Hans-Joachim Klimkeit, *Buddha: Leben und Lehre* (Stuttgart: Kohlhammer, 1990), 169ff.; and Frauwallner, *Geschichte*, 1:176.

9. Frauwallner, *Geschichte*, 1:166.

10. Ibid., 1:170.

11. Lambert Schmithausen, "Die Vier Konzentrationen der Aufmerksamkeit: Zur geschichtlichen Entwicklung einer spirituellen Praxis des Buddhismus," *Zeitschrift für Missions- und Religionswissenschaft* 60 (1976): 241–66.

12. Frauwallner, *Geschichte*, 1:179.

13. Still unsurpassed in the field of religious phenomenology is Friedrich Heiler, *Das Gebet* (Munich: Reinhardt, 1923).

14. Gustav Mensching, *Buddha und Christus—ein Vergleich* (Stuttgart: Deutsche Verlagsanstalt, 1978; abbreviated new ed., Freiburg: Herder, 2001), 174–75.

15. Heiler, *Buddhistische Versenkung*.

16. Ulrich Luz remarks at this point, "We know nothing about the state of Jesus' emotions!"

17. Heiler, *Gebet*, 494.

18. Herbert Braun, *Jesus: Der Mann aus Nazareth und seine Zeit* [Jesus of Nazareth: The Man and His Time], rev. ed. (Gütersloh: Mohn, 1989), 220–29.

19. Ibid., 225–26.

20. Ibid., 228.

21. See the response in chapter 3.

22. Braun, *Jesus*, 229.

23. For an extended analysis, see Ulrich Luz, *Matthew 1–7: A Commentary* (Minneapolis: Fortress Press, 1992), 367–89.

24. The text reflects the wording of Matthew 6:9–13. The words in parentheses are absent from the parallel, slightly different version in Luke 11:2–4. This short version is probably closest to the original Aramaic prayer spoken by Jesus.

25. Hugo M. Enomiya-Lassalle, *Zen Meditation für Christen* (Munich: Barth, 1983), 198.

11. Monks and Laity in Early Buddhism

1. Richard Gombrich, *Theravada Buddhism: A Social History from Ancient Benares to Modern Colombo* (New York: Routledge & Kegan Paul, 1988), 87.

2. Karl Seidenstücker, *Pāli-Buddhismus in Übersetzungen,* 2nd ed. (Munich: Schloss, 1923), 341–42.

3. Hermann Oldenberg, *Reden des Buddha: Lehre, Verse, Erzählungen* (Freiburg: Herder, 1993), no. 106.

4. Cf. Oliver Freiberger, *Der Orden in der Lehre. Zur religiösen Deutung des Saṅgha im frühen Buddhismus* (Wiesbaden: Harrassowitz, 2000), 164.

5. Martin G. Wiltshire, *Ascetic Figures before and in Early Buddhism: The Emergence of Gautama as the Buddha* (New York: de Gruyter, 1990); cf. the review by Steven Collins in "Problems with Pacceka-Buddhas," *Religion* 22 (1992): 172–78.

6. Max Weber, *Gesammelte Aufsätze zur Religionssoziologie,* vol. 2, *Die Wirtschaftsethik der Weltreligionen—Hinduismus und Buddhismus,* 5th ed. (Tübingen: Mohr, 1972).

7. Stanley Tambiah and Gananath Obeyesekere have criticized this thesis, but Heinz Bechert defends it. Their contributions are in Wolfgang Schluchter, ed., *Max Webers Studie über Hinduismus und Buddhismus* (Frankfurt: Suhrkamp, 1984).

8. Weber, *Gesammelte Aufsätze,* 2:230.

9. Stanley Tambiah, "Webers Untersuchungen des frühen Buddhismus," in Schluchter, *Max Webers Studie,* 204–46.

10. On this, see Rita Kloppenborg, *The Paccekabuddha: A Buddhist Ascetic* (Leiden: Brill, 1974); but see also the sharp critiques of this book by Richard Gombrich in *Orientalische Literaturzeitung* 74 (1979): 78–80; and by Willem de Jong in *Indo-Iranian Journal* 18 (1976): 322–24.

11. Gananath Obeyesekere, "Exemplarische Prophetie oder ethisch geleitete Askese: Überlegungen zur frühbuddhistischen Reform," in Schluchter, ed., *Max Webers Studie,* 247–92.

12. The emphasis on the ancient equipment rule for the itinerant preachers as a prohibition on earning in Matthew 10:9–10 is especially impressive: A "laborer" is only worthy of his "food," not of a "wage" (thus the older version in Luke 10:7).

13. In the Eastern Orthodox churches, whose episcopacy is made up of unmarried monks, there are special conditions that I cannot discuss in detail here.

14. Cf., e.g., Mark 10:35–45; Matt 18:1–20; 23:8–12; 1 Cor 12:12–31; and John 15:13–15.

12. Jesus and the Church

1. Cf. Alfred Loisy, *L'évangile et l'église* (Bellevue: chez l'auteur, 1903), 2nd ed., Paris, 155.

2. The second occurrence, Matthew 18:17, is obviously a community construction and interprets the word *church* as meaning "local community."

3. "Babylon" is code for Rome.

4. Nevertheless, two recent Protestant commentaries—W. D. Davies and Dale C. Allison, *The Gospel According to St. Matthew* (Edinburgh: T&T Clark, 1991), 2:615; and Donald A. Hagner, *Matthew 14–28* (Dallas: Word, 1995), 466—cautiously admit the possibility that the saying originated with Jesus.

5. Ulrich Luz, *Das Evangelium nach Matthäus (Mt 8–17)*, 3rd ed. (Neukirchen-Vluyn: Neukirchener Verlag; and Düsseldorf: Benziger Verlag, 1999), 478–79.

6. Gerd Theissen, *Soziologie der Jesusbewegung* (Munich: Kaiser, 1977), 14–26, translated by John Bowden as *Sociology of Early Palestinian Christianity* (Philadelphia: Fortress Press, 1978). The "sympathizers" who lived settled lives are contrasted with the "itinerant charismatics" or "itinerant radicals."

7. This is established by Luke 13:31–32.

8. In the Qumran community, there was also a leadership group of twelve men, and that probably also had to do with the twelve tribes of Israel (1QS 8, 1–4).

9. 2 Esdras 13:39–47; cf. Syriac Baruch 78–87.

10. Cf. especially the parallel material in F. Gerald Downing, *Christ and the Cynics* (Sheffield: JSOT, 1988). According to John Dominic Crossan, *Jesus: A Revolutionary Biography* (San Francisco: HarperSanFrancisco, 1994), 553, Jesus himself was a "peasant Jewish Cynic."

11. Compare, e.g., the feeding in Mark 6:34–44 with 2 Kings 4:42–44; the healing of a leper in Mark 1:40–45 with 2 Kings 5; the raising of a dead girl in Luke 7:11–17 with 1 Kings 17:17–24 and 2 Kings 4:18–36.

12. Martin Hengel, *Nachfolge und Charisma* (Berlin: Töpelmann, 1968), 16–17, translated by James Greig as *The Charismatic Leader and His Followers* (New York: Crossroad, 1981).

13. Theissen, *Sociology of Early Palestinian Christianity*.

14. Mark 6:8 (permission for a staff); Mark 6:9 (permission to wear sandals); Matt 10:9–10 (simple prohibition on acquiring anything while traveling).

15. On this, see Gerd Theissen, "Legitimation und Lebensunterhalt," in *Studien zur Soziologie des Urchristentums,* ed. idem (Tübingen: Mohr, 1979), 201–30, translated by Margaret Kohl as *Social Reality and the Early Christians: Theology, Ethics, and the World of the New Testament* (Minneapolis: Fortress Press, 1992); and Wolf-Henning Ollrog, *Paulus und seine Mitarbeiter* (Neukirchen-Vluyn: Neukirchener Verlag, 1979).

16. Cf. especially Mark 8:34–38; Matt 10:5–39; 16:24–27; Ign. *Eph.* 1.2; Ign. *Magn.* 9.1–2; and Ign. *Rom.* 4.2; 5.3, etc.

17. Pseudo-Clement, *Letters to Virgins,* English translation in *Ante-Nicene Fathers* 8 (Peabody, Mass.: Hendrickson, 1994), 55–66.

18. Pentecost cannot simply be seen as the "birthday" of the institutional church, as Luke depicts it, although experiences of the Spirit may well have played an essential role in its creation and discovery of its identity. On the whole subject, see the cautious presentation by Jürgen Roloff, *Die Kirche im Neuen Testament* (Göttingen: Vandenhoeck & Ruprecht, 1993), 58–85.

19. For the "unity" of the church in the New Testament, see Christian Link, Ulrich Luz, and Lukas Vischer, *Sie aber hielten fest an der Gemeinschaft: Einheit der Kirche als Prozeß im Neuen Testament und heute* (Zurich: Benziger, 1988).

20. For Paul's idea of the people of God, see Wolfgang Kraus, *Das Volk Gottes* (Tübingen: Mohr [Siebeck], 1996).

21. Roloff, *Die Kirche im Neuen Testament,* 18.

22. *Vin* I.5.12–7.10; cf. Hans-Joachim Klimkeit, *Buddha: Leben und Lehre* (Stuttgart: Kohlhammer, 1990), 91–92.

23. Cf. Ulrich Luz, "Das 'Auseinandergehen der Wege,'" in *Antijudaismus— christliche Erblast,* ed. Walter Dietrich et al. (Stuttgart: Kohlhammer, 1999), 62–64; and James D. G. Dunn, *The Partings of the Ways* (London: SCM; Philadelphia: Trinity Press International, 1991), 18–36.

24. Details can be found, for example, in Günter Lanczkowski, *Begegnung und Wandel der Religionen* (Düsseldorf: Diederichs, 1971).

25. On this, see Gottfried Küenzlen, *Der Neue Mensch: Eine Untersuchung zur säkularen Religionsgeschichte der Moderne* (Munich: Fink, 1994).

26. For more detail, see Axel Michaels, *Der Hinduismus: Geschichte und Gegenwart* (Munich: Beck, 1998), 85ff.

Sources and Bibliography

Only a few basic titles and those frequently cited are included here. Other recommended literature is cited in the endnotes. For a continuously updated critical bibliography of Buddhism, see "Materialien" at www.sai-heidelberg.de/IND/index.htm.

Buddhism

Primary Sources

For Buddhist texts, as a rule the *Pāli* canon is based on that of the Pali Text Society (PTS), London. German translations, when used, are given in parentheses. *AN, DN, MN, SN,* and *Vin* are cited by volume (Roman numerals), page, and line number; *It, Mil,* and *Ud* by page and line number; *Sn* by verse number or page and line number; and *Dhp* by verse number.

AN   *Anguttara-Nikāya*, edited by Richard Morris and Edmund Hardy. 5 vols. London: PTS, 1885–1900. Vol. 6 (indexes by Mabel Hunt and C. A. F. Rhys Davids). London: PTS, 1910.

Dhp   *Dhammapada*, edited by Suriyagoḍa Sumaṅgala Thera. London: PTS, 1914.

DN   *Dīghanikāya*, edited by T. W. Rhys Davids and J. Estlin Carpenter. 3 vols. London: PTS, 1810–1911.

It   *Itivuttaka*, edited by Ernst Windisch. London: PTS, 1889.

Mil   *Milindapañha*, edited by Vilhelm Trenckner. London, 1880.

MN   *Majjhima-Nikāya*, edited by Vilhelm Trenckner and Robert Chalmers. 3 vols. London: PTS, 1888–99. Vol. 4 (indexes by C. A. F. Rhys Davids). London: PTS, 1925.

PTS   Pali Text Society, London.

SN   *Samyutta-Nikāya*, edited by Leon Feer. 5 vols. London: PTS, 1884–98. Vol. 6 (indexes by C. A. F. Rhys Davids). London: PTS, 1904.

Sn   *Suttanipāta*, edited by Dines Andersen and Helmer Smith. London: PTS, 1913.

Ud   *Udāna*, edited by Paul Steinthal. London: PTS, 1885.

Vin   *Vinayapiṭaka*, edited by Hermann Oldenberg. 5 vols. London: PTS, 1879–83.

Anthologies

Frauwallner, Erich, trans. *Die Philosophie des Buddhismus*. 4th ed. Berlin: Akademie-Verlag, 1994.

Mehlig, Johannes, trans. *Weisheit des alten Indien*. Vol. 2, *Buddhistische Texte*. Leipzig: Kiepenheuer, 1987.

Mylius, Klaus, trans. *Gautama Buddha. Die vier edlen Wahrheiten: Texte des ursprünglichen Buddhismus*. Leipzig: Reclam, 1983.

Nyanatiloka, trans. *Das Wort des Buddha: Eine systematische Übersicht der Lehre des Buddha in seinen eigenen Worten*. 4th ed. Konstanz: Christiani, 1978. Also translated into English by Nyanatiloka as *The Word of the Buddha: An Outline of the Teaching of the Buddha in the Words of the Pali Canon*. Kandy, Sri Lanka: Buddhist Publication Society, 1968.

Oldenberg, Hermann, trans. *Reden des Buddha: Lehre, Verse, Erzählungen*. Freiburg: Herder, 1993.

Rahula, Walpola. *What the Buddha Taught*. 2nd ed. New York: Grove, 1974.

Schmidt, Kurt, trans. *Buddhas Reden: Majjhimanikaya. Sammlung der mittleren Texte des Pali-Kanons*. Reinbek by Hamburg: Rowohlt, 1961.

Seidenstücker, Karl, trans. *Pāli-Buddhismus in Übersetzungen*. 2nd ed. Munich: Schloss, 1923.

Literature on the Historical Buddha

Bareau, André, et al. *Die Religionen Indiens.* Vol. 3, *Buddhismus, Jinismus, Primitivvölker.* Stuttgart: Kohlhammer, 1964.

Bechert, Heinz, and Richard Gombrich, eds., *Der Buddhismus.* Munich: Beck, 1989. Originally published as *The World of Buddhism* (London: Thames & Hudson, 1984).

Bechert, Heinz, et al., eds. *Der Buddhismus,* vol. 1. Stuttgart: Kohlhammer, 2000.

Conze, Edward. *Der Buddhismus: Wesen und Entwicklung.* 8th ed. Stuttgart: Kohlhammer, 1986. Originally published as *Buddhism: Its Essence and Development* (New York: Harper & Brothers, 1959).

Frauwallner, Erich. *Geschichte der indischen Philosophie,* vol. 1. Aachen, Germany: Shaker, 1953. Translated by V. M. Bedekar as *History of Indian Philosophy.* Vol. 1, *The Philosophy of the Veda and of the Epic: The Buddha and the Jina; The Samkhya and the Classical Yoga-System.* Delhi: Motilal Banarsidass, 1973.

Gombrich, Richard. *Der Theravada-Buddhismus: Vom alten Indien bis zum modernen Sri Lanka.* Stuttgart: Kohlhammer, 1997. Originally published as *Theravada Buddhism: A Social History from Ancient Benares to Modern Colombo.* New York: Routledge & Kegan Paul, 1988.

Klimkeit, Hans-Joachim. *Buddha: Leben und Lehre.* Stuttgart: Kohlhammer, 1990.

Lamotte, Étienne. *History of Indian Buddhism: From the Origins to the Śaka Era.* Louvain-la-Neuve, Belgium: Université Catholique de Louvain, Institut Orientaliste, 1988. Original French edition published in 1958.

Oldenberg, Hermann. *Buddha: Sein Leben, seine Lehre, seine Gemeinde* (1881). 13th ed. Stuttgart: Cotta, 1959. Translated by William Hoey as *Buddha: His Life, His Doctrine, His Order.* Delhi: Indological Book House, 1971.

Panikkar, Raimundo. *Gottes Schweigen. Die Antwort des Buddha für unsere Zeit.* München: Kösel, 1992. English: *The Silence of God: The Answer of the Buddha.* Maryknoll, N.Y.: Orbis, 1989.

Regamey, Constantin. "Der Buddhismus Indiens." In *Christus und die Religionen der Erde* 3, edited by Franz König, 229–317. Freiburg: Herder, 1956.

Schumann, Hans-Wolfgang. *Der historische Buddha: Leben und Lehre des Gotama.* Köln: Diederichs, 1982. Translated M. O'C. Walshe as *The Historical Buddha: The Times, Life, and Teachings of the Founder of Buddhism.* New York: Arkana, 1989.

Thomas, Edward Joseph. *The Life of Buddha as Legend and History* (1927). 6th ed. New York: Knopf, 1960.

Vetter, Tilmann. *The Ideas and Meditative Practices of Early Buddhism.* Leiden: Brill, 1988.

Waldschmidt, Ernst. *Die Legende vom Leben des Buddha.* Berlin: Volksverband der Bücherfreunde, Wegweiserverlag, 1929.

Zotz, Volker. *Buddha.* 4th ed. Reinbek by Hamburg: Rowohlt, 1996.

Christianity

Primary Sources

Biblical texts

Translations are from the German, with reference to the New Revised Standard Version Bible, © 1989, Division of Christian Education of the National Council of the Churches of Christ in the United States of America.

Aland, Barbara, and Kurt Aland, et al., eds. *Novum Testamentum Graece.* 27th ed. Stuttgart: Deutsche Bibelstiftung, 1993.

Elliger, Karl, and Wilhelm Rudolph, eds. *Biblia Hebraica Stuttgartensia.* 4th ed. Stuttgart: Deutsche Bibelgesellschaft, 1990.

Die Heilige Schrift des Alten und des Neuen Testaments. Zurich: Zwingli, 1955.

Early Jewish writings

Kümmel, Werner Georg, et al., eds. *Jüdische Schriften aus hellenistisch-römischer Zeit.* 5 vols. Gütersloh: Mohn, 1973ff.

Josephus

Niese, Benedict, ed. *Flavii Iosephi Opera.* 6 vols. New printing. Berlin: Weidmann, 1955.

Qumran texts

Lindemann, Andreas, and Hennig Paulsen, eds. and trans. *Die Qumran-Essener: Die Texte vom Toten Meer.* Tübingen: Mohr, 1992.

Garcia Martinez, Florentino. *The Dead Sea Scrolls Translated. The Qumran Texts in English.* Translated by Wilfred G. E. Watson. 2nd ed. Leiden, New York, and Cologne: Brill; Grand Rapids: Eerdmans, 1996.

Nag Hammadi texts

Lüdemann, Gerd, and Martina Janssen, commentary and trans. *Die Bibel der Häretiker: Die gnostischen Schriften aus Nag Hammadi.* Stuttgart: Radius, 1997.

Robinson, James M., ed. *The Nag Hammadi Library in English.* 3rd ed. San Francisco: Harper & Row, n.d. (Brill, 1988).

Literature on Jesus

Allison, Dale C. *Jesus of Nazareth: Millenarian Prophet.* Minneapolis: Fortress Press, 1998.

Becker, Jürgen. *Jesus von Nazaret.* Berlin: de Gruyter, 1995. Translated by James E. Crouch as *Jesus of Nazareth* (Berlin: de Gruyter, 1998).

Borg, Marcus. *Jesus, a New Vision: Spirit, Culture, and the Life of Discipleship.* San Francisco: HarperSanFrancisco, 1991.

Bornkamm, Günther. *Jesus von Nazareth.* 15th ed. Stuttgart: Kohlhammer, 1995. Translated by Irene McLuskey and Fraser McLuskey, with James M. Robinson, as *Jesus of Nazareth* (London: Hodder & Stoughton; New York: Harper, 1960).

Braun, Herbert. *Jesus: Der Mann aus Nazareth und seine Zeit.* Rev. ed. Gütersloh: Mohn, 1989. Translated by Everett R. Kalin as *Jesus of Nazareth: The Man and His Time* (Philadelphia: Fortress Press, 1979).

Bultmann, Rudolf. *Jesus.* Die Unsterblichen: Die geistigen Heroen der Menschheit in ihrem Leben und Wirken, vol. 1. Berlin: Deutsche Bibliothek, 1926.

Crossan, John Dominic. *Jesus: A Revolutionary Biography.* San Francisco: HarperSanFrancisco, 1994.

Flusser, David, with R. Steven Notley. *Jesus.* 3rd ed. Jerusalem: Hebrew University / Magnes, 2001.

Gnilka, Joachim. *Jesus von Nazaret.* Freiburg: Herder, 1990.

Horsley, Richard A. *Jesus and the Spiral of Violence: Popular Jewish Resistance in Roman Palestine.* Minneapolis: Fortress Press, 1987.

Jeremias, Joachim. *Neutestamentliche Theologie I: Die Verkündigung Jesu.* Gütersloh: Mohn, 1971. Translated by John Bowden as *New Testament Theology* (London: SCM, 1971).

Kee, Howard Clark. *What Can We Know about Jesus?* Cambridge: Cambridge University Press, 1990.

Meier, John P. *A Marginal Jew: Rethinking the Historical Jesus.* 3 vols. to date. New York: Doubleday, 1991–.

Roloff, Jürgen. *Jesus.* Munich: Beck, 2000.

Sanders, E. P. *The Historical Figure of Jesus.* New York: Penguin, 1995.

Schweitzer, Albert. *Geschichte der Leben-Jesu Forschung* (1906). 9th ed. Tübingen: Mohr, 1984. Translated by W. Montgomery as *The Quest of the Historical Jesus,* edited by John Bowden (London: SCM; Minneapolis: Fortress Press, 2001).

———. *Reich Gottes und Christentum,* edited by Ulrich Neuenschwander. Tübingen: Mohr, 1967. Posthumous collection. Translated by L. A. Garrard as *The Kingdom of God and Primitive Christianity* (London: Black; New York: Seabury, 1968).

Theissen, Gerd. *Der Schatten des Galiläers.* 13th ed. Gütersloh: Mohn, 1993. Translated by John Bowden as *The Shadow of the Galilean: The Quest of the Historical Jesus in Narrative Form* (London: SCM; Philadelphia: Fortress Press, 1987).

Theissen, Gerd, and Annette Merz. *Der historische Jesus: Ein Lehrbuch.* Göttingen: Vandenhoeck & Ruprecht, 1997. Translated by John Bowden as *The Historical Jesus: A Comprehensive Guide* (Minneapolis: Fortress Press, 1998).

Vermes, Geza. *Jesus the Jew: A Historian's Reading of the Gospels.* London: Collins, 1973.

———. *The Religion of Jesus the Jew.* London: SCM; Minneapolis: Fortress Press, 1993.

Wengst, Klaus. *Jesus zwischen Juden und Christen.* Stuttgart: Kohlhammer, 1999.

Literature Comparing Christianity and Buddhism

Aufhauser, Johannes B. *Buddha und Jesus in ihren Paralleltexten.* Bonn: Marcus & Weber, 1926.

Bechert, Heinz, and Hans Küng. *Christentum und Weltreligionen: Buddhismus.* Rev. ed. Munich: Piper, 1995.

Brück, Michael von, and Whalen Lai. *Buddhismus und Christentum.* Munich: Beck, 1997.

Bsteh, Andreas, ed. *Der Buddhismus als Anfrage an christliche Theologie und Philosophie.* Mödling: Verlag St. Gabriel, 2000.

Edmunds, Albert J., and Masuharu Anesaki. *Buddhist and Christian Gospels.* 3rd ed. Tokyo: Yūhōkwan, 1905.

Garbe, Richard. *Indien und das Christentum: Eine Untersuchung der religionsgeschichtlichen Zusammenhänge.* Tübingen: Mohr, 1914. Translated by Lydia Gillingham Robinson as *India and Christendom: The Historical Connections between Their Religions* (La Salle, Ill.: Open Court, 1959).

Mensching, Gustav. *Buddha und Christus—ein Vergleich.* Stuttgart: Deutsche Verlagsanstalt, 1978. Abbreviated new ed. (Freiburg: Herder, 2001).

Index